Worldly Spirits, Extra-Human Dimensions, and the Global Anglophone Novel

Worldly Spirits, Extra-Human Dimensions, and the Global Anglophone Novel

Hilary Thompson

BLOOMSBURY ACADEMIC
LONDON • NEW YORK • OXFORD • NEW DELHI • SYDNEY

BLOOMSBURY ACADEMIC
Bloomsbury Publishing Plc, 50 Bedford Square, London, WC1B 3DP, UK
Bloomsbury Publishing Inc, 1385 Broadway, New York, NY 10018, USA
Bloomsbury Publishing Ireland, 29 Earlsfort Terrace, Dublin 2, D02 AY28, Ireland

BLOOMSBURY, BLOOMSBURY ACADEMIC and the Diana logo are trademarks of
Bloomsbury Publishing Plc

First published in Great Britain 2023
This paperback edition published 2025

Copyright © Hilary Thompson, 2023

Hilary Thompson has asserted her right under the Copyright, Designs and Patents Act,
1988, to be identified as Author of this work.

For legal purposes the Acknowledgments on p.vii constitute an extension
of this copyright page.

Cover design: Eleanor Rose
Cover image © Gita Govinda Kowlessur

All rights reserved. No part of this publication may be: i) reproduced or transmitted
in any form, electronic or mechanical, including photocopying, recording or by means
of any information storage or retrieval system without prior permission in writing from
the publishers; or ii) used or reproduced in any way for the training, development or
operation of artificial intelligence (AI) technologies, including generative AI technologies.
The rights holders expressly reserve this publication from the text and data mining
exception as per Article 4(3) of the Digital Single Market Directive (EU) 2019/790.

Bloomsbury Publishing Plc does not have any control over, or responsibility for,
any third-party websites referred to or in this book. All internet addresses given
in this book were correct at the time of going to press. The author and publisher
regret any inconvenience caused if addresses have changed or sites have ceased
to exist, but can accept no responsibility for any such changes.

The author and publisher gratefully acknowledge the permission granted to reproduce
copyrighted material in this book. The third-party copyrighted material displayed in the
pages of this book is done so on the basis of fair use for the purposes of teaching,
criticism, scholarship or research only in accordance with international copyright laws,
and is not intended to infringe upon the ownership rights of the original owners.

A catalogue record for this book is available from the British Library.

A catalog record of this book is available from the Library of Congress.

Library of Congress Cataloging-in-Publication Data

Names: Thompson, Hilary (Professor of English), author.
Title: Worldly spirits, extra-human dimensions, and the global Anglophone
novel / Hilary Thompson.
Description: London ; New York : Bloomsbury Academic, 2023. |
Includes bibliographical references and index.
Identifiers: LCCN 2023020522 (print) | LCCN 2023020523 (ebook) |
ISBN 9781350373815 (hardback) | ISBN 9781350373853 (paperback) |
ISBN 9781350373822 (pdf) | ISBN 9781350373839 (epub)
Subjects: LCSH: American fiction–21st century–History and criticism. |
Canadian fiction–21st century–History and criticism. | Animals in literature.
| Animism in literature. | Spiritualism in literature. |
LCGFT: Literary criticism.
Classification: LCC PS374.A54 T48 2023 (print) | LCC PS374.A54 (ebook) |
DDC 823/.9209–dc23/eng/20230818
LC record available at https://lccn.loc.gov/2023020522
LC ebook record available at https://lccn.loc.gov/2023020523

ISBN: HB: 978-1-3503-7381-5
PB: 978-1-3503-7385-3
ePDF: 978-1-3503-7382-2
eBook: 978-1-3503-7383-9

Typeset by RefineCatch Limited, Bungay, Suffolk

For product safety related questions contact productsafety@bloomsbury.com.

To find out more about our authors and books visit www.bloomsbury.com
and sign up for our newsletters.

Contents

Acknowledgments	vii
Introduction	
Interanimisms: Spirits, Species, and Dimensions of Planet-Thinking	1
Part One: Ripples	
1 Spirited Creatures: The Weretigers and their Worlds in Yangsze Choo's *The Night Tiger*	33
2 Creaturely Dimensionism: Unbearable Worlds in Azareen Van der Vliet Oloomi's *Call Me Zebra*	54
Part Two: Portals	
3 Provincializing Dimensionism: The Paranormal Ontario of André Alexis's *Days by Moonlight*	99
4 Foreseeable Futures: Avataric History in Amitav Ghosh's *Gun Island*	135
Part Three: Spirals	
5 Expected on Earth: Distributive Redemption in Zeyn Joukhadar's *The Thirty Names of Night* and Tanya Tagaq's *Split Tooth*	187
Recalling Gaia: A Note in Ending	203
Notes	206
Bibliography	213
Index	222

Acknowledgments

This book's journey has been helped by many hands, many minds. The writing experience has had a lateral hourglass shape—full of light and expansiveness at the beginning and end with a narrow passage through the center. As the journey's come out of its tunnel vision stage, I've been especially grateful for the wonderfully supportive and creative team at Bloomsbury: Lucy Brown and Aanchal Vij who've overseen the process with such positivity and care, the anonymous reviewers whose attentive readings flagged important spots for improvement, Ayesha Hussain, Moira Eagling, and Merv Honeywood as the book went into production, and Gita Govinda Kowlessur, who brought her bright artfulness to the cover. Many thanks, too, to Sam Durrant for being a such a critically kindred spirit as a reader and for inviting me to converse about this project with the Animist Engagements group. Through the middle stages when I was sheltering in place on sabbatical or working remotely upon return, I was supported first by Bowdoin College through its Faculty Research Fellowship in 2019–20 and then, in a different way, by the 75 State Street and Northern Light Hospice teams in Portland who cared for my father in his last months with such kindness and compassion. Bowdoin affords me the opportunity to work with inspiring students as I direct their independent projects on everything from the poetics of symbiosis to epigenetics and intergenerational memory, the rhizome and queer ecology, the affect of gratitude, or the lyrically hybrid forms of memoirs. In addition to thanking my supportive community of colleagues in the English department, I extend thanks to these students, particularly Benjamin Felser, Molly Moore, Mishal Kazmi, Mitchel Jurasek, Clayton Wackerman, and Hannah Kim. Moreover, the creative camaraderie of Vyjayanthi Selinger, Jeff Selinger, Paul Hoffman, and Rachel Sturman has been absolutely essential, as have been the steadfast friendships of Linda Sinclair, Leila Virtanen, Sarah Miles, and Michele Tepper. Heartfelt thanks go to my family, especially to Gail, Evan, Rebecca, Andrew, Beatrice, and to the enduring spirit of my father, his wit without bounds. And to Belinda Kong, hero of heroes, who models using fierceness for good, and who steered me towards Dimensionism, may we always muse together among the multiverses, having and sharing our visions.

Introduction

Interanimisms: Spirits, Species, and Dimensions of Planet-Thinking

Animated Spirits, Uncanny Animals

What is the "beyond" invoked by the much-used academic phrase "beyond the human"? While its repetition often signals the importance of nonhuman species, research into diverse modes of beholding the nonhuman frequently encounters more expansive realms. In a chapter of *Braiding Sweetgrass: Indigenous Wisdom, Scientific Knowledge, and the Teachings of Plants* called "Learning the Grammar of Animacy," biologist Robin Wall Kimmerer provides a telling example. Having come across a word that, had history taken another course, she might have inherited—*Puhpowee*—the Anishinaabe term for "the life force of mushrooms" that allows them to spring up overnight, she bemoans the boundedness of Western scientific terminology, but watches her world expand:

> You'd think that biologists, of all people, would have words for life. But in scientific language our terminology is used to define the boundaries of our knowing. What lies beyond our grasp remains unnamed.
>
> In the three syllables of this new word I could see an entire process of close observation in the damp morning woods, the formulation of a theory for which English has no equivalent. The makers of this word understood a world of being, full of unseen energies that animate everything.
>
> 49

Likewise, contemporary fiction has broadened and intensified turns towards realms of indeterminate animating forces, with recent works attending, often conjointly, to not only a variety of nonhuman species but also spirit beings. Contemporary fiction's depiction of animals specifically can serve as an illustrative example of this shift. Wendy Doniger remarks in her epilogue to the 2012 volume *Animals and the Human Imagination*, "We know very well how to make animals vanish. We have made so many species vanish from the earth" (349). And for Haruki Murakami in the late twentieth century, the elephant of his perhaps most famous short story was notable for disappearing. As the narrator of his tale "The Elephant Vanishes" eulogizes at its close, "People seem to have forgotten that their town once owned an elephant ... The elephant and keeper have vanished completely. They will never be coming back" (327). For more recent global anglophone fiction, however, animals, much like Kimmerer's mushrooms, are becoming notable for appearing—in odd ways, unexpected times, and unusual places. This book argues that current studies of the nonhuman in contemporary fiction might best engage with the increasingly unusual way that animals and the intimations of the extra-human they evoke have been appearing by situating this phenomenon at the intersection of two dynamic forces: dimensionism and animism.

If, as Jean-Christophe Bailly has urged, we acknowledge that "the world in which we live is gazed upon by other beings" (15), that it is in fact a vast array of other species' perceptual worlds, then it becomes not only radically multiple but also multiply dimensional. Theories of world literature have also recently called not only for more inclusive definitions of "the world" but for recognition of multiple lived worlds with multiple dimensions, and in this respect these theories can be usefully put into conversation with a significant precursor. Briefly in the 1930s, the poet Charles Sirató called for artistic practices that could meditate on their own media, pushing them towards incorporating awareness of other media and hence encompassing unaccustomed dimensions. The Einstein-inspired movement he named "Dimensionism" rallied under its banner many artists we associate with surrealism and expressionism. Its forward-thinking formula and credo was N+1, where N stands for an art form's total number of acknowledged dimensions and +1 gestures towards a further dimension, an added medium, into which each art form might expand.

Also writing in the early twentieth century was another thinker who reconceived dimensions, but in relation to animals: the founder of ethology, Jakob von Uexküll, whose work has been taken up across several disciplines. Uexküll, as I'll discuss in Chapter 2, asked us to stop analyzing animal behavior according to human-centered perceptual standards, but rather to see our perceptual world as one "bubble" in which we are at the center and any other species' world we might examine as another bubble in which that species is central. As the ever more popular academic descriptors "*beyond* the human" and "*more* than human" attest, recent theoretical engagements with the nonhuman generally and nonhuman concerned works of fiction in particular can be analyzed for their similarly expansionist aesthetic appeal. Accordingly, I argue that recent nonhuman-themed novels such as the ones I consider in this book can be read not simply for their engagements with plants and animals, but also as crafting their own dimensionisms (the small "d" indicating multidimensional creative endeavors beyond Sirató's movement). This interpretation is bolstered not only by all the novels' interest in intangible spirit realms, for which nonhuman species often serve as avatars and portals, but also by particular works' either engaging explicitly with the 1930s and alluding to Einstein (*The Night Tiger*), their addressing the related artistic movement of surrealism (*Call Me Zebra*), or their incorporating important gestures to other art forms and media (*Days by Moonlight, Gun Island, The Thirty Names of Night,* and *Split Tooth*).

At the same time, these contemporary novels also merge what I am calling their nonhuman-oriented dimensionist impulse with an awareness of the violent effects of colonialism, globalization, and especially ecological devastation. And it is at this juncture where an intuition of domains beyond the human meets with a sense of multiple planetary threats that uncanny animals are most likely to emerge, seeming at once otherworldly and the mark of increasingly uncertain states of the world. Indeed, the very presence of out-of-place creatures can seem to speak for itself, as in Amitav Ghosh's *Gun Island* which I discuss in Chapter 4, where characters perceive unusual animal sightings as both proverbial "signs from the universe" and evidence of animals' altered migration patterns and habitat disruption amidst climate change. While such ecologically minded use of the uncanny in global anglophone fiction has been usefully discussed in relation to the gothic and the spectral, and the works I analyze do at times dwell on the dead and on haunting, in appealing to the extra-human, I focus more on spirits than ghosts, expanded notions of life as opposed to simply realms of the undead.[1] Nonhuman spirits in general and uncanny animals in particular do more than haunt. The forces and realms beyond embodied human life that these novels invoke ask to be taken not simply as critiques of past and current policies and politics, spectral calls for justice, but also on their own terms. Less about unsettled scores and more about reconfigurable playing fields, they open up possibilities and ask us to consider thought and life in new ways. To understand the larger context in which these particularly animated spirits emerge, it's useful to think, as the texts I analyze in this book suggest we should, of our planet as thinking through and with us, an us in the most expanded of senses.

Returning to the Surface: Planet-Thinking Across Dimensions

We can find an early yet subtly influential model for this thoughtful earth and its multidimensional modes of communication, ones that ask us to engage as much with surfaces as with depths, in one of the most canonical texts of literary theory,

Walter Benjamin's "The Storyteller." If environmentally aware approaches to writing frequently return to the concept of the story, it's fitting to note that this oft-cited theoretical essay on the form has had a dramatic one.[2] And crucial to its story, and hence key to its relevance for theories of planet-thinking, is its contemplation of the earth itself, not simply as stable substratum, but as dynamic strata. Samuel Titan in his introduction to *The Storyteller Essays* describes Benjamin's classic essay as a text of counterintuitive destiny. Now a cross-disciplinary syllabus favorite, "The Storyteller" was composed, he notes, in austere circumstances: the Nazis had seized power, its exiled author was financially constrained, and its publication venue was "the very last issue of an eccentric Swiss review, which counted a mere thirty-five subscribers at the time." Nevertheless, despite its "obscure beginnings," the essay's rise to academic fame testifies to its "remarkable reversal of fate" (vii). Retranslated and reissued in this 2019 *New York Review of Books* Classics Original volume, the essay appears in the middle of a matrix that suggests, as the back cover details, an expanded—and even meta—narrative:

> What might be called the story of *The Storyteller Essays* starts in 1926, with a piece Benjamin wrote about the German romantic Johann Peter Hebel. It continues in a series of short essays, book reviews, short stories, parables, and even radio shows for children. This collection brings them all together to give readers a new appreciation of how Benjamin's thinking changed and ripened over time, while including several key readings of his own—texts by his contemporaries Ernst Bloch and Georg Lukács; by Paul Valéry; and by Herodotus and Montaigne. Finally, to bring things around, there are three short stories by "the incomparable Hebel" with whom the whole intellectual adventure began.
>
> Benjamin, *Storyteller Essays*

The wide-ranging, fate-changing adventure of the volume comes full circle yet gives the essay not merely a prior or afterlife, but also a set of parallel ones, the suggestive model for which might be the concentric circles rippling out across the earth described in the fourth chapter, "The Lisbon Earthquake."

In this radio broadcast Benjamin tries to conjure for his listeners a hard-to-imagine catastrophe, one that has had subtle aftereffects for European philosophy and in turn has, I suggest, inflected theories of the global debated amongst those who study world literature and especially the global anglophone novel. While many have railed, as I detail in Chapter 2, against a "flat earth" style of imagining the global and have seen it as the deleterious effect of colonialism and globalization, others have found merit in thinking in and through collapsed dimensions.

Benjamin's attempt to conjure a historic earthquake, the conceptions of the earth it implies and the spatial configurations it uses, makes for not only a useful counterpoint to important if familiar criticisms of the superficial flatness of globalization's two-dimensionally imagined earth; it's also an often forgotten precursor with a line of quiet influence worth attending to now. Recent global anglophone novels display a stunning ability to imagine worlds multidimensionally, moving both up and down scales and inspiring us to revisit flat figurings too easily dismissed as reductionist. Bringing Benjamin into conversation with philosopher Michael Marder, postcolonial theorist Gayatri Spivak, and novelist Amitav Ghosh suggests a multidimensional planetarity and underscores the ways that censuring imaginative recourse to a single plane becomes questionable if thinking in the name of our planet entails accounting for the untold complexity of multiple perspectives.

Indeed, according to Marder, the earth itself is hard to think about. In a time when so many academic studies engage the nonhuman, the beyond the human, or the more than human, whether under the heading of animal studies, plant studies, or the more capacious category of multispecies thought, turning to the earth itself, as Marder does in his essay "For the Earth That Has Never Been," makes sense. Yet when Marder does make this turn, it's in negative terms, with his essay attesting to a philosophy, identity, definition, and morality that have never been. He lays out these "never-beens" in four core theses: "1) that there has never been a philosophy of the earth; 2) that the earth has never been itself; 3) that the earth has never been defined; and 4) that the earth has never been moral" (60). If these theses seem to join hands to throw a colossal wrench at politics in the name of Gaia in the time of the Anthropocene, that's because Marder has deep reservations about many applications of this mythic-scientific mixture. In particular, he scrutinizes Bruno Latour's ironically zealous attempts, captured for Marder in Latour's lecture title "Gaia, a (Finally Secular) Figure for Nature," to disenchant the Greek earth goddess so that she might become the object we face as we make a grand recognition of our post-humanity, or ourselves as, in Marder's paraphrase, "collective human (or post-human) subject in the mirror of industrial waste engrained into the body of the earth" (63). Without using a specifically psychoanalytic idiom, Marder is sensitive to the charged oscillations between good mother figure and good-disguised-as-bad object that take place in such ecologically minded imaginings of Gaia. One can leave his essay thinking that we fail to conceive of the liminality of the earth in less reified, more useful ways because we fail to see how unfixed, vague, and contradictorily layered our imagination of the earth really is. Musing, for example, at the locution "planetary geology" used for the study of the matter of other heavenly bodies, he notes the second word's prefix makes any other planet we might settle "another earth" (69). And if this terminology places our supposed ground in the heavens above us, then likewise, reference to our planet's "subterranean, chthonic regions" implies that the proverbial earth below us holds another, an under-earth that is a potentially teeming "underworld" of "dark forces" (67). How to engage the earth as this obscure confusion of levels and layers, this nexus of seeming malapropisms and complexities? Marder weighs the merits of naming the explicit intellectual engagement he hopes for with the earth-inspired terms "terraphilia," "geophilia," and, of course, "geophilosophy." In doing so, he looks for an approach that, like Hegelian dialectics, acknowledges the elusiveness of the "sophia" it pursues, a sophia that is "nothing substantive in itself," but rather "the mediatedness of mediation, a middle conscious of its place." Holding an equally elusive "geo" in similar regard, he hopes geophilosophy can name a "courage to admit to our unity with earth and thought fracked, disemboweled, and filled with our garbage, even as we are filled with them," so that we can "be on the earth that has never been" (74). Marder's geophilosophy that must traverse regions of profound doubt and questioning, such geoskepticism, comes to seem like an environmentally beleaguered Orpheus who, returning to the surface, must push past layers upon layers of landfill.[3]

This orphic earth that has never been might seem in line with Spivak's difficult to grasp concept of planetarity, a notion that underwrites many contemporary critiques of the global that then become relevant for those studying the global anglophone novel.[4] And Sangeeta Ray has argued that attending to postcolonial literature with Spivak's "planet-thought" in mind can counter common misperceptions of that literature as arriving at environmental consciousness belatedly. Instead, with both awareness of past visions and critical foresight, Ray shows postcolonial literature to have long sketched out its own "imaginative eco-graphies" beyond Eurocentric notions of nature (428). In a last line that helps show the connection I mean to evoke with the term "planet-thinking," a possible bridge between Spivak's "planet-thought" and Marder's "plant-thinking" (which I'll come to shortly), she calls for "a planetary reader ... interested in the rhizomatic spread of ... roots, emphasizing the poetics, politics, and aesthetic of relation presented in the possibility of taking up the planet as subject of a radical comparative reading project" (434). Ray cites Ghosh's writing of the early 2000s, particularly his 2004 novel *The Hungry Tide*, as exemplary of this critically aware and intertwined approach, but Ghosh's critiques of colonially inherited cartography in his 1988 novel *The Shadow Lines* also provide a way to think about both Spivak's planetarity and the liminality of Marder's earth. There, as in much of Ghosh's work, we can see the traces of Benjamin, as though his prose lives just below the surface of Ghosh's. The best way to see these thinkers' ideas and the story of planet-thinking they advance as dynamic geophilosophical strata is to cite them in layers, moving through Benjamin to Ghosh to arrive at Spivak before returning to Marder.

In his essay "The Storyteller," Benjamin considers the appropriate scale for tracking the evolution of oral and written narrative forms and proposes a deep, and deeply earthly, analogy: "One must think of the rhythms in which epic forms are transformed as comparable to the rhythm of the geological transformations the earth's surface has undergone over millennia" (53). Benjamin's appeal to geological rhythm suggests a kind of perceptual attunement beyond the mere registering of sights in one's direct line of vision, and it is to this kind of attunement that he also appeals in his description of the Lisbon earthquake. In this twenty-minute radio broadcast of 1931, Benjamin works to make a disaster of one hundred and seventy-six years prior real to his listeners. In the Lisbon earthquake of 1755, he perceives not just the horrific elements he claims would be common to many natural disasters: "One house collapses after another, one family perishes after another. The terror that spreads with the engulfing flames and flooding water; the darkness, the pillaging and the cries of the injured, and the wails of those looking for their family members—" (17). Instead, while noting Lisbon's forgotten significance as an imperial and commercial hub comparable, he claims, to twentieth-century London and Chicago, Benjamin underscores the far-reaching effects and uncanny premonitions of the event, thus stretching this catastrophe outward in space as well as forward and backward in time. Remarking that the quake was felt "across Europe, even as far away as Africa, and it has been calculated that its most distant tremors spanned the enormous surface area of two and a half million square kilometers," he further details:

> Its strongest tremors extended from the coast of Morocco on the one side to the coasts of Andalusia and France on the other. The cities of Cádiz, Jerez, and Algeciras were almost completely destroyed. According to one eyewitness, the towers of the cathedral in Seville trembled like reeds in the wind. Still, the most powerful shocks spread through the sea. Powerful waves were felt from Finland to the Dutch East Indies, and it was calculated that the shocks spread with unbelievable speed through the ocean, traveling from the coast of Portugal to the mouth of the Elbe in just a quarter of an hour.
>
> 18–19

It came to seem significant that weeks before the quake, Europe experienced bizarre phenomena and cataclysmic weather. In Switzerland steam had emerged from the earth creating a strangely red-colored haze and then purple rain, and in Spain "the ground near Cádiz was covered with masses of worms that had crawled out of the earth" (19). Perhaps we forget this event, yet Benjamin notes it was not only terrestrially devastating but also registered in natural philosophy, leaving none other than the great transcendental thinker Immanuel Kant spellbound. "Although he never left his hometown of Königsberg either before or after," Benjamin tells us, "he zealously collected every account of the earthquake he could find, and the short study he wrote about it formed, no doubt, the beginnings of scientific geography in Germany. Certainly the beginnings of seismology" (19).

Benjamin's description of the Lisbon earthquake's wide, yet easily forgotten, concentric reach and his particular interest in its covering an "enormous surface area" make this text seem a fitting precursor for perhaps the most discussed passage in Ghosh's landmark 1988 novel, *The Shadow Lines*. In a climactic and unsettling meditation, an unnamed narrator wonders why riots that spread across Asia in 1964, from Srinagar to Calcutta and Khulna, can become completely forgotten to history, even within less than two decades, and not just for Westerners, but forgotten also to those in Calcutta who were affected by them at the time. In the text's famous atlas and compass scene, the narrator contemplates the riots' scale by experimenting with different circles, first placing the point of the compass on Khulna and the pencil on Srinagar, a radius of 1,200 miles. He draws a circle that

> cut through the Pakistani half of the Punjab, through the tip of Rajasthan and the edge of Sind, through the Rann of Kutch, and across the Arabian Sea, through the southernmost tow of the Indian Penninsula, through Kandy, in Sri Lanka, and out into the Indian Ocean until it emerged to touch upon the northernmost finger of Sumatra, then straight through the tail of Thailand, running a little north of Phnom Penh, into the hills of Laos, past Hué in Vietnam, dipping into the Gulf of Tonking, then swinging up again through the Chinese province of Yunnan, past Chungking, across the Yangtze Kiang, passing within sight of the Great Wall of China, through the Inner Mongolia and Sinkiang, until with a final leap over the Karakoram Mountains it dropped again into the valley of Kashmir.
>
> 226–7

Noting of this circle "more than half of mankind must have fallen within it," the narrator tries to draw a circle of equivalent span but centered in Europe. Randomly choosing Milan as center but maintaining the 1,200-mile radius, he finds that this circle passed through Helsinki in Finland, Sundsvall in Sweden, Mold in Norway, above the Shetland Islands, and then through a great empty stretch of the Atlantic Ocean until it came to Casablanca. Then it travelled into the Algerian Sahara, through Libya, into Egypt, up through the Mediterranean, where it touched on Crete and Rhodes before going into Turkey, then on through the Black Sea, into the USSR, through Crimea, the Ukraine, Byelrussia and Estonia, back to Helsinki.

227–8

The epiphany for the narrator is the culmination of his subsequent thought experiment: asking himself what event could occur "near the periphery of that circle" and "bring the people of Milan pouring out into the streets," he claims he can "think of none. None, that is, other than war" and adds, "It seemed to me, then, that within this circle there were only states and citizens; there were no people at all" (228).

It's a similar epiphany that Spivak wants to convey in "Imperative to Re-imagine the Planet" when she says that conceiving of ourselves as "planetary creatures" (*Aesthetic* 339) is radically different from beholding the globe, but also insists in her preface to the reprinted address, "Like the subaltern, planetarity has been altogether misunderstood; as something like community, thinking of the world's resources, or yet, at the extreme, sustainability" (335). Just as Ghosh's narrator looks for circles of significance by tracing over the surface of the atlas, Spivak claims that with her concept of "planetarity," she has "proposed the planet to overwrite the globe." And this because the globe is itself an overbearing fabrication:

> Globalization is achieved by the imposition of the same system of exchange everywhere. It is not too fanciful to say that, in the gridwork of electronic capital, we achieve something that resembles that abstract ball covered in latitudes and longitudes, cut by virtual lines, once the equator and the tropics, now drawn increasingly by other requirements—imperatives?—of Geographical Information Systems. The globe is on our computers. It is the logo of the World Bank. No one lives there; and we think that we can aim to control globality. The planet is in the species of alterity, belonging to another system; and yet we inhabit it, indeed are it. It is not really amenable to a neat contrast with the globe.
>
> 338

States and citizens, but no people. Computer screens and bank symbols, with no one living there. Both thinkers want to say we think we know ourselves on mapped macro scales, but there's something we fail to take in. When the way we think about mapped space makes it a ghost town, the earth on which we live out our stories disappears. Ghosh's narrator notes, "By the end of January 1964 the riots had faded away from the pages of the newspapers, disappeared from the collective imagination of 'responsible opinion', vanished without leaving a trace in the histories and bookshelves." But especially interesting is his metaphor for this oblivion: "They had dropped out of memory into the crater of a volcano of silence" (226). In the same way that Benjamin's description of the Lisbon earthquake, preceded by strange natural phenomena and then vastly destructive in its effects, ripples across times, Ghosh's volcanic image resonates with the past as well as with a text Ghosh himself was to write much later. It's volcanism to which Kant attributed, mistakenly we now know, the phenomenon of earthquakes, but it's also a group of Indonesian volcanic islands to which Ghosh turns in *The Nutmeg's Curse* (2021). And there he tells a story of seventeenth-century omnicidal extractivist colonialism and its assault on an Indigenous people who perceived its volcanic landscape as spiritually alive. What's particularly striking here, though, in this volcanic reference from *The Shadow Lines* is that even if we've dropped through its layers, we're back to the earth's surface—or the characteristic compounding of earthly surfaces implied by Marder's phrase, "subterranean, chtonic regions." We might question, then, whether it's truly the globe that's an imposition, with its lines drawing into relation oceans and continents, or whether instead the oversight is our own forgetting of a tradition, a way we've subliminally been thinking of "the earth that has never been" or the planet, seen from a perspective of alterity that won't allow it to conform to a neat opposition with the globe, as we've spun our most cataclysmic stories. Why else when we've wanted to recount upending events, reawaken our senses to something whose effects we still carry, do we so often unfold stories that focus on surface areas and seem to stretch out the earth along them? The two-dimensional imagination itself might not be what's traumatic. Rather, our recourse to it might mark one way the planet we inhabit thinks through us, one we could attend to, were we attuned enough, in stories of transformations beyond cataclysms. Imaginatively returning to the surface might stand, then, as a small emblem for a reinvigorated multidimensional mode of planetary thought, one that can engage expansive realms and relationships beyond strictly human stories of conquest or commerce.

Avatars and Arts of Interanimism

Narrative, then, with its capacity to make artful use of an imaginative range of dimensions, might be a key resource for sustaining a planetary sense of animacy. The idea of planetarity we see traces of in Benjamin onwards becomes especially vital in recent anglophone fiction, as though this fiction conceives of itself as a prime vehicle for such animation. The notion, for example, that such beyond-the-human forces as plate tectonics might be considered as engaging in thought-provoking, perhaps thoughtful, exchange with us as they assert themselves in our lives, mold and leave marks in our stories, interests not only Marder but also, as we'll see in Chapter 4, Ghosh. And a key influence Ghosh cites is the anthropologist, Eduardo Kohn. In *How Forests Think*, Kohn claims, "all living beings, and not just humans, think, and . . . all thoughts are alive." And for Kohn, this idea suggests that "the world is enchanted":

> What I mean is that the world beyond the human is not a meaningless one made meaningful by humans. Rather, mean-ings—means-ends relations, strivings, purposes, telos, intentions, functions and significance—emerge in a world of living thoughts beyond the human in ways that are not exhausted by our all-too-human attempts to define and control these. More precisely the forests around Ávila [the site of Kohn's fieldwork in Ecuador's Upper Amazon] are animate. That is, these forests house other emergent loci of mean-ings, ones that do not necessarily revolve around, or originate from, humans. This is what I'm getting at when I say that forests think.
>
> 72

If thought for Kohn is living beings' act of interpreting environmental information or signs as these beings strive towards their various ends, then his definition of thought can be called biosemiotic. No surprise then that he cites the theories of not only the semiotician Charles Sanders Peirce but also Uexküll, a founding figure for biosemiotics as well as ethology to whom I turn in Chapter 2. But Kohn's strain of biosemiotic thought also moves him towards animism. And "animism" is a term that, as many who use it note, originates in the hostile eyes and mouths of colonial ethnographers, and thus often requires delicate cross-cultural negotiations.

Kohn's particular conception of animism converges with recent impulses in contemporary anglophone fiction both in its capacious scope (nonhuman life generally) and in one of its specific interests (nonhuman animals that regard humans). What he calls "living thought" is especially well represented not merely by animals but particularly by those beings that trouble simplistic divisions between human and animal, the hybrids we call were-animals. In keeping with his interest in biosemiotics and intersubjective encounters, Kohn explains the logic by which the people he studies, the Runa, use the term "puma," not simply for jaguars, but for those beings who can be recognized as predators generally, those who don't succumb to becoming prey, those who, for example, sleeping in the forest face up rather than down might avoid a jaguar attack by being perceived as selves who can return "the feline's gaze" (92):

> Because the jaguar exemplifies the quintessence of predation, it is known simply as puma. Runa who survive encounters with such predators are by definition, then, runa puma, or were-jaguars (the term *Runa* is not only an ethnonym; it also means "person" ...). One survives, then, by not being noticed as prey by a puma. But in the process one also becomes another kind of being, a puma.
>
> 93

This is a key context in which Kohn's concept of animism and his consideration of were-jaguars first emerge. Thus for him animism is what might be called "interanimism" in the sense that it is radically intersubjective or interpersonal, at its core an interspecies attribution of selfhood. In this regard, interanimism can never be singular; it always implies recognition of other perceptual worlds and their attributions of animacy. It's important to note, though, that Kohn differentiates and delimits his use of the term "animism" from other common usages. He distances himself from older conceptions and what he calls the question of "classical animism," which, far from a multispecies endeavor, merely involves inquiring into the principles and practices of so-called "natives" in their broad attributions of animacy to entities the "West" deems inanimate: "The case of the jaguar troubles this project; if jaguars also represent us we cannot just ask how it is that some of us humans happen to represent them as doing so" (94). Kohn also distances himself from the practice of ascribing life to such objects as stones, for example, even if some animists whom anthropologists study do. His animism, which he proposes as a foundation for what he frequently calls "anthropology beyond the human," is one in which nonhuman life forms can be seen as making meaning, demonstrating living thought, and thoughtfully beholding us. Where Kohn converges with recent anglophone fiction, and where what I am calling his interanimist anthropology provides a resource for reading such fiction, is in making the were-animal especially exemplary: "One might say that the animal person is the model of the universe for animists, whereas for us [the mechanist "West"] it is the machine" (94). It is the idea of this "universe for animists" with all the perceptual dimensions it implies that has become increasingly important for global anglophone fiction's approach to the nonhuman. And it is with the goal of comparatively and dialogically attending to texts that engage with such universes that I extend my use of the term "interanimisms."[5]

We can usefully distinguish this emergent approach in anglophone fiction by noting its apparent vulnerability to critiques of anthropocentrism as well as questions of fetishism and, in that regard, contrasting it briefly with earlier turn-of-the-millennium animal-themed texts as well as with another important philosophical initiative of Marder's: phytocentrism. This conception of the animal as hybrid avatar for human imaginings of more than human animacy might easily run afoul of turn-of-the-millennium critiques of seemingly human-centered conjurings of animals. Turning to the big cats of poetry, J. M. Coetzee's Elizabeth Costello, for example, debated in *The Lives of Animals* the merits of Rainer Marie Rilke's panther against Ted Hughes's jaguar and praised the latter's more embodied, less idea-driven approach: "With Hughes it is a matter—I emphasize—not of inhabiting another mind but of inhabiting another body. That is the kind of poetry I bring to your attention today: poetry that does not try to find an idea in the animal, that is not about the animal, but is instead a record of an engagement with him" (51). Her objection to animals as vessels, to forms of meaning-making that make animals "stand for human qualities" or else make them a "stand-in for something else" (50) might seem at odds with the animistic animal and especially with the hybrid human-animal as standard-bearer for interanimism. For animal-themed anglophone fiction in the decades after the turn of the millennium, such critiques and the concern with animal alterity they raise remain forceful and can put urges toward animism in an awkward position. In order to register these concerns while still exploring a heady and lively multiverse of perceptual worlds, recent fiction frequently turns not so much to a key influence for turn-of-the-millennium considerations of creatureliness, Franz Kafka,[6] but to one of his uniquely imaginative inheritors, Jorge Luis Borges. As I suggest in Chapter 1 and in Chapter 2, his felines, both in *Dreamtigers* and "The God's Script," artfully balance considerations of animals as portals to worlds of multiple meanings with unflagging recognition of their otherness. At an intersection of lucid dreaming and awareness of his own circumscribed position, Borges conjures tigers that stand for other tigers, the wild ones he can never fully call forth, and thus his texts make themselves imperfect vessels for tigers, make tigers vessels for the idea of further literature, and record the engagement. His works demonstrate an awareness of ethical objections such as Costello's, but also use this awareness to spur a dimensionist unfolding, as though after every conjured a tiger there should follow a further tiger, requiring enhanced, enriched, and expanded modes of conjuring, but still leaving truly wild tigers at large.

The interanimist animal also addresses a concern Marder voices on behalf of plants, key figures in my third chapter, even if focus on this animal and on animism seem to diverge initially from his proposed phytocentrism. In "For a Phytocentrism to Come," Marder argues against both biocentrist ecology and zoocentrist animal studies as modeling exemplary anti-anthropocentric philosophies. Marder groups many calls for planetary ecological awareness under the heading of "biocentrism" and sees them as invoking a vast and amorphous "nature" we are encouraged to somehow respect. But such calls risk erasing specific differences as well as conflating the distinct Greek concepts, seen in the prefixes of the words *biocentrism* and *ecology*, of "bios" and "oikos." For Marder, we all too easily (and sloppily) make ourselves at home in a blanket concept of natural life to which we're supposedly paying homage. "The singularity of its [such promoted respect's] recipients is all but lost," he warns, "as their qualitatively distinct forms of life evaporate into the ideality of nature, the ecosphere, or indeed *bios*" (3). If such biocentrism is too generalizing and broad, the animal-focused approach he calls "zoocentrism" is too narrow and covertly specific, since it typically makes its case by turning not really to all animals, but to those animals whose sentience, suffering, and hence interests are most similar to our own. At the root of this problem seems to be Aristotle's diminished conception of life and specifically his devaluing of plant life, which for Marder "slips between the cracks of *bios* and *zoe*" and, according to the Aristotle he quotes, is life that merely appears to be living (5). Rescuing plant life and reiterating his argument from *Plant-Thinking, A Philosophy of Vegetal Life*, Marder claims a philosophy centered on the form of life exemplary in but not exclusive to plants—the ability to grow—offers new promise:

> Admittedly, animals are often assumed to be the rightful representatives of life as such. But this synecdochic substitution is illegitimate, in that it excludes non-animal living beings, notably plants. Only growing beings are in a position to represent all other creatures that, in addition to their respective modes of vitality, share vegetal life.
>
> 6–7

Centering a philosophy of life on plants, these unfixed, ever-growing entities, makes for a much more other-oriented and less rigidly centralized program, Marder hopes.

But Matthew Hall raises an important counterpoint, one that allows us to acknowledge yet reconfigure Marder's arguments while also meditating on the potential perils of invoking animism. Hall expresses the significant concern that in his strict attempts to combat anthropocentrism, Marder dismisses animism and attributions of personhood to plants, seeing such ways of thought as harmfully fetishistic or human-centered. And the question of unacknowledged ties to fetishism haunts recent reclamations of animism generally. Hall counters Marder by asserting that the highly relational animist conception of personhood, which we might see also in what I am calling Kohn's interanimist notion of selfhood (and about which I'll have more to say below), need not be understood as based on the human and then projected onto or extended to nonhuman others. For Hall, as a reader of studies of animism and author of *Plants as Persons*, other foundational principles than the West's notoriously exceptional concept of the human motivate his project. "An open, relational stance, an attentiveness to the behaviour and characteristics of living beings, an emphasis on connection rather than separation and the recognition and the re-telling of genealogical kinship are all aspects of animistic approaches to personhood that have influenced and informed my understanding of plant personhood," he writes (8). For the scholars and believers of animism Hall cites, personhood is not grounded in human being but seen in multiple beings' forming of relationships. Accordingly, if we were to use but modify Marder's style of argumentation, we might look not so much for a form of life that works well as broad representative by exemplifying creaturely growth, but rather for a figure that can represent intercreaturely relationships by being itself hybrid.[7] In this sense, the were-animal does not need to be seen as typifying a zoocentrism that disguises or presupposes entrenched forms of anthropocentrism; instead it might point up a universe, or multiverse, of moveable centers, mobile intentions, and multiple beholdings. And as I explore in more detail in Chapter 3, anglophone fiction that engages centrally with plants needn't forbear using them in tandem with uncanny animals. Indeed, André Alexis's *Days by Moonlight* shows ways an anthropomorphic plant and a female lycanthrope might combine forces to make a radically life-altering assemblage, one whose power can both heal and eclipse the subjects who bear it.

Yet animism is neither a culturally innocent nor culturally specific concept. A colonially inherited term, "animism" is tied to the practices Edward Said critically and famously referred to in *Orientalism* as "imaginative geography," and as Sam Durrant and Philip Dickinson warn, "The very word animism ... or at least its most familiar operative definition suggests a reflex of (often disavowed) anthropological judgment, and risks reinscribing the onto-epistemological fracture that the entire apparatus of colonial anthropology sought to painstakingly assemble" (4). As a historically tainted name for a phenomenon attributed, first pejoratively then restoratively, to various others, it is inherently cross-contextual. If discussions of specters with their unsettled scores are hounded by thoughts of economy, reengagements with animism with their beyond-the-West quests seem haunted by colonial anthropology. (Indeed, Ghosh, seemingly seeking an alternative, prefers to call for "cosmopolitan vitalist" rather than animist politics in *The Nutmeg's Curse*, and although I retain the word "animism" precisely because it has generated so much engagement, the novels I examine fit well with his paradigm.) Both lines of thought, economic and anthropological, can converge on the fetish, and whether it refers to a stance toward labor and objects or to specific Indigenous practices, the term "fetishism" itself is often used in academic discussions to elicit fears and evoke caution. Accordingly, a brief consideration of the surprising way questions of the object and technology arise in debates about animism can illuminate contemporary anglophone fiction's modes of animist engagement and suggest viable paths for the concept's reclamation, ones that entail a conjoint appeal to dimensionism.

Marder is not the only one to raise the question of fetishism with regard to animism. In his sharply skeptical essay "Is There Such a Thing as Animism?" (the title itself interesting for its thing-focus), Darryl Wilkinson retraces the term's roots, as do many others, to Victorian anthropology generally and Sir Edward Tylor specifically, who, Wilkinson writes, "in his foundational work *Primitive Culture* defined animism as the earliest religious condition of humankind" and deemed it "a self-evidently false belief system" (290; 292). Not only have contemporary ecological appeals to animism had to redeem it from this imputation of benighted backwardness, but, according to Wilkinson, they have also had to selectively reclaim Indigenous traditions, leaving aside the less ecologically amenable practices of fetishism:

> The exploitation, habitat destruction, and extinction of other species are, after all, among the most classic of environmentalist concerns. By contrast, personhood accruing to items of human manufacture, as is the case in fetishism, has limited relevance to the environmentalist agenda, since these are not considered "natural" entities at all. Fetishism might offer something to art conservators perhaps, but for nature conservationists, animism is evidently much more pertinent.
>
> 297

Wilkinson relates the resistance to reclaiming the perceived vitality and personhood of things to the discomfort of revisiting inverse practices that entail the removal of "human capacities from any instance of the biologically defined species *Homo Sapiens*, even though there are plenty of indigenous models for that as well" (299), that is, various forms of human sacrifice and slavery. On the one hand, the excesses of human exceptionalism lead the nonhuman to appear as uncanny and inspire us to reconsider animism; on the other, animism seems to have always been construed as uncanny and can threaten us with dehumanization in the extreme.

This same tension emerges in debates, sparked by Anne Allsion's *Millennial Monsters: Japanese Toys and the Global Imagination* (2006), over contemporary Japan's supposedly "techno-animist" culture, but these debates can also lead us to think more creatively about animism's potential techniques. While some, following Allison, argue for Japan's love of animation, its cute "kawaii" toys and games, and even its advances in robotics as a continuation of a Shintoist belief in diverse animating spirits that can inhabit the material world, others worry about selective rescriptings of the history of Shintoism and the dangers of fetishism (as fixation on objects, objectification of humans, and erasure of the politics of labor).[8] Japan is cited as an example of influential anthropological and philosophical ideas—"nature-culture," "multinaturalism," and "actor-network theory" among them—that even a Western-centric Latour might learn from but is also seen as the site of agenda-driven, politically motivated narratives of such alternative (non)modernities. Among these arguments over whether what is called animism exists, whether a new hybrid techno-animism exists, or whether such an imagined Japan truly exists, Fabio R. Gygi makes a particularly inventive and relevant intervention. Citing precise Japanese contexts and procedures via which objects—swords, calligraphy brushes, and tea jars, for example—are deemed to take on life, he argues, "My point is that the impression of animism here does not rest on an ontology in which things are already alive, but on a sophisticated technology of ritual animation," and he further stresses, "It is not that we understand what is animate and what is inanimate in fundamentally different ways, but that there is in Japan a long history of concrete technologies that transform inanimate things into animate objects" (100). In other words, the formulation "techno-animism" underrates the role of the "techno," as practice and procedure, in animism itself in Japan and perhaps beyond. And this point might mean that what is relevant for Wilkinson's "art conservators" might be relevant as well for those who would reclaim animism. Whether we want to see animism anthropologically as an ontology, taking up the burden of all the uncanniness that can entail, any reclamation of animism will involve what Gygi calls an animating technology. Or, in Durrant and Dickinson's formulation regarding any "new animism," if "one cannot simply overturn the Enlightenment," then "animism becomes something like a tactic," a "response" rather than a redaction of the legacies of colonial modernity (13–14). Animism might be seen, then—and this is crucial for contemporary anglophone fiction—as an art, a technique, or a process rather than used, without critical self-reflection, as a label to strictly delimit a time, place, or people.

It is in this spirit—at once knowing and tempered—that Isabelle Stengers offers her highly textual approach in "Reclaiming Animism," an essay that navigates the perils of the Western tradition it claims to inherit as well as those dangers inherent in characterizing its perceived others. And although Melanesian ethnographer Jadran Mimica includes Stengers in a list of names with fetishistic value, cult intellectuals whose ready-made interpretations of the West are all too often taken for granted—Derrida, Deleuze, Foucault, Irigaray, Kristeva, Le Douff, Habermas, Bourdieu, Rorty, Taylor, Žižek, Butler, Serres, Latour, and Badiou constituting the others—Stengers can nonetheless be read as performing in her brief essay the core point Mimica posits: "there is no knowing without an N number of correlative modes of un/knowing" (204). Mimica's concern is with the misunderstandings and misrepresentations that occur when ethnographers describe diverse lifeworlds with terms arising within specific, insufficiently analyzed Western contexts: "It would be easy to demonstrate that many a self-avowed anthropologist who appeals to the post-modern critics of Western ontological tradition would have difficulties to explicate the meaning of such basic concepts as 'substance,' 'form,' or 'essence' all of which frequently figure as the routine concepts in anthropological discourse about any culture" (220). Beyond not properly knowing their Western metaphysics, such researchers can characterize others' beliefs as "supernatural" and sense of selfhood as relational but neglect the specific history of the dichotomy between nature and supernature and even the philosophical provenance from Nietzsche onwards of the relational self to which, as we've seen, both Hall and Kohn appeal. Forgetting the emergence of core ideas within a so-called Western tradition, we risk displaying as much nescience as knowledge when we find them anew in others' worlds, hence "N" for Mimica is a single figure of both + and −, knowing and unknowing.

If any reclamation of animism with its attendant appeals to such concepts as a relational or distributed self needs to know as much about its own inheritances as it does about others' lifeworlds, then Stengers' insistence on speaking more about her own tradition than Indigenous others' makes sense. "Reclaiming Animism" is ostensibly a reflection on ecological philosopher David Abram, a pioneering advocate for the "more-than-human" and someone much more comfortable speaking about various Indigenous traditions and opposing them to developmental narratives of Western society. But in moving his initiatives towards a more radically alternative rereading of the West and in turning towards Deleuze and Guattari to do so, Stengers models a textual "technology of animation," to use Gygi's phrase, that converges with Dimensionism. Key to her approach is Deleuze and Guattari's concept of the rhizome, and it is this idea, one highly influential for Marder's plant-thinking, that, looking beyond Stengers and back to *A Thousand Plateaus*, we will see was originally defined using a Dimensionist idiom.

Although Stengers supports Abram's desire to reclaim animism, her appeal to the creatively enactive style of thought the rhizome represents allows her to reconfigure Abram even as she supports him. Far more critical of technology and written text in particular than either Gygi or Stengers is, Abram argues for the restoration of our lost sensuous connection to an animate earth. In an especially revealing moment, he plays rhetorically, as we will later see Alexis do, with the metaphoric shadows evoked by the word "eclipse." He holds writing, particularly alphabetic script, responsible for enabling abstract senses of space and time that sever stories from specific places, from the sense of an enfolding and living earth. In a chapter of his 1996 work *The Spell of the Sensuous: Perception and Language in a More-Than-Human World* called "Space, Time and the Eclipse of the Earth," he writes, "It would seem, then, that the conceptual separation of time and space—the literate distinction between a linear, progressive time and homogeneous, featureless space—functions to *eclipse* the enveloping earth from human awareness" (italics in the original). Aesthetically appealing to Einstein, as a Dimensionist artist such as Marcel Duchamp would (who, as we'll see in Chapter 2, found inspiration in an Einsteinian view of eclipses as a confirmation of spacetime), he adds, "Only when space and time are reconciled into a single, unified field of phenomena does the encompassing earth become evident, once again, in all its power and its depth, as the very ground and horizon of all our knowing" (131). As we will see in Chapter 4, Ghosh will echo Abram's concern at the potentially deleterious power of written texts. Yet in *The Nutmeg's Curse* he will also question whether Abram's argument, "clouded by a kind of technological determinism," gives the alphabet itself rather than colonial history too much agency, as though "alphabetical literacy [is] a technology that can achieve certain effects on its own, almost passively" (211). Ironically, in its very animation of technology, Abram's argument for the eclipsing alphabet risks overshadowing as much as illuminating causes for the occlusion of the earth's animacy. Abram's argument and imagery can thus be seen as performing both awareness and nescience, or Mimica's un/knowing. In light of such lively tension, it's easy to understand why, in addressing Abram's book, Stengers retains the idea of textual animacy even as she both approaches and avoids claiming animism.

Stengers invokes philosophy as a form of possible "textual animism" in which one can feel, even in writing philosophy as Alfred North Whitehead's proverbial "footnotes to Plato," "the text as an animating power," yet at the same time she veers away from simply, as she says, "using this [possibility] to delocalize myself, to feel authorized to speak about animism." Instead, she owns the history of thought that has made so-called animism its other and looks for alternative resources for approaching animism from within this philosophical tradition. Eschewing a view of proper noun "Science" as an epic narrative of arborescent growth and linear progress, one responsible for conquering and disenchanting the world, she presents scientific practice as an adventure based on situated experiments and achievements. "An experimental achievement may be characterized as the creation of a situation enabling what the scientists question to put their questions at risk, to make the difference between relevant questions and unilaterally imposed ones," she explains and adds, "What experimental scientists call objectivity thus depends on a very particular creative art, and a very selective one, because it means that what is addressed must be successfully enrolled as 'partner' in a very unusual and entangled relation." This adventurous science is intensely creative, connective, and expansive, since "the answers that follow from such achievements should never separate us from anything, because they always coincide with the creation of new questions, not with new authoritative answers to questions that already mattered to us." Such a self-consciously adventurous science would neither cast a blanket entity called "animism" as its other, nor would it position itself as uniquely able to "verify" animist "beliefs." In an effort to convey a counterfactual sense of a world in which a narrative of scientific adventure prevails and, we infer, makes science akin to animism, Stengers cites the rhizome:

> Instead of the hierarchical figure of a tree, with Science as its trunk, what we call progress would perhaps have had the allure of what Gilles Deleuze and Félix Guattari called a rhizome, connecting heterogenous practices, concerns, and ways of giving meaning to the inhabitants of this earth, with none being privileged and any being liable to connect with any other.

This emblematic use of a dynamic plant system allows us to interweave Dimensionism and textual animism by returning not only to experimental artist and impresario Charles Sirató but also to Indigenous plant biologist Robin Wall Kimmerer, whose beloved sweetgrass is, as she meaningfully describes, rhizomatic. If Sirató called for art forms to take on new dimensions by mixing their media, expanding their universes according to an ongoing practice of the formula N+1, Brian Massumi advises something similar in his Translator's

Foreword to *A Thousand Plateaus*. "Most of all," he hospitably tells us, "the reader is invited to lift a dynamism out of the book entirely, and incarnate it in a foreign medium, whether it be painting or politics" (xv). While this advice seems to follow Sirató's formula, in their first section "Introduction: Rhizome," Deleuze and Guattari invert N+1 in calling for a new relation between the book and the world. They object to a binary logic of subject and object according to which either the book reflects the world and follows a basic bifurcating root or tree structure whereby "the One becomes two" (5) or the book supplants the world as though secondary roots flourish in place of a damaged primary one. Instead, truly embracing the multiple rather than the merely binary would mean taking away the +1 that unfolds by first positing N:

> The multiple *must be made*, not by always adding a higher dimension, but rather in the simplest of ways, by dint of sobriety, with the number of dimensions one already has available—always $n-1$ (the only way the one belongs to the multiple: always subtracted). Subtract the unique from the multiplicity to be constituted; write at n−1 dimensions. A system of this kind could be called a rhizome.
>
> 6

But lest we simply oppose the Deleuzo-Guattarian rhizome defined as n−1 to Dimensionism's program, it's wise to consider Marder's point in *Plant-Thinking* that "non-anthropocentric thinking of difference" need not adhere to the principle of non-contradiction. "Mirroring the plants' heteronomy, its ontological dependence on something other than itself, such as the light," he adds, "plant-thinking is so closely entwined with its other (i.e., with non-thinking) that it does not maintain an identity *as thinking*." Rather, according to Marder, such thinking "rejects the principle of non-contradiction in its content and in its form, in that, at once thinking and not thinking, it is not at all opposed to its 'other'" (164). As with Mimica's dual N of un/knowing, both relations of N to 1, plus and minus, can be part of rhizome-thinking. Thus, when Deleuze and Guattari sum up the rhizome's features, they stress its logical, natural, and dimensional flexibility:

> Let us summarize the principal characteristics of the rhizome: unlike trees or their roots, the rhizome connects any point to any other point, and its traits are not necessarily linked to traits of the same nature; it brings into play very different regimes of signs, and even nonsign states. The rhizome is reducible neither to the One nor the multiple. It is not the One that becomes Two or even directly three, four, five, etc. It is not a multiple derived from the One, or to which One is added (n+1). It is composed not of units but of dimensions, or rather dimensions in motion. It has neither beginning nor end, but always a middle (*milieu*) from

which it grows and which it overspills. It constitutes linear multiplicities with n dimensions having neither subject nor object, which can be laid out on a plane of consistency, and from which the One is always subtracted ($n-1$).

21

Taking scientific inspiration from biology rather than physics, Deleuze and Guattari arrive at a lively dimensionist multiverse that recreates Sirató's expansionist imperative as a more mobile palimpsest through which we can read N + and − 1 together. And this move clears the way not only for the imaginative uses of the planar we see in key examples of planet-thinking, but also for the arts of interanimism we see expressed in recent global anglophone fiction, fiction at once worldly and spirited.

We can see this multiverse and the appeal of the extra-humanly viewed human it offers in two final examples that illustrate two main tendencies in the novels I analyze: the first turns to the dynamics of predation as it envisions a multiply hybridized human and the second works through practices of reclamation as it illuminates a newly crystallized human.

If Kohn's were-jaguar is the product of human stories of pumas' human-directed gazes, then it is the emblem of a cross-species theory of other minds, an entertaining of other perspectives that Kohn's key influence Eduardo Viveiros de Castro has called, as if naming an art movement, "perspectivism." Adding ethnography to the other scientific adventures, whether originating in physics or ethology, that have inspired dimensionisms yields an enhanced multiverse of metamorphic intersubjectivities, as Viveiros de Castro's brief catalogue of his ethnographic archive reveals:

> Typically, in normal conditions, humans see humans as humans and animals as animals; as to spirits, to see those usually invisible beings is a sure sign that the "conditions" are not normal. Animals (predators) and spirits, however, see humans as animals (as prey), to the same extent that animals (as prey) see humans as spirits or as animals (predators). By the same token, animals and spirits see themselves as humans: they perceive themselves as (or become) anthropomorphic beings when they are in their own houses or villages and they experience their own habits and characteristics in the form of culture—they see their food as human food (jaguars see blood as manioc beer, vultures see the maggots in rotting meat as grilled fish etc.), they see their bodily attributes (fur, feathers, claws, beaks) as bodily decorations or cultural instruments, they see their social systems as organised in the same way as human institutions are (with chiefs, shamans, ceremonies, exogamous moieties etc.).

197

What might be said to think through "us" not only in such accounts but also in their collecting and being placed alongside each other? One could infer a longing for a distributed species self, a sense of the "human"—with the word likely hiding a myriad of other languages' words that do not precisely equate to it—that is multidimensional because multiply beheld, multiply beholdable.

Moving then to the planet, we might wonder, if we were to see it at a macro level as sentient and organized, how would it perceive us? The question of whether we can tangibly experience a version of ourselves not only beheld by the earth but beheld by it gratefully becomes almost a quest for Kimmerer. Devoted to acts of cultural and botanical restoration as well as a philosophy of thankful reciprocity, she poses her question to a member of a clan, the Bear Clan, known for keeping medicinal knowledge. Discussing the Mohawk tradition of regularly giving a "Thanksgiving Address" that expresses gratitude to the earth for all it gives, she asks, "has the land ever been known to say thank you in reply?" (259). Met with silence, Kimmerer's question lingers throughout her chapter "Putting Down Roots" as she describes bringing the difficult to cultivate and formerly thriving plant sweetgrass to a reestablished Mohawk community. Disrupted by pavements and hard to propagate by seeds, sweetgrass, Kimmerer explains, "has its own way of multiplying." It's a way Deleuze, Guattari, and Marder might love:

> Every shiny green shoot that pokes up above ground also produces a long, slender white rhizome, winding its way through the soil. All along its length are buds, which will sprout up and emerge into the sunshine. Sweetgrass can send its rhizomes many feet out from the parent. In this way, the plant could travel freely all along the riversides. This was a good plan when the land was whole.
>
> 262

This ability of a plant to thrive far from parents to which it remains nonetheless connected is implicitly contrasted with the chapter's description of Indigenous children taken from families and forcibly assimilated in far-off residential schools. Offering a further positive example of connection, Kimmerer tells us that beyond the ecological conditions favoring the plant's restoration, "there is yet another dimension to sweetgrass' requirements. The most vigorous stands are the ones tended by basket makers" (262). It's in the midst of digging in the dirt of Mohawk country in New York state as she plants the sweetgrass she has cultivated, sweetgrass to be used again for traditional basket making, that Kimmerer's shovel hits on a crystal, a Herkimer diamond:

> It is nearly the size of an egg. With a muddy thumb I rub away the dirt and a glassy surface is revealed, then another and another. Even beneath the dirt it

> gleams as clear as water. One face is rough and cloudy, another abraded by time and history, but the rest is brilliant. There is light shining through. It is a prism and the fading light refracts, throwing rainbows from within the buried stone.
>
> 266

And this she takes to be the earth's answer to her quest and question. Consulting again with her formerly silent friend, Kimmerer is gratified when he says, "This is the way the world works ... in reciprocity," and closes her hand around the quartz, adding, "This is for you" (267). It's an ending that tempts us toward a perspectival conclusion: if the earth beholds basket weavers, it's as multifaceted stones that light can move through.

Overview and Terminology

The first two chapters contained in "Part One: Ripples" explore the way that two striped animals, the tiger and zebra, lend themselves to becoming figures of human–animal hybrids, their bodily forms and mobile lines suggesting unsettled and unsettling worlds. A little fancifully, I think of the curved striations displayed on these emblematic animals' skins as suggestive of Einsteinian warped space and as an animally embodied version of Deleuze and Guattari's rhizome. As with Donna Haraway's celebration of the tentacular in *Staying with the Trouble*, sinuous natural images of lateral outreach have appeal for a reclaimed interanimism conceived as moving across multiple dimensions. The following two chapters of "Part Two: Portals" explore what it might be like to travel a sinuous route across these dimensions. Tracking characters whose senses are awakened to subtle realms, these novels open up other worlds as the culmination of their protagonists' quests, either across local land in search of a legendary plant or across continents and oceans in search of the truth behind a mythic snake goddess legend. The final fifth chapter contained, along with a brief afterword, in "Part Three: Spirals" turns to the question of time, placing Indigenous thinker Kyle Whyte and his concept of "spiraling time" into conversation with Benjamin's philosophy of messianic time, a model of messianism often set aside in both world literature and ecocritical discussions that favor of Derrida's famous and seemingly more secular "messianic without messianism." Both spiraling and messianic time enable vital conversations between ancestors and descendants, providing ways to imagine redemption and hope. This notion of an enhanced conversation, both between an Indigenous and a European thinker and across generations, informs my reading of two novels concerned with restoring inherited histories that are riddled with erasures.

My selection of novels, as I'll further elaborate below, moves from settings in British Malaya, modern Iran, Syria, India, contemporary Europe and North America, and my authors, when not Indigenous North American, are members of various diasporas: Asian, Middle Eastern, and Caribbean. This selection is by no means meant to represent an exhaustive survey, but in choosing my texts, I have been interested in the ways these differently located voices—ones that cover a political range including positions before the nation, outside the nation, peripheral within the nation, and crisscrossing over multiple nations—articulate visions of the multidimensional and imagine extra-human perspectives from such varying positions. And while in choosing novels published between 2018 and 2020 I had initially followed a presentist urge, trying to capture a trend I saw rapidly emerging in an era that's been called one of great acceleration, I now see this choice differently. Published in the time just before COVID-19's outbreak, this selection has come to seem a crucial archive of past presciences, of foreknowings without a foregone conclusion. If the COVID-19 pandemic has involved a collective witnessing of mass death and contemplative experiences born of mourning and confinement, much contemporary literature that imagines spirit beings and spirit realms that lie beyond embodied human life will be attributed to this crisis. Resisting what might be called disaster determinism, I find it important to recognize the multiple imaginative paths writers were already on, the many realities they intuited without the pandemic's having (yet) occurred. Readers may find in my chosen novels an intimacy with death, an anxiety in the face of difficult to localize threats, a sense of the instability of the human/nonhuman border, even a concern with the precariousness of attempts at communal immunity, but these should serve as reminders of elements of a world from which a crisis like the pandemic was yet to emerge, was one of many possibilities. It's perhaps a testament to both the foreseeability of 2020's future and writers' expansive imaginative capacities that many were already reconceiving the human's relationship to the borders between life and death in such creatively resonant ways before the pandemic unfolded.

The book's chapters follow a two-part structure in which an initial section situates the chosen literature in larger relevant theoretical conversations and the second section focuses on close textual analysis. The conversations most pertinent to these quite recent novels often come not from a canon of established criticism, but rather from author interviews, book reviews, and diverse theories—of world literature, spirit worlds, dimensionist art, biopolitics, and the nonhuman. These writers' intellectual and lived trajectories move across borders and many evince a sensibility that could be called cosmopolitan, in the sense that they look to merge revolutionary or surrealist European thinkers with such other traditions as Confucianism, Hinduism, and a variety of spirit beliefs. Accordingly, I engage an international range of theoretical interlocutors in discussing them, while quoting liberally from interviews to let authors speak for themselves. While my focus is on global anglophone fiction, many current interpretive models come from theorists who prefer the ideas of a "world" and "world literature" to notions of a globe. To accommodate discussion of them as well as of influential works of fiction in translation, my terminology must make occasional use of the terms "world" and "world literature," often situating specific features of the global anglophone novel against this backdrop. To highlight a turn beyond strictly material manifestations of the "more than human," a turn that attends to unseen forces and worlds beyond the ones of our customary dimensions, I use the term "extra-human" and at times contrast it with the nonhuman. But this "extra" should be taken as flexible, gesturing toward what can move through, around, and beyond the human rather than anything conceived as absolutely apart from it. So, for example, a novel in which a dolphin researcher cultivates a friendly rapport with a particular dolphin, as Piya does in Ghosh's *Gun Island*, might show its interest in the nonhuman. But a book in which a snake bite lends its recipient uncanny intuitive powers and awareness of spirits, as happens to Piya's ward Tipu in the same novel, merges interest in the nonhuman with interest in realms of the extra-human.

Chapters

Chapter 1, "Spirited Creatures: The Weretigers and their Worlds in Yangsze Choo's *The Night Tiger*," introduces a spirit continuum for contemporary fiction; the prominence of popular forms and genre instability in such recent fiction; the importance of the were-animal; and the relevance of dimensionism for understanding Malaysian Chinese American author Choo's rendering of its world. A consideration Pheng Cheah's insightful essay "Worlding Literature: Living with Tiger Spirits," which situates Indonesian writer Eka Kurniawan's novel in translation *Man Tiger* within a discussion of Heideggerean worlding in contrast to more static models of world literature, allows me to compare *Man Tiger* and *The Night Tiger*. While Cheah aptly underscores problems with the label "magical realist" for any work that engages with Indigenous lifeworlds, I tease out a Borgesian quality to Choo's tiger apparitions and a hybrid Confucian–Einsteinian one to the way one of her spirit characters describes the traditional model of the human becoming warped and stretched. Given this dimensionist aesthetic impulse in *The Night Tiger*, I ask whether the description "surrealist" is necessarily as problematic as the oft-used label "magical realist" can be.

Chapter 2, "Creaturely Dimensionism: Unbearable Worlds in Azareen Van der Vliet Oloomi's *Call Me Zebra*," brings the other-dimensional world figured by spiritual animals in Chapter 1 home to the human, particularly the human who has no stable home. This chapter picks up the conceptual thread of surrealism I tease out at the end of Chapter 1 and presents 2018 as the year of two significant explicit returns to surrealism: Iranian American author Van der Vliet Oloomi's publication of the novel *Call Me Zebra* and Vanja V. Malloy's curation of the exhibit "Dimensionism: Modern Art in the Age of Einstein." Before turning to *Call Me Zebra* and the dazzlingly multidimensional "Matrix of Literature" its surrealism-inspired heroine imagines, I give a fuller portrait of Dimensionism's agenda. Outlining the sweeping terms of Sirató's manifesto, I compare its bold language to the rhetoric of such recent appeals as those of postcolonial historian Dipesh Chakrabarty, who exhorts us to expand our sense of history by declaring our era of human-made climate change the Anthropocene. In addition, I highlight the manifesto's understanding of art as an enactive form of world-making, noting its similarity to Cheah's concept of "worlding literature" that I introduce in Chapter 1. After giving a brief overview of calls for a reconsideration of the concept of "the world" implied by the category "world literature," I stress the recent move towards recognition not only of plural worlds but of plural dimensions, much like those of Zebra's proposed matrix. Noting that in discussions of multiple literary worlds, fabled animals are often invoked as figures signaling readers' transportation to another realm, I bring both such world literature theories and Uexküll's conception of the multiplicity of animals' perceptual worlds to bear on a close analysis of *Call Me Zebra*. Uexküll's ties to antisemitism and early Nazism make a discussion of biopolitics relevant, since the plurality he could conceive of in relation to animal worlds became harmfully hierarchical and exclusionary when he applied his theories to human politics. As a wandering Iranian exile, Van der Vliet Oloomi's self-named heroine Zebra can be seen, I argue, as simultaneously typifying the Arendtian refugee's recourse to the spiritual; as dwelling in the perceptual world of the out-of-place Uexküllian animal; and, finally, as taking the transcendental nature of Borges's fabulous tigers to a farcical extreme best described in Mikhail Bakhtin's famous theory of the carnivalesque. Van der Vliet Oloomi's novel illustrates the geopolitical crises that can push one to conceive of oneself as a multidimensional animal and the burden, taken to pathetic limits, of inhabiting this expansively creative but also creaturely position.

Chapter 3, "Provincializing Dimensionism: The Paranormal Ontario of André Alexis's *Days by Moonlight*," picks up the concept of Bakhtin's carnivalesque with which I close Chapter 2 and applies its dynamically upending momentum to the structural games and satirical critiques of Trinidadian Canadian author André Alexis. Here alternative dimensions and initiation into a spirit world enable those who bear the ambivalent burdens of their nation's awkward attempts at inclusion to arrive at a re-envisioned sense of belonging. Eschewing realism, Alexis's novel depicts a bizarre Southern Ontario road trip in which traveling companions Alfred Homer, an avid botanist, and his mentor Professor Morgan Bruno, a literary scholar, merge their respective quests—for a fabled indigenous medicinal and psychotropic plant named "five fingers" and a vanished Canadian nature poet, John Skennen—and question dominant narratives of Canadian culture along the way. If *Call Me Zebra* portrays the multidimensional consciousness of a deracinated dissident to multiple nations, *Days by Moonlight* turns to the subtle experiences of alienation from within the nation. Homer and Bruno's road trip becomes a tour of absurd local institutions and offensive if well-meaning town festivals. Likewise, and on a metatextual level, if *Zebra* imagines herself as belonging to a multidimensional literary matrix, Alexis imagines *Days by Moonlight* as part of an expansive intertextual network of literary influences and as a member of a novel series in which it puzzlingly comes both fourth and fifth. Claiming that in his "Quincunx Cycle," the five novels' relation to each other resembles the five dots on one side of a die and that the central dot text needs to be written last, Alexis invites analogies to hypercubes and tesseracts as well as associations with the spinning and flipping toys that Bakhtin links to carnival energy. Alexis's subtle sense of both structure and satire thus makes a consideration of alternative, pre-Sirató and pre-Einstein, geometrical theories of higher dimensions relevant. And fittingly, these theories were often linked to spirituality movements. Highlighting the underrecognized dimensionism that is also built into Bakhtin's theories—both of the chronotope and the ambivalent nature of carnival—and then comparing Bakhtin's discussion of carnival with Giorgio Agamben's in *State of Exception*, I read Alexis as satirizing the historically settler colonial yet currently multicultural nation Canada via its eccentrically quaint capital province Ontario. Operating as a carnival festival's mock sovereign, Ontario oscillates between attempts at subversion and inclusion. Its official multiculturalism both spawns evermore complex center/periphery power dynamics and seems to create an ethos of stalled-out carnivalesque energy. Yet the stalemate between subversion and inclusion that Alexis humorously depicts in his strange tale also allows for alternative, higher-dimensional forms of empowerment. Those who feel the most wistfully attenuated senses of longing and belonging become, via their uncanny experiences with anthropomorphic plants and apparitional were-animals, those who inherit the magical power to channel the land's animacy.

Chapter 4, "Foreseeable Futures: Avataric History in Amitav Ghosh's *Gun Island*," analyzes Ghosh's most recent novel, arguing for its importance on four levels: metatextual, political, philosophical, and ecological. As a capstone work, *Gun Island* crystallizes Ghosh's views on the efficacy of literary fiction as well as culminates his own oeuvre of fiction and what I propose is a Bay of Bengal trilogy covering the Kolkata and Sundarbans region and including *The Calcutta Chromosome* and *The Hungry Tide* as precursors. Politically, the novel proposes ways to navigate our era of hyper defense of biological and national borders in the face of perceived threats of contamination and disintegration, whether from disease, refugees, or climate crises—a formation Roberto Esposito has called "the immunity paradigm." Philosophically, I argue that *Gun Island* attempts to make room for hope for the future with its rendering of Benjamin's messianic time in more lateral, pluralist, and embodied terms. Here multiple characters take on avataric functions so that almost any character can serve for any other as a fortuitous channel of a spirit's-eye view of current events as well as past history. And finally, ecologically, the novel is relevant for current discussions of planetary animism through its use of the nonhuman and extra-human to intimate a macro view of our planet itself as a living system with intelligence, agency, and multiform modes of communicating with us. Tracking unusual animal and human migrations as its traveling protagonists decipher a legend of a beleaguered merchant and a menacing snake goddess, Ghosh's novel is cosmopolitan, ecological, and at times gothic, yet in resisting subordinating uncanny apparitions—whether of nonhuman species or extra-human entities—*entirely* to ecological explanations, advocacy for Indigenous beliefs, or critiques of geopolitics and late capitalism, it resists simple classification as *only* eco-cosmopolitan or ecospectral. While amenable to these important paradigms, it also lets spirit dimensions simply be, and in that way, I believe, portends much fiction to come.

Finally Chapter 5, "Expected on Earth: Distributive Redemption in Zeyn Joukhadar's *The Thirty Names of Night* and Tanya Tagaq's *Split Tooth*" acknowledges the way many of the novels I analyze, with the exception of *Call Me Zebra,* reach out to Indigenous cultures, whether historical, spiritual, or botanical, yet hedge when it comes to directly representing them. Alexis's novel, in particular, might be interpreted along two lines. On the one hand, it bespeaks a desire, one Ghosh describes in relation to the Banda Island community of Lonthor in *The Nutmeg's Curse*, to syncretically engage spirit belief and feel almost indigenized by the land itself. On the other, it conforms, albeit somewhat parodically, to a pattern Indigenous Canadian writer Joshua Whitehead calls the "Indigiqueer idyll." Considering the dual pressures much (but not all) contemporary literary fiction faces, as in a time many call the Anthropocene, it's asked to imagine alternative worlds, yet in a time that's also filled with postcolonial reckoning, it might feel unable to draw heavily on some of the planet's richest traditions for doing so, I turn to Indigenous scholar Kyle Whyte. Claiming that the apocalyptic conditions imagined in relation to the Anthropocene have already been endured by many Indigenous peoples, Whyte also argues that the counterfactual narrative conventions associated with genres, such as science fiction, that lie outside strictly literary fiction are already customary in Indigenous storytelling. Whyte challenges us to see ourselves as not alone in our era, but rather as moving through an ever-curving time he calls "spiraling time." Spiraling time allows us to think of ourselves as always in the midst of a gathering of ancestors and descendants and to engage both groups in dialogue as we weigh ethical questions. I bring Whyte's words into conversation, not only with Benjamin's thoughts on the expectations of past generations, but also with two literary works that might exemplify this spiraling time and temporally distributed sense of community and redemption: Zeyn Joukhadar's *The Thirty Names of Night* and Tanya Tagaq's *Split Tooth*. While the first tracks a Syrian immigrant community in America, an erased queer family history, a rare ibis, the vanished visual artworks portraying it, and a contemporary narrative of trans becoming, the second mixes pictures, poems, legends, and coming-of-age memories with a strong awareness of Nunavut's history of anti-Indigenous violence and intergenerationally passed-down trauma. They both bring together multiple media as well as the nonhuman and the extra-human to conceive of protagonists as held in an energetic net, a form of contact that extends across species, generations, and the bounds of death.

Part One

Ripples

1

Spirited Creatures: The Weretigers and their Worlds in Yangsze Choo's *The Night Tiger*

1. The Span of Spirits

Spirits span a spectrum in contemporary world literature from the uncannily stateless to the intensely autocthonous. This spectrum's ends can be marked with two intertextual pairs as poles: first, Hannah Arendt's descriptions of spiritually inclined liminal political subjects and Azareen Van der Vliet Oloomi's 2018 novel *Call Me Zebra*, and second, Pheng Cheah's animal spirit amenable concept of "worlding literature," which he outlines with reference to Eka Kurniawan's novella *Man Tiger* (2004, English translation 2015). Between these provisional poles, each of which I will describe briefly below, lies a richly ambiguous and ever more popular territory, one peopled with resilient extra-human entities of unclear status and provenance. This is the realm of Yangsze Choo's 2019 anglophone novel *The Night Tiger*. Its world is one of particularly pronounced and pervasive uncertainty, a quality that is best perceived comparatively. Whereas other recent novels that engage with both animality and spirit realms may seem to fit the theoretical models suggested by Arendt or Cheah very well, *The Night Tiger* is compellingly elusive. Neither radically worldless nor worlded, it calls for a theory that is at once more expansive and more flexible.

If, as Hannah Arendt wrote in 1943, "Refugees driven from country to country represent the vanguard of their peoples" (274), the refugee figure's significance for novels concerned with cosmopolitanism is unsurprising. Yet in this satiric essay, "We Refugees," Arendt also suggested an even more cosmic inclination for refugee consciousness. There she outlines the terms of an almost natural alliance between the refugee and the realm of spirituality. In doing so, she zeroes in on the Second World War Jewish refugee's peculiar attitude toward time. In a world of wide-ranging camps where hell is no longer restricted to theology and fable, it becomes impossible to speak of one's past, even amongst one's peers, without seeming to imply ingratitude for the present, for one's new home. Instead, along with compulsory forgetting, a compulsory orientation to the future takes hold. But the refugee needs more assurance than usual in grasping this future and so turns to the occult:

> After so much bad luck we want a course as sure as a gun. Therefore, we leave the earth with all its uncertainties behind and we cast our eyes up to the sky. The stars will tell us—rather than the newspapers—when Hitler will be defeated and when we shall become American citizens.
>
> 265

Believing more in personal fate than in one's psyche, Arendt and these refugees look also to "the lines of our hand or the signs of our handwriting" rather than to psychoanalysis, which no longer entertains even the "bored ladies and gentlemen of high society." Equally demystified for such elites are ghost stories, since "it is real experience that makes their flesh creep." For both refugees and high society, "There is no longer any need of bewitching the past; it is spellbound enough in reality. Thus, in spite of our outspoken optimism, we use all sorts of magical tricks to conjure up the spirits of the future" (266). More a critical comment than an earnest proposal, Arendt's essay nonetheless links magical thinking with refugee status, or more broadly, with a sense of nation-state dysphoria epitomized by the refugee, in a way that, as we'll see in Chapter 2, Van der Vliet Oloomi's protagonist Zebra would find second nature. If the refugee's flights lend themselves easily to mystical fancies, the cosmopolitan novel's heavy investment in networks of circulation "beyond the nation" makes it a readymade vehicle for speculations beyond the merely material, however satirically cast.[1]

Yet at the other end of a world literature continuum from *Call Me Zebra* and a view of it as typifying Arendt's sense of magical thinking born of geopolitical disillusionment are the tiger spirits of Indonesian novelist Eka Kurniawan. Analyzing their world as conjured in *Man Tiger*, Pheng Cheah decries banal, Eurocentric, and globally reductive views of the world and its art "that cannot hospitably admit cultures that have not been completely disenchanted or purged of magic, worlds in which spirits dwell with human beings." Instead, Cheah offers "*worlding literature*," a mode of reading texts with phenomenological sensitivity for their ways of making and dwelling in worlds, ones that may not conceive of the relations between nonhuman and human in merely Western secularist terms. Among the additional features of *Man Tiger* that draw Cheah's interest is its own lack of interest in "globalization and global circuits of exchange" or "the global character of literary production in its formal dimensions"

("Worlding" 87). It is a text that demands *more* than a global reading. Yet at the same time, its translated appearance in English more than a decade after its original publication (and Cheah refers to the original, noting issues of translation, particularly with its title) brings it into conversation with recent trends in the global anglophone novel and leaves us with the question of how to pursue this conversation without losing sight of worlding.

Van der Vliet Oloomi's Zebra, as I will later argue, can be read as a hyperbolically Arendtian refugee figure and Kurniawan's text, especially when read in the original, might become a perfectly exemplary work for worlding literature, but so many recent works of anglophone fiction leave us with less distinct claims. Between the satirical enchantments of *Call Me Zebra* and the magical yet ordinary worlding of *Man Tiger*, we might place the uncertain strategies of Yangsze Choo's *The Night Tiger*. Described on her website as a "fourth generation Malaysian of Chinese descent," a Harvard graduate, and someone who, "Due to a childhood spent in various countries . . . can eavesdrop (badly) in several languages" (*Yangsze Choo*), Choo is enjoying current popularity. While her first novel *The Ghost Bride* (2013) has been produced as a Netflix miniseries, her second novel, *The Night Tiger*, was chosen as the April 2019 selection for Reese Witherspoon's Hello Sunshine book club. And indeed, as befits the work of an academically inclined multilingual lurker, her book reaches out to many bases. At once a medical mystery, murder mystery, ghost story, and romance, this anglophone fiction of 1930's Malaysia, or British Malaya, presents a world in which spirits dwell with humans, humans are highly concerned with networks of exchange, and the novel itself is far from unknowing when it comes to recent trends and longstanding traditions in the forms of the English language novel. It isn't merely that to understand this novel we have to take spirits seriously, as Cheah exhorts us to in the case of Kurniawan's text. It's also that we should entertain the prospect of such spirits moving along both orthodox and unforeseen lines. We have to see spirit belief itself transmigrating. Now hosted in global anglophone novels that are increasingly merging with the popular forms we call "genre fiction" (mystery, fantasy, romance, young adult stories), diverse spirit beliefs and the troublings of the nonhuman/human boundaries they entail are urging us to further reconceive of the "worldliness" of world literature. Indeed, in such novels it might seem that the more popular, mobile, or worldly in David Damrosch's admittedly controversial sense the text becomes, the more it can engage otherworldliness.[2]

All this might also seem what was meant by "magical realism" in literature at the end of the twentieth century, and indeed it's difficult not to discuss current trends in light of illustrious predecessors. Some readers may hear, for example, echoes of Gabriel García Márquez's *Chronicle of a Death Foretold* in the style and narrative pacing of *Man Tiger*. Cheah, however, has strong words for those who pursue such lines of "global" literary analysis:

> Studying the novel as global literature involves looking at literary precursors and influences and the global circulation of literary genres, forms, and techniques. In this vein, Kurniawan's writing has been dubbed as magical realist and surrealist because of its fantastic elements, which are mixed with supernatural elements from Indonesian storytelling traditions. In the North Atlantic popular press, his work has been likened to that of Gabriel García Márquez, Salman Rushdie, and William Faulkner as well as Mark Twain, Nikolai Gogol, Fyodor Dostoyevsky, and Herman Melville. This reductive approach enables Western critics to remain within their comfort zone and sanctions ignorance about local languages, social life, culture, and context, that is, the knowledge produced by area studies.
>
> "Worlding" 100

Cheah goes on to cite Kurniawan's self-proclaimed Indonesian influences, including literary writers, pulp fiction, and popularized versions of Hindu epics. Yet also intriguing is the remark of Kurniawan's he quotes in which he questions our usual accounts of magical realism: "We rarely identify Kafka as a magical realist writer, despite the fact that there are many fantastical elements in his works. And why are the comic characters from DC and Marvel not called magical realism, even though they have plenty of fantastic elements?" (qtd. in Cheah, "Worlding" 100). Although Kurniawan goes on to say he is influenced by Indonesian horror and martial arts fiction, he leaves open the possibility that he thinks about Kafka and American comics as well. And indeed, just before the lines Cheah quotes from the interview, Kurniawan states,

> I don't mind that people associate my writing with Márquez' or Faulkner's. Undoubtedly, they are my favorite writers. I read their books (not just theirs, but Gogol's, Melville's, and Cervantes'), and I would able [sic] to look around, to have a bit of perception that people I know and history I am familiar with could be narrated in different ways. The society tends to simplify it as "magical realism," just because of how it shows up, both fantastically and realistically.
>
> Kurniawan, "Eka"

Cheah is right to caution about reductionist approaches and Kurniawan rightly points out inconsistencies in the use of the label "magical realist." Yet Kurniawan could also be read as wanting to argue for a capacious intertextuality that is not reducible to a capricious "magical realism." In this light, what is especially distinctive about recent novels as they knowingly take up the fantastic, especially in comparison with many past inheritors of Kafka, is not their way of forcing readers to comply with their narrative conceits and decisions, but rather their myriad ways of leaving readers in states of indecision.

To this end, the mystery is endlessly useful. *Man Tiger* opens with our knowing that our protagonist, the mild young Margio, has admitted to killing the town's older womanizer, Anwar Sadat, but we are unable to fathom his reason. Margio himself claims that it is not truly his doing but rather that there is a tiger inside him who is responsible. And we are told that Margio is the latest descendant of a family line whose men are accompanied by tiger spirits. The narrative backtracks through Margio's family and village history, and the whole manner and motive for the murder seem more and more incredible, a complete stretch, until the novel's final lines. These lines, however, work mostly to conjure the affect in the moment right before the killing; we are still left with quandaries concerning the nonhuman and human, ones that are far less easily contained than Margio is in his prison cell. As Cheah states, "the perpetrator's identity is radically undecidable" ("Worlding" 100). If *Man Tiger* is more a "whatdunit" than a whodunit, *The Night Tiger*, also concerned with Southeast Asian tiger spirits, in this case called "weretigers," follows suit. *Man Tiger* is originally entitled *Lelaki Harimau* and *The Night Tiger* translates *harimau jadian* as "weretiger," but an easy equation of these two texts' animating tigers akin to using "wolfman" and "werewolf" synonymously is not possible. The two novels treat their core spirits differently, and the *harimau jadian* is not the only spirit animal in the latter text. What's particularly intriguing about *The Night Tiger* is its crisscrossing trajectory across spirit realms as well as across realms of human and nonhuman animality. Along with entertaining a belief in human possession by animal spirits, the novel explores burial customs requiring the integrity of the human body, mystical name and number significances, and the destinies of human souls—both in this life and after. In other words, the novel gives a wide range of dimensions in which stories that are nonetheless human-centered can play out. While *Man Tiger* is a tightly woven narrative that only appears to digress as it reaches its goal, *The Night Tiger* is a sprawling hybrid unable to settle on a single aim. Amidst a complex colonial setting inhabited also by diverse diasporas, the novel uses its multiple plotlines involving multiple spirits and multiple species to put past conceptions of the human to the test. It is as though formerly accepted dimensions and traditions no longer provide human being with stability and integrity. Colonial and commercial expansion has enabled an intermingling of worlds in which models of the human that once gave it distinctive coherence have become stretched and warped. The ethereal tiger, with its gaze, bulk, paws, and wavering stripes, embodies a vision of this altered universe that seems to look back on us asking if we're prepared to cross over.

2. Trailing Tigers

The Night Tiger opens with a premise that is also a promise: faithful servant boy Ren agrees to retrieve the long-missing finger of his dying master Dr. MacFarlane within the prescribed forty-nine days after his burial and before his soul will be doomed to haunt the earth. While Ren's chapters are narrated in the third person, largely alternating chapters are narrated by the young dance hall girl, Ji Lin, who filches the missing finger from an ill-fated customer. This customer has himself illegally obtained the finger, preserved in a vial and formerly kept for study at a hospital, via a black market that trades in thought-to-be talismanic items. After the press reports this businessman's mysterious and untimely death, Ji Lin struggles to discover the finger's rightful place in order to return it. In a near parallel plot path, Ren follows MacFarlane's deathbed instructions to locate the finger, leading him to eventually meet Ji Lin. While the plot's machinery is set in motion by the need to restore integrity to a dead human body, many other severed fingers are encountered along the way, not all of them belonging to the hospital pathology storeroom that once housed Dr. MacFarlane's lost digit. This seemingly macabre fixation on dismembered human fingers has everything to do, however, with spirits and animals, and especially animal spirits. It is as though nothing exists in a merely material state in this novel. In addition to attaching particular significance to names and the names of numbers in Chinese, the novel's characters dwell in a world of three core potential beliefs: the physical peculiarity or maimed limb as the sign of the were-animal; the talismanic and/or medicinal power of relics from both human and nonhuman animal bodies; and the distinctiveness of the human hand. Amidst these at times contradictory yet at times converging beliefs and the worldviews they entail, the mystery and its mysterious offshoots unfurl.

At the plot's foundation is Dr. MacFarlane's belief that he is inhabited by a tiger spirit and that when overcome, he roams the land committing murders in weretiger form, an allotment of the tiger spirit that contrasts starkly with Kurniawan's. In *Man Tiger*, tiger spirits, often female, act as protective companions to the men who inherit or "marry" them, and they often serve to empower Indonesians against oppressors. As Ma Muah, the village storyteller, summarizes, "many a man in the hamlet had a tigress of his own. Some married one, while others inherited a tigress, passed down through the generations. [Margio's]

Grandpa had one from his father, which before had belonged to his father's father, and so on right on up to their distant ancestors. No one remembered who was the first to marry the tigress" (40). Told that "If a man couldn't control his beast, it could turn so violent that nothing could restrain it once enraged" (41), Margio becomes fascinated with such tigers' legendary powers:

> He had often heard of his grandfather's prowess, and that of elders in other hamlets: how they resisted Dutch efforts to abduct the best young men for forced labor in the Land of Deli. Bullets had no effect on them, nor did the samurai swords of the Japanese, who came later, and if they got angry, their white tigresses came out from their bodies to attack. They expelled the gangs of Darul Islam guerrillas roaming the jungle. Ma Muah said that this was all because of the elders' elemental friendship with the tigresses, who became family through wedlock.
>
> 42

As defenders in ever more localized struggles, the tiger spirits seem to take up a particularly gender-based cause when Margio inherits his grandfather's tigress and it rises up as Margio becomes enraged at the town womanizer's trifling with his much-abused mother. While Cheah prefers, and rightly so, not to read the tigress merely metaphorically, the inward progression of the targets of the tigresses' defensive actions does mirror a traditional trajectory of postcolonial fiction, as struggles for national independence often give way to concern over the turmoil and inequities, not least gender inequities, in the postcolony. In this way, *Man Tiger* might be read as retaining a concern with geopolitics and gender politics, and hence with political allegory. The relation of the tiger spirit, as well as local spirit belief, to the colonizer is much more ambiguous in Choo's text, however.

In many ways *The Night Tiger* reads like a knowing colonial fiction, one almost indulging in its tropes. The eccentric Dr. MacFarlane, for example, is depicted as a well-meaning paternalistic master, one who gives Ren English language and medical instruction, but one who "goes native" to his and others' peril. Fascinated by local animal legends, Dr. MacFarlane goes on investigative expeditions, some of them with his colleague the surgeon William Acton. On one such excursion, the one in which the doctor mysteriously loses his finger, they meet and photograph a young man who, like MacFarlane, is missing the groove above his upper lip. Discussing the photo later with Ren, Dr. MacFarlane explains that upon seeing him, the young man became excited and called him *abang* or older brother. "He said this missing upper lip groove is the sign of a weretiger," reports Dr. MacFarlane. Others in his hamlet supposedly recount witnessing the young man's habit of slowly transforming into a tiger while walking off into the forest to hunt. Days later he would return, revert to human form, and "vomit up the undigested bones, feathers, and hair of everything he had eaten" (141). As Ren recalls uncannily similar recent behavior from Dr. MacFarlane, the doctor adds that a "deformed paw" is the "other sign of the weretiger," elaborating, "Whether it's a front or hind leg, there's always one that's defective. When I lost my finger on that trip, the *pawang* told me to bury it with me so I could be made whole again—a man. I didn't believe it at the time" (142).

But the missing or defective limb is not only a sign associated with the term *harimau jadian* or weretiger. Tracking down his former master's finger, Ren seeks employment in the house of William Acton, MacFarlane's past expedition companion. Seeing a tiger skin spread out on Acton's floor and told of Acton's own tiger fascination, Ren hears that Acton is "keeping it for a friend who told him it was *keramat*," although disbelief is expressed that "a *keramat* tiger could ever be shot." Ren recalls his knowledge of seemingly supernatural *keramat* animals, how "he once saw the tracks of the elephant Gajah Keramat. It was a famous beast, a rogue bull that had ranged from Teluk Intan up to the Thai border. Bullets were magically deflected from Gajah Keramat's hide, and he had the uncanny ability to sense an ambush." Such animals are considered sacred, able "to come and go like a phantom," and, again, they are "always distinguished by some peculiarity, such as a missing tusk or a rare albino color," yet "the most common indicator is a withered or maimed foot" (26). In his early days of employment with MacFarlane, Ren had told him of the famous *keramat* elephant, much to MacFarlane's enchantment. Years later, seeing the tiger skin on Acton's floor, Ren worries, rightly, that it was in pursuit of this supposedly *keramat* tiger and other *harimau jadian* weretigers that MacFarlane lost his finger and encountered the young man whose upper lip and bizarre hunting excursions resembled MacFarlane's own later accounts of himself.

For the other, less captivated, colonizers, such spirit beliefs are profoundly nonsensical. We see a mixture of attitudes in Acton as he writes in a letter home:

> Malaya, with its mix of Malays, Chinese, and Indians, is full of spirits: a looking-glass world governed by unsettling rules. The European werewolf is a man who, when the moon is full, turns his skin inside out and becomes a beast. He then leaves the village and goes into the forest to kill. But for the natives here, the weretiger is not a man, but a beast who, when he chooses, puts on a human skin and comes from the jungle into the village to prey on humans. It's almost exactly the reverse situation, and in some ways, more disturbing.

> *There's a rumor that when we colonials came to this part of the world, the natives considered us beast-men as well, though nobody has said that to my face.*
>
> 56–7

And later, discussing with Ren the story of the weretigers of Korinchi, site of an expedition with MacFarlane, Acton recounts a peddler who was mistakenly captured and then killed in a weretiger trap, all the while not believed when he adamantly proclaimed his humanity. Acton concludes philosophically:

> "The conditions for a man to become a tiger seem to contradict each other. He either has to be a saint or an evildoer. In the case of a saint, the tiger is considered *keramat* and serves as a protective spirit, but evildoers are also reincarnated as tigers as punishment. And let's not forget the *harimau jadian*, who aren't even men, but beasts who wear human skins. They're all contradictory beliefs, and so I'd classify them as folktales."
>
> 78

Malaya is shown to be a place of multiple intermingling Indigenous, imported, and indeterminate traditions that radically upset colonial conceptions of the human, not just by inverting them and giving animal spirits primacy, but also by relativizing them. To the European outsider, there seems to be no single standard for the mingling and migrating of humans and nonhuman animals in both spirit and physical form. Likewise, potential analogies to colonialism proliferate. The colonizer, as alien invader, may be understood in Malayan terms as a rapacious and rogue spirit beast. Or, as in MacFarlane's case, it may be the colonial settler who "goes native" who desires to see himself as such a were-animal. Or yet again, and more in line with Kurniawan's tigresses, the sacred *keramat* animal, deflecting bullets, may represent native or local strength. Choo cleverly puts many instances of ethnographic commentary into the thoughts and words of colonizers who are both drawn to spirit animals and driven to categorize them as well as the belief systems around them. Yet, although we see much of the obsession with spirit animals through colonial eyes, Choo refuses to relinquish these animals' significance for the various other communities of Malaya.

In viewing tiger spirits through colonial eyes and presenting such forms of spirit belief as especially complex and confusing, Choo follows a trend in both Malaysian anglophone fiction and Southeast Asian historical and cultural studies. As Stuart Miller, interviewing her for *Harvard Magazine,* reports, Choo "reached back into her childhood, reading historic traveler's tales about Malaysia by Isabella Bird and R. H. Bruce Lockhart." And likewise, fellow Malaysian Chinese writer Zen Cho states in an interview for Barnes and Noble that not only does she consider her fantasy novel *Sorcerer to the Crown* to be informed by colonial ethnography, but also that she's not alone in making creative use of such sources:

> I told Zedeck Siew, who is a fellow Malaysian writer of the weird, that this is my Skeat book. (Walter William Skeat's ethnographic treatise on Malay folklore, *Malay Magic*, is becoming something of a bible for Malaysian Anglophone speculative fiction writers ...). You could get into the weeds talking about how weird it is that Malaysian writers are drawing on the work of a British colonial administrator to write Malaysian fiction. But that's what it's like being from a former colony.
>
> qtd. in Cunningham

Unsurprisingly, Choo's colonial characters MacFarlane and Acton seem to echo European accounts such as the ones contemporary historian Peter Boomgaard collects and sifts through in his 2001 study *Frontiers of Fear: Tigers and People in the Malay World, 1600–1950*. Just as Acton does, Boomgaard will initially draw on his archive to propose separate tiger categories—the protective village tiger, the selectively poaching tiger, the ancestral spirit tiger, the tiger familiar, the cemetery guarding tiger, etc.—only to then quote colonial voices expressing perplexity or to express perplexity himself as these categories merge. Amid a Southeast Asian survey of accounts of tigers as bearers of ancestral human souls, he, for example, remarks:

> Beliefs regarding "human" tigers in Malaya either were more varied and more complicated or else the European reports regarding these beliefs were more confused than for Java, Bali, and Sumatra. It is certainly possible that these beliefs were, indeed, more varied given the existence of various tribal groups in addition to the settled Malays.
>
> 171

Boomgaard suggests that such accounts became even more confounded as, beyond the late nineteenth century, Europeans moved further inland and confronted the idea that tigers could carry not merely the souls of ancestors but also those of shamans:

> Later on, as the British penetrated into the tribal inland areas, reports came in on shamanic tribal beliefs. Later researchers stressed that Malay beliefs concerning tigers were incredibly confused and complicated. Evans [one explorer], driven to distraction by all these stories, at one point exclaimed: "For all I know all tigers may be thought to be human beings who have assumed an animal shape."
>
> 172

Boomgaard himself, faced with the complexity of Southeast Asia, seems at times in doubt about particular beliefs' provenance and identity. Discussing the Sumatran idea that bad people become tigers after death, he suggests the notion is "A Hindu belief in Muslim guise" (177). Or describing lost souls who might become vicious tigers because their families have not made adequate offerings to help them in their afterlife journeys, he remarks, "This sounds very much like an animistic explanation, not a Hindu one" (178).

In moving at times not just from the coast to the tribal inland, but from Islam to Hinduism, and from Hinduism to animism, Boomgaard's inferences not only underscore Southeast Asia's complexity, but they also follow a logic that, however potentially justified in some cases, still needs to be approached with caution. While Choo describes a nexus of spirit belief, often making use of a colonial lens, she also dwells on Malayan Chinese characters. And Chinese influence, as Margaret Chan points out, can be dangerously misrecognized and mischaracterized in Southeast Asia. As her key example, Chan proposes a link between Javanese and Indonesian divinatory games with basket figures and fifth-century Chinese spirit basket divination rituals, noting the longstanding presence of the Chinese in Southeast Asia. In doing so, she counters past research with its "asymmetrical privileging of Indic influences to the almost total exclusion of the Chinese voice," a biased approach she claims is tied to "early European Sinophobia." And this Sinophobia has been dangerously bolstered by anti-Semitism, since, as she details, "The Europeans of the seventeenth to nineteenth centuries compared the Chinese disparagingly with the Jews, and this analogy contributed to indigene resentment of Chinese communities" (96). Chan cautions her readers that "any attempt to ascribe origins of folkloric figures can at best be speculative" (104). She cites the anthropologists Clifford Geertz as well as Wim M. J. van Binsbergen to argue instead for the significance of "cultural involution," whereby artefacts and rituals can become ever more elaborate over time while still retaining important core features. For Chan, "cultural involution can endow a borrowed item so completely with the recipient symbolism and cosmology that the resultant product cannot be other than uniquely localized" (107). Chan's arguments point to the difficulty and danger in using simple dichotomies, for example, between imported and indigenous or diasporic and local, to categorize many Southeast Asian beliefs and practices. Her conception of cultural involution suggests a world in which it's just as unwise for scholars to call any particular belief or practice one faith in another's guise as it is for colonial settlers faced with startling creatures to say they know for certain who they really are beneath their apparent shapes.

It's perhaps in this spirit that Choo favors the indeterminate, refusing to decide on the question of spirit animals' existence and pursuing a concomitant, and culturally complex, open-ended inquiry into concepts of the human. MacFarlane's core hope that he can redeem his human moral and spiritual integrity by restoring his body to wholeness is paradoxically derived from his expeditions, a belief he is told by a village *pawang* or shaman. Such wholeness is threatened in the novel by the strange circulation of preserved body parts, a traffic that involves many of the Chinese Malayan characters, and here what the colonizers deem superstition and what they deem science both play a role. Indeed, it's often difficult to discern a difference between relic and specimen, fetish and medicine. When, for example, Ren first sees Acton's decorative tiger skin, his thoughts migrate effortlessly across these categories: "Tiger eyes are prized for the hard parts in the center, set in gold rings and thought to be precious charms as are the teeth, whiskers, and claws. A dried and powdered liver is worth twice its weight in gold as medicine. Even the bones are taken to be boiled down into jelly" (26). While Acton might classify these cures as "folk medicine," the reality of his hospital's pathology storeroom is not so different. A hub for illicit body part trafficking, one that might seem to gesture anachronistically toward contemporary organ trading, it is a space where no "specimen" is safe. In a plot sub-strand that explains the manner in which MacFarlane's originally donated digit goes missing, a criminal ring specializing in black market sales of talismanic items sells specimens stolen from the pathology storeroom. In philosophical terms, this commerce leads to a dispersal and circulating of the fragments of the human that science is storing. In other words, the basic separation between the human as a distinctive being and the human as organic life that is necessary for medicine, what Giorgio Agamben has called "the caesura" or moveable border between human and animal or animal and vegetative life, has now become both multiply fractured and blurred.[3] Parts take on more and more alienated types of aura, and human and animal become difficult to distinguish.

At the same time, a Chinese philosophical belief is used to secure the human being as having an identity distinct from nonhuman animals—a doctrine of Confucian virtues underscored by characters' names. Ji Lin tells us early on that her name is a Cantonese version of what would in Mandarin be "Zhi Lian," with "the character *zhi*, or knowledge," as "one of the five Confucian Virtues," along with "benevolence, righteousness, order, and integrity," because the "Chinese are particularly fond of matched sets and the Five Virtues were the sum of qualities that made up a perfect man" (15). This bit of information initiates a puzzle for readers who begin to look for the rest of the set. Three other members are easily filled in. When Ji Lin's mother becomes a widow and a matchmaker finds her a suitable second husband, he comes with a son named Shin, or *xin* when written, the character designating the Confucian Virtue of integrity (16–17). Not surprisingly, Ren's name also denotes a virtue, "the greatest of the five Confucian Virtues. It means human-heartedness: the benevolence that distinguishes man from beast" (40). And Ren, too, was part of a matched set, a twin rescued from a fire with his brother Yi and then sent as toddlers to live in an orphanage. Because the matron there names Ren "for humanity and *Yi* for righteousness" but "stopped at two of the Five Virtues," Ren is left forever wondering, "What about the others: *Li*, which is ritual, *Zhi*, for knowledge, and *Xin*, for integrity?" (23). Although Yi has tragically died before the novel's action, Ren still feels his twin's spirit accompanying him through life and visiting him in dreams. But as though fulfilling an orphan's wish to reunite with lost family, the novel also plots a course along which Ren will rendezvous with Ji Lin and Shin. Thus, four out of five virtues are quickly accounted for with the novel's Chinese characters, and they, all in their own ways wanting to restore the missing finger, are brought into concert. More difficult to bring into coordination is the missing fifth virtue, *Li*.

Although MacFarlane's preserved finger is restored to his gravesite after many travails, the question of Li's identity and the crisis in human virtue implied by the broken-up set require recourse to other realms, and these issues are never truly resolved. The narrative has to move beyond the Chinese characters, the Chinese language, and even the realm of the living in its consideration of the missing fifth virtue. But plot sub-strands involving material mysteries and crimes with human motives as well as agents are also involved. Just as *Man Tiger* does, *The Night Tiger* weaves a mystery around a repeated womanizer. But while Kurniawan's novel focuses on the local figure of Anwar Sadat, Choo's work requires William Acton to fit the part and to prey particularly on various Asian women. The death of the ill-fated businessman in whose pocket Ji Lin had found MacFarlane's missing finger occurs not because he is involved in the illicit traffic in specimens, but because he has accidentally witnessed one of Acton's liaisons. When Acton inherits Ren as a servant from dead colleague MacFarlane, he too is depicted as a benevolent master, acknowledging and encouraging Ren's gifts for medicine. Yet when Acton's supposedly secret improprieties threaten to become public (and this to the English colonial community, not the already knowing Malayan communities), deaths uncannily occur, with some of them looking strangely like the work of man-eating tigers. But far from the animal violence of either tigers or tiger spirits, these murders that are so convenient for the preservation of Acton's reputation are authored by the Englishwoman, Lydia, who wishes to become his fiancée. Because these murders uphold Acton's social standing and eligibility for marriage within his group, they can be seen as tied to ritual, customs, and cultural standards, an oppressive version of order or *Li*. And indeed, as colonials abroad who have had their names at one time or another translated into written Chinese, both William and, it is later revealed, Lydia know their names contain *Li*. Towards the end of the novel, when Ren mentions this to his new master, Acton asks, "Does it make us a good match, then?" The questions of who is the true final virtue and whether the existence of two *Lis* makes for a matched set or rather an eerie overabundance, as though the hypertrophy of English order will never make up for the loss of Confucian righteousness that vanished with Yi, hang in the air. Ren replies to Acton's question that he doesn't know, and we are told, "He's confused. Which of them is the mysterious *Li* then? Or perhaps he's been mistaken and neither of them is" (353). This is, however, Acton's final conversation, as Ren has unintentionally poisoned his tea, bolstering it with "medicine" from Lydia that is in fact lethal and intended for another. Thus, the habitual womanizer meets his end, but not in the grip, despite Lydia's monstrous acts, of an actual tigress spirit.

And much of the novel is double-edged or indecisive in this way. Just as we never see tiger spirits acting definitively in *The Night Tiger*, Ji Lin and Ren have the sense that there is something wrong with the five virtues, as though the traits that represent the human are not operating appropriately. While the bulk of the novel's murders are explained as human crimes, the novel still never fully disenchants or disengages the spirit realm. Both Ren and Ji Lin, for example, are shown to be sensitive to the presence of Ren's departed, but not fully gone, twin Yi. Often in dreams, they see him on a train, near a station, or along a riverbank, and they communicate with him. When Ji Lin discovers that Yi, far from trying to fully cross over and leave these limbo-like zones behind, has in fact been hoping to be reunited with Ren sooner rather than later, she castigates him for this lack of his named virtue, righteousness. Yi cries and speculates, "Maybe we're all cursed. We should have all been born together in the same family, or even as the same person, not separated like this by time and place." And Ji Lin muses to herself in agreement, "The five of us should have made a kind of harmony. After all, weren't the Confucian Virtues supposed to describe a perfect man? A man who abandoned virtue lost his humanity and became no better than a beast." Before the dream fades, Yi makes a final warning, "It's all a problem with the order—the way things are being bent and rearranged. The further each of us strays, the more everything warps," and adds ominously, "And the fifth one is the worst" (235). If readers need more encouragement to link the five exemplary Confucian Virtues with the five fingers of the human hand, Ji Lin and the specimen trafficker make this explicit. Late in the novel as the characters' paths converge, Ji Lin, too, wonders whether William Acton "really was the fifth one of us," and muses, "I imagined the five of us making a pattern. A set that fit together naturally like the fingers on a hand. The further we strayed, the more the balance in our worlds distorted. Less human, more monstrous. Like the claw of a beast" (251).

Here we see the influence of contemporary Confucian scholar Tu Weiming with whom Choo studied at Harvard. An explicitly cosmic and multidimensional thinker, Tu looks to Confucian thought for ethical models of being human in today's global capitalist and ecologically imperiled world. Choo recalls in her Kindle Notes and Highlights on Goodreads' website:

> Many years ago as an undergraduate, I took a class in Confucianism. Little did I know how useful and interesting it would be later! At the time, I had some vague idea of finding out more about this mysterious Confucius, whom everyone seemed to quote without particularly understanding. We were lucky enough to have as our professor Tu Weiming, one of the foremost scholars of neo-Confucianism, and in addition to the main lecture, he personally led a small tutorial conducted in Chinese for those of us who could read Chinese. Sitting in that small tutorial room with Professor Tu and a few other students, a fascinating world view unfolded: one in which your own personal morality (and responsibility for it) reflected outwards and even shaped society, including the balanced relationships between people. I've never forgotten that class, and years later when it came to naming the characters in *The Night Tiger*, I quickly wrote down the five Confucian virtues.

Fittingly, Choo recalls this experience as one in which from the vantage point of a "small tutorial room" a "world view unfolded," since Tu advocates for an understanding of Confucianism that is both holistically integrated and ever expansive. Resisting the "marketization of society" (79) as well as "exclusive dichotomies, such as body/mind, spirit/matter, mental/physical, and flesh/soul," he proposes understanding Confucianism as a humanism unrestricted by secularism. For him, "spirituality is embedded in the lifeworld" (94), and humans have an active world-making role to play. "A human being ... is an observer, appreciator, partner, and co-creator of the evolutionary, indeed the cosmic process," Tu outlines, and, just as human experience in this Confucianism radiates out across multiple dimensions, so, he argues, "Human responsibility must be expanded from the self, family, community, nation, world, nature, and ultimately to the 'great transformation' of the cosmos" (89). For Tu, the "five core values in the Confucian tradition—humanity, righteousness, propriety, wisdom, and trust—are not merely Asian values, but universal values rooted in East Asian theory and practice" (91). In terms that, as we'll see in Chapter 4, converge with Amitav Ghosh's, he advocates for a capacious understanding of an "anthropocosmic" Confucianism, particularly in an era when the human "capacity to destroy our environment has enhanced our awareness that the 'global village' is also a lifeboat for human survival," and he suggests a sense of our "connectedness" can further "a vision of cosmopolitanism" (93–4).

Yet however much the novel's errant five virtues might suggest a world defaulting on cosmic Confucian responsibilities, the handlike vision of them becomes associated also with Malay belief. The hospital orderly (and, as it turns out, linchpin in the specimen trade), Koh Beng, when asked by Ji Lin about finger superstitions, replies:

> "Well, the Malays say that each finger has a personality: the thumb is the mother finger, or *ibu jari*. Then you have the index finger, *jari telunjuk*, which points the way. The third finger, *jari hantu*, is the ghost finger, because it's longer than the others. The fourth one is the ring finger; in some dialects they call it the nameless one. The little finger is the clever one."
>
> 264

Ji Lin seems to link Koh Beng's speech to Yi's warning, reflecting, "The idea of fingers having personalities troubled me, as though they were five little people" (264–5). This reference to Malay belief raises unsettling possibilities related to but also beyond Yi's concern for the five virtues' straying and Ji Lin's vision of this warped pattern as a monstrously clawlike human hand. One might wonder whether Koh Beng's speech suggests that a Confucian conceptual mechanism for distinguishing the human from the nonhuman is faltering, not only amidst hyper-materialism and predatory market forces, but also against the cultural complexity of Malaya, as forms of anthropocentrism or anthropological exceptionalism, however cosmic, mingle with forms of animism. Indeed, the idea of individually animated digits is presented as distinctly disturbing. And the circulation of specimens that take on talismanic life and then come to fateful ends of their own underscores this. It seems fitting, then, that in Koh Beng's inventory, the fourth and fifth are unnamed and in the novel's Confucian roundup, the fifth is split. Taxonomy fails on both hands.

Yet this Confucian mechanism already shifts in its numbers, with significant consequences for its anthropomorphic interpretations. In an oft-quoted passage, Mencius states, "Slight is the difference between man and the brutes. The common man loses this distinguishing feature, while the gentleman retains it"

(IV.B.19, 131). He famously attributes man's distinctive potential for goodness to four qualities, the "hearts" or "germs," rather than the later five virtues, noting that whoever lacks even one of them is "not human": "The heart of compassion is the germ of benevolence; the heart of shame, of dutifulness; the heart of courtesy and modesty, of observance of the rites; the heart of right and wrong, of wisdom. Man has these four germs just as he has four limbs" (II.A.6, 83). Intriguingly, the movement from four to five allows for a movement in Choo's novel from limbs to hands, and this shifting emphasis allows also for a consideration of a modern globalized world's gothic orientalist reference points. Describing Hollywood's Fu Manchu and his monkeylike affinities, Mel Y. Chen notes a line of thinkers—Steve Baker, Jacques Derrida, and Martin Heidegger—who have meditated on the question of whether the human hand uniquely exhibits the ability to grasp, and this with creative intellectual as well as manual consequences. A dvd cover displaying Fu Manchu holding a monkey, displaying its paws over his own hands, inspires Chen to muse, "The paws suggest that all that Fu Manchu grasps is animalistic in nature, or that animality itself drives his will to knowledge and to creativity," and further that his transgressive "interior animality" renders him "porous along many axes of difference" (120). If Tu and Choo hold out hope for a Neo-Confucian anthropocosmic human, the orientalist Fu Manchu reveals an early twentieth-century brutish counterpart, a multiply warped gothic double. Countering such specifically Sinophobic villainizing, however, Choo distributes guilt and this sense of humanist panic across multiple characters and purposely plays up the text's colonial elements.

The Night Tiger knows how to conjure a sense of horror, particularly colonial horror, but also how to make fun of itself for doing so. Like a lucid dream, it is highly self-aware. In a bizarre twist in an already elaborate plot, Ren at one point gets mistaken for a tiger in the night and shot, requiring him to lose a finger and stay in the hospital. Attended to not only by Acton, but also by Lydia who volunteers there, Ren finds himself confronted with her trolley of reading material. When she at first gives him an alphabet book, Acton objects, knowing Ren's more advanced reading abilities. In a flamboyant moment of intertextuality, we're told, "She hands over a book with a girl's name, Jane Eye or something like that. *Who's Jane and what's wrong with her eye?* Ren thinks. There's another one, a slim volume that slips out. *Heart of Darkness*. But Lydia seizes it swiftly, 'Oh no, dear. Not that one'" (257). Again, as with the decorative tiger skin, Ren's thoughts immediately turn to medical concerns and turn a body into parts. The frequent go-to novel for discussions of colonialism and English literature, *Heart of*

Darkness emerges here as a parapraxis, an unfortunate slip that must immediately, if also noticeably, be censored. Not only does Choo's novel make a playful show of covering its literary tracks, but it also makes a shout-out to its predecessor, her first novel *The Ghost Bride*. For readers of that novel, Acton's older servant Ah Long will readily recall the ghost-seeing servant Old Wong, and Choo craftily makes this link explicit. When Ren wakes from a dream of Yi and discusses ghosts with Ah Long, the older servant claims that his uncle was able to see them, explaining and summing up Choo's first novel in doing so: "He was a cook in a household in Malacca. A lot of peculiar things happened in that house, he said. They had a beautiful daughter who was supposed to marry a dead man." And he clinches the connection, stating, "They wanted her to become a ghost bride" (181). We could see such games with intertextuality and metatextuality as Pascale Casanova does, features akin to magical realist motifs, stock devices in fiction that circulates well in a world literature market.[4] But these moments also seem part of *this* novel's distinctive character, its wish to disaggregate its constituent parts, reflecting on them, and gesturing toward a further dimension that would reconfigure and host them.

Even granting the novel its due as popular fiction and a degree of license as quasi-genre fiction, it's difficult to contain within one type of generic contract. While Lydia is responsible for many of the deaths of those who would threaten William Acton's reputation and Koh Beng for the deaths of those who might bring his specimen dealings to light, Dr. MacFarlane's nighttime expeditions are never clarified. Was he delusional or actually possessed as he went off roaming? Likewise, the after death communications from Yi to Ren and Ji Lin are never demystified, but they are also contained within dreams. For Ren, his extrasensory intuitions from Yi render him what many would call posthuman, that is, both animallike and technicized, since these intuitions are frequently described as giving Ren a cat sense and as coming to him like radio signals (94–5). While these were stronger when both twins were alive and Ren was said to have "often felt this sixth sense" (94), later they come and go, existing in a more tenuous way after Yi's death. Thus, the novel insists on the possibility of another dimension, a vantage point from which to see the warp of a pattern that was meant to hold, but it keeps this dimension at a remove.

If it's the dream state that allows access to this part of the pattern that exists beyond waking human life, it's fitting that Ren's strongest dream vision occurs after his shooting, when he had followed his cat sense to retrieve MacFarlane's finger and was mistaken for a tiger. As he sleeps feverishly in the hospital, his dream unfolds:

> Ren closes his eyes. Behind them, another landscape unfurls, bright and burning like a fever dream. And there it is, the tiger that he's feared for so long. It stands before him, unbelievably large. Lean muscular bulk tapering into a twitching tail. This isn't the moth-eaten, forlorn tiger skin that's stretched out on the floor of William's study, or the wraithlike white creature Ren has imagined, wandering in the jungle with Dr. MacFarlane's face. It's simply a huge bright beast. An animal that he cannot comprehend. Surprisingly, Ren feels no fear, just an overwhelming sense of relief. *So that's what you are*, he thinks, though it seems undignified to address it.
>
> 237–8

When the tiger snarls and turns, Ren sees the railway station in the distance and wants to follow, to explore this realm. The finally revealed spirit tiger is clearly linked to the afterlife, a realm that's distant but far from sealed away by a secure barrier between life and death.

By contrast the tigress that comes to Margio is intimate and even domestic, making Margio's usual world otherworldly:

> The tigress had come to him, lying beside him on the surau's warm rug, while the universe outside froze. As his grandfather had said, the tigress was white as a swan or a cloud or cotton wool. How unbelievably happy he was, for the tigress was more than anything he ever owned. He thought about how she would hunt with him, helping to corral the wild pigs that ruined the rice fields, and, if he ever got slack when one or two boars charged, she would protect him from the worst. It had never occurred to Margio that the tigress would turn up on such a damn cold morning, surrendering herself to him like a girl. Look how the tigress lay down, still licking the tips of her paws, tongue flickering. For a moment she seemed like a giant domestic cat, grandly aristocratic and huge. Margio looked deep into her face, so lovely to him, and the boy fell profoundly in love.
>
> 43

In one way, Choo's and Kurniawan's tigers are opposed: one animating the spirit of death and beckoning from this other side, the other crossing over into life and becoming a vital companion. But noting this opposition tempts us with a further question: is there a sense of worlding that would encompass them both?

Foreworlds

While Margio could not have predicted the cold morning or feminine demeanor of the tigress, he recognizes her instantly because she matches his grandfather's description. Likewise, Ren's tiger in no way recalls Acton's trophy skin or

MacFarlane's tortured face, the possessing colonizer or his possessed counterpart. But Ren instantly knows this "huge bright," if incomprehensible, "beast." The visions, really visits, are epiphanic because they are charged with foreknowing, as though a dormant force has been activated. The tigers are spirits of the future that come to fulfill a promise, provide a reunion. A spirit force that can take tiger form is undeniably part of Margio's and Ren's world; they recognize immediately these tigers they have dwelled on for so long. But they also embody worlds one can't have, fully or presently, as Margio's imprisonment and Ren's continued life show. If they overwrite and reconfigure a real, contorting it from a vantage point that still can't be brought into easy harmony with existing conditions, is it merely reductionist to call them surreal? They manifest a dimension that, while lurking somewhere, also appears as an unusual addition. Far from grounds for complacent dismissal, the name "surrealism," as we'll see in the next chapter, might enable us to contemplate art that manifests multiple dimensions in relation to multiple disciplines.

Because these tigers, while dwelt with, are not easily accommodated, they also recall the restless human hand, whose fingers are either too autonomous to be coordinated or so thoroughly rogue as to make the whole clawlike. And, as though referring to extra dimensions, this unstable quality is attributed to "the missing fifth." About the effects of expansion that the missing fifth represents, the words of Yi's warning and Ji Lin's interpretation are telling: "It's all a problem with the order," says Yi, "the way things are being bent and rearranged. The further each of us strays, the more everything warps" (235), and Ji Lin decides, "The further we strayed, the more the balance in our worlds distorted" (251). This is worlding that is admittedly fantastical, but in being fantastical, quite self-aware. And yet not entirely uniform, since what for Yi is an *order* of things is for Ji Lin a balance in *worlds*. In Kurniawan's and Choo's fictions, it isn't just that we're getting a world *as such* à la Heidegger, whose philosophy, as we'll see in Chapter 2, crucially informs Cheah's, and respectfully watching its lived making. It's that we're getting worlds. But at the same time, when the tigers, both foreseen and surprising, finally visit, they force a question, not just of plurality, but of primacy. The tiger makes its witnesses reconsider and expand their habitual number of lived dimensions. Both Margio and Ren think of the beast as "huge" and somehow more than what has come before. But the tiger also acts as a singularly supreme agent in manifesting this vision.

And this, as we'll see with *Call Me Zebra*, is a paradox of surrealism, specifically its recently retrieved offshoot Dimensionism. As curator Vanja V. Malloy explains, Dimensionism sought art that could "Imagine a place in which time is not constant, cosmic space is warped (or non-Euclidean), and it's infinitely expanding" (1). In eschewing a strict Euclidean separation of space and time, this Einsteinian art invoked relativity and a fourth dimension of spacetime. We can perceive the reverberations of this shake-up in Choo's novel of this same period, the 1930s. It's as if the text asks what in an era of infinitely expanding, warping space and a newly conceived fourth dimension can hold together a Confucian definition of man. In appearing to respond from the other side, Choo's dream tiger is as unsettling as Jorge Luis Borges's "dreamtigers." Borges reports that while in childhood he worshipped "that striped, Asiatic, royal tiger," when he tried to conjure it years later in lucid dreams, it brought only frustration: "Oh, incompetence! Never can my dreams engender the wild beast I long for" ("Dreamtigers" 24). As in his poem "The Other Tiger," every imagined tiger, dreamt or poeticized, necessitates a further, undomesticated one, "The other tiger, that which is not in verse" (71). Singular and additive, the pursued other tiger recalls Dimensionism's core imperative, its call for all art forms, all artistic media, to invoke an extra medium and thus a further dimension. Encapsulating in a formula a paradox of primacy and plurality, singularity and progressive increase, it sums up and represents the number of an art form's existing dimensions as N and then calls for whatever further dimension can ensue as $+1$: All art forms should conform to a principle of $N+1$. But both Borges and Dimensionism leave open a question, one that Kurniawan's and Choo's tigers impose and on which *Call Me Zebra* will further expand, the question of how $N+1$ is lived by characters whose worlds' dimensions have never been fully settled, colonially or cosmically. It's as though the tigers mark worlds with extra dimensions, but dimensions without "N."

2

Creaturely Dimensionism: Unbearable Worlds in Azareen Van der Vliet Oloomi's *Call Me Zebra*

1 New Dimensionisms

Surreal Returns

Two artistic events occurred in 2018 that made significant returns to surrealism: Vanja V. Malloy's organization of the exhibition and catalogue *Dimensionism: Modern Art in the Age of Einstein* and Azareen Van der Vliet Oloomi's publication of her second novel *Call Me Zebra*. Intrigued in 2010 by a brief mention of Dimensionism in Linda Dalrymple Henderson's *The Fourth Dimension and Non-Euclidean Geometry in Modern Art,* curator Malloy reports spending eight years researching its founder, the Hungarian poet Charles Sirató, and his 1936 Dimensionist Manifesto ("Introduction" 1). An art movement that had quickly gained momentum, with manifesto signatures from such figures as Hans Arp, Alex Calder, Robert Delaunay, Sonia Delaunay-Terk, Marcel Duchamp, Wassily Kandinsky, Joan Miró, Francis Picabia, and Sophie Taeuber-Arp, Dimensionism lost momentum and its full moment in history equally quickly, as Oliver A. I. Botar explains, due to Sirató's health problems, the onset of the Second World War, and Hungary's subsequent political turmoil (44–5). Yet this lost art movement is notable, not only for its manifesto's powerful signatories, but for its foresightful engagement with science, particularly quantum physics. Botar suggests that while Dimensionism's reliance on Sirató to explain its scientific basis may have been the movement's weakness, still, its core document, the first manifesto, has likely had an oblique afterlife, "a powerful, though indirect effect on the art world," that we can see in postwar art that plays with dimensions (46–7). While surrealism's complex understandings of the relation of art to politics, dream worlds to waking ones, have never ceased to spark debate, the explicit artistic engagement with science from its offshoot movement Dimensionism provides a timely new avenue of exploration.

This recovery of an artistic appeal to dimensions is especially timely for world literature. Scholars of this capacious, yet contested field can take little for granted, as they debate not only the purview but the very meaning of the term "world literature," questioning whether there's intractable bias in definitions of the world; whether we ought to think rather in terms of multiple worlds; and whether concomitant with this plurality, we should attend to the ways various artistic practices are not merely representations of the world but forms of world-making. Recently, Haun Saussy and Ryan Johnson have each proposed multidimensional models of world literature as ways to move beyond potential stalemates and perceived insufficiencies in discussions based on the term "world." The retrieval of Dimensionism, with its radical interdisciplinarity—both across art movements and intellectual fields of its day—is suggestive. Not only is this intellectual movement of historical interest as we look back on surrealism's era, but aspects of its core principles may have become especially applicable now, particularly to recent global anglophone novels. If the expansion of literary studies to a supposedly world scale, a move often imagined in simple spatial terms, inspires criticism of lingering Eurocentrism, conceiving of artistic expansion as dimensional presents an intriguing alternative vision, one that Van der Vliet Oloomi addresses with gusto. Both recent revisions of world literature theory and Van der Vliet Oloomi's Zebra take issue with oppressive conquests of space, ideological forces that flatten worlds either conceptually or literally. But Zebra's narrative testifies to the ways the experience of violent flattening is endured and the multifarious extra-dimensional perceptions that can ensue. As she unfolds her story, it becomes as difficult to summarize as the movement from point A to B or vice versa—a journey to the west or homecoming of a daughter of the east—as it is to contain within one aesthetic mode or genre. Far from giving us the world-making of a single settled or traversed world, it evokes a complex ontology of myriad possible realms reflecting and distorting each other. Not only this, but it gives us a heroine brought comically low by her attempts to manifest this ontology in every moment of her lived experience. In rendering multidimensionality both bathetic and creaturely, *Call Me Zebra* reveals its dimensionism to be not simply avant-garde but part of a planetary politics fit for our time.

Manifesting New Dimensions

A work that won the 2019 Pen/Faulkner award for fiction, *Call Me Zebra* was described in telling terms by the prize panel. Upon bestowing the award, judges Percival Everett, Ernesto Quiñonez, and Joy Williams proclaimed:

> [O]nce in a while a singular, adventurous, and intellectually humorous voice appears that takes us on an inescapable journey. Azareen Van der Vliet Oloomi's *Call Me Zebra* is a library within a library, a Borges-esque labyrinth of references from all cultures and all walks of life. In today's visual Netflix world, Ms. Van der Vliet Oloomi's novel performs at the highest of levels in accomplishing only what the written novel can show us.
>
> "Announcing"

Singular, hyper-literary, omni-cultural, and needing to unfold in a realm beyond Netflix, *Call Me Zebra* in this paean becomes an ur-novel for a new era, particularly one habituated to streaming visual content. The story of an intellectual Iranian family who must flee after the 1979 revolution and whose sole surviving daughter, influenced by surrealism, decides to write a manifesto, *Call Me Zebra* is as zestful and forward-looking as its praise suggests. But it also casts its eyes back to the 1930s, to the surrealism of the Spanish Civil War era, and has points in common with the story of Charles Sirató. Both Zebra, as she decides to be known, and Sirató are thwarted by their home nations' politics as well as their ongoing concerns for their own well-being, yet they remain vastly ambitious, and their artistic visions stand out for their cosmic proportions. While Sirató expounded a dimensionally expansionist program for all art, Zebra puts stock in a transhistorical "Matrix of Literature." In its very grandiosity, however, *Call Me Zebra* is also self-consciously farcical, poking fun at every turn at its heroine's hyperbole, an inflationary rhetoric that threatens to alienate any potential companion. It's as though the novel takes Dimensionism's expansionist imperative to always unfold an art form in a further dimension, expressed in the formula $N+1$, and further contorts it, turning it, if not on its head, on its side. As $N+1$ is continually subjected to what Mikhail Bakhtin has called a "sideways glance," we are left with key questions. What precisely is this realm of skewed dimensionism, how is it lived, and what community if any might be possible within it? What new models does *Call Me Zebra* suggest for world literature and what forms for the global anglophone novel as it continually revels in warping its unfolding dimensions, staging the persistent question of what we might call $Z+1$?

In asking how Van der Vliet Oloomi's text illuminates ways to reclaim forms of dimensionism (the small "d" referring here to potential variants beyond Sirató's original vision), ones that are useful for contemporary theories of world literature, it's helpful to revisit the original Dimensionism's terms alongside current calls to conceive of world literature as multidimensional. As we will see, although the Dimensionist Manifesto, appearing in subsequent editions in Hungarian as well as originally in French, is rhetorically exorbitant right from the start, its intentions are broadly inclusive, even cosmically so, and its vision is strangely prescient.

In its first 1936 version published in French in Paris, the manifesto identifies Dimensionism as an unconscious impulse in European art as well as in the European spirit, one that has now erupted into conscious practice due to new theories of relativity:

> Dimensionism is a general movement of the arts. Its unconscious origins reaching back to Cubism and Futurism, it has been continuously elaborated and developed since by all peoples of Western civilization.
>
> Today the essence and theory of this great movement bursts with absolute self-evidence.
>
> Equally at the origin of Dimensionism are the European spirit's new conceptions of space-time (promulgated most particularly by Einstein's theories) and the recent technical givens of our age.
>
> Sirató 170

While this appeal to "Western civilization" and the "European spirit" read awkwardly in our time, especially in relation to global fiction, the appeals to a "general movement of the arts" and a reconceptualization of spacetime are meant to evoke a broad-based phenomenon, almost cataclysmically so:

> We must accept—contrary to the classical conception—that Space and Time are no longer separate categories, but rather that they are related dimensions in the sense of the non-Euclidean conception, and thus all the old limits and boundaries of the arts d i s a p p e a r [sic].
>
> This new ideology has elicited a veritable earthquake and subsequent landslide in the conventional artistic system. We designate the totality of relevant artistic phenomena by the term "DIMENSIONISM."/Tendency or principle of Dimensionism. Its formula: "N+1."
>
> 170

Sirató goes on to explain this formula, in all capitals, as the arts collectively becoming "ANIMATED BY A NEW CONCEPTION OF THE WORLD" and individually as each art form having "ABSORBED A NEW DIMENSION." In practical terms, this means literature's "leaving the line and entering into the plane," as in graphic poems; painting's "quitting the plane and entering space," as in spatial and mixed-material constructions; and sculpture's "stepping out of closed immobile, dead forms" in order to become open, mobile, kinetic, and thus to engage four-dimensional spacetime. This final artistic transformation is followed by the proclamation: "And after this a completely new art form will develop: Cosmic Art," following "The Vaporization of Sculpture," after which, "Instead of looking at objects of art, the person becomes the center and subject of creation," seemingly dissolving boundaries between creators, materials, and receivers (170–1).

While the manifesto's mode is undeniably grandiose, speaking for a formerly unconscious spirit and reclaiming various arts and art movements on its own terms, still, there are striking parallels with intellectual impulses today. The rhetoric used to expand definitions of the human and elicit recognition of the Anthropocene, for example, is surprisingly similar. We might recall Dipesh Chakrabarty's terms in his much discussed essay "The Climate of History: Four Theses." Here he, too, speaks of necessary disciplinary and dimensional expansion as he declares: "The crisis of climate change calls on academics to rise above their disciplinary prejudices, for it is a crisis of many dimensions" (215). He applies this logic to our very conception of ourselves, our history, and our forms of agency:

> To call human beings geological agents is to scale up our imagination of the human. Humans are biological agents, both collectively and as individuals. They have always been so. There was no point in human history when humans were not biological agents. But we can become geological agents only historically and collectively, that is, when we have reached numbers and invented technologies that are on a scale large enough to have an impact on the planet itself.
>
> 206–7

In an era of widely acknowledged human-made climate change, we expand the dimensions of human agency, seeing ourselves collectively as a geological force, a supposedly radical scaling up from mere biological terms. Biology effectively becomes N and geology +1 for the collective human imagination. As with Sirató's hailing of advances in theoretical physics, this perilous advance in human agency is made possible by scientific and technological innovation. Not only is this recognition of planetary geological impact a further dimension that our conceptions of the human must move into, but it is as unsettling as a fourth dimension of spacetime is to the space and time of a Euclidean vision. Indeed, this awareness calls for a collapsing of two temporalities: "Geological time and the chronology of human histories [have] remained unrelated. This distance between the two calendars, as we have seen, is what climate scientists now claim has collapsed" (208). Both thinkers, moreover, speak cataclysmically, moving quickly from the Western to the cosmic or universal. Sirató may use a geological metaphor for a revolution in the imagination, hailing "a veritable earthquake and subsequent landslide," but Chakrabarty makes a complementary move, seeing a radical conceptual unsettling reflected in our very geological status. For Chakrabarty, viewing human history not simply in past human-centered and nature-opposed terms but also as the story of our increasingly planetary geological impact means "A fundamental assumption of Western (and now universal) political thought has come undone in this crisis" (207). Whether it is relativity or looming climate catastrophe that causes this expanded view of the human and disappearance of disciplinary boundaries, both the call for Dimensionist art and Anthropocene-aware history speak in similarly vast, epochal terms, perceiving a current shakeup at our very foundations.

Beyond the revolutionary phrasing of the manifesto and its recent analogues, also of contemporary interest is its call for an artwork's beholder to become the "center and subject of creation." Along with dimensional expansion and boundary dissolution, there is an important recognition of world-making here, one that allows us to bring Dimensionism into closer conversation with models of world literature. As we saw in Chapter 1, Pheng Cheah proposes the term "worlding literature" as a preferable alternative to "world literature," which comes tainted with a Eurocentric past and persistently elitist present. "Worlding" is preferable for Cheah because it draws attention to an active process of world constitution rather than simply "taking the world for granted" ("Worlding" 87). In *What Is a World? On Postcolonial Literature as World Literature*, Cheah argues that what is key for unlocking the perception of world literature as world making is an element also taken for granted in typical discussions of the world: time. Getting to the foundation of the idea of world, he maintains, "*World*, however, is originally a temporal category. Before the world can appear as an object, it must first *be*. A world only is and we are only worldly beings if there is already time" (2). While the forces of colonial domination and capitalist globalization have taken Europe as temporally central, as in the notorious Greenwich Mean Time, this merely betrays that their "mapping of the world by temporal calculations is premised on a conceptualization of the world as a spatial category, an object of the greatest possible extension that can be divided into zones of quantitatively measurable time" (2). Just as Dimensionism mobilizes awareness of spacetime to undo the constraints of a Euclidian space/time division, Cheah works against oppressive spatializations of time in our concepts of the world. Restoring the crucial role of time at the very foundation of the idea of world is the almost geological and dimensional shakeup needed to reveal a more radical sense of worldliness than globalization will allow.

An important further effect of returning attention to time's foundational role in the concept of world is an opening up of world literature to spirit. Cheah reclaims the word "normative" to describe visions of world history and world literature that seek to move towards ever more ethical political community, or cosmopolitanism. Both the colonialist mapping of the world in strict center–periphery spatial relations and global capitalist fixations on core–periphery commercial circulation efface this potential. The first offers one-way world-making forever frozen in spatial terms and the second is caught in a contradiction that Cheah cites Marx for illuminating:

> As Marx pointed out, the globalization of capital creates the material conditions for a community of the greatest possible extension. However, the capitalist world-system also radically undermines the achievement of a human community of global reach, that is, a genuine unity of the world. For Marx, the world is a normative category that exceeds the global market.
>
> 2

For Cheah, if we wish to approach this genuine human community of the world, we need to struggle against reductionist spatial and temporal mappings, a struggle he outlines as one of "world" against "globe." Returning to world literature's founding figure, Goethe, Cheah sees him as advocating for this literature's role as "the diverse manifestations and expressions of an ideal universal humanity" and for the exchange of such literature as one that, in manifesting this ideal, also "generates a spiritual world that transcends spatial networks" (6). While Cheah may not wish to return to Goethe's precise formulations or another century's models of spiritualism, still, far from eschewing normativity in world literature, he proposes a new version of it. His conception of worlding literature as restoring time to space, dissolving strict boundaries between world and making, and moving towards more ethical forms of human political community, ones that require us to conceive of the world in terms not reducible to the material circulations of global capitalism, is thus highly compatible with Dimensionism's artistic imperatives. Nonetheless, Cheah does not explicitly theorize dimensions and he differentiates himself from current world literature thinkers who do in one crucial respect: he objects to thinking of world literature texts as creating "possible worlds."

Haun Saussy and Ryan Johnson, by contrast, each advocate for viewing world literature in dimensionally enhanced ways, and they do so to extend considerations of literary worlds as possible worlds. Cheah credits Thomas Pavel with initiating this approach that in his gloss "argues that literature creates a world, a totality with its own consistency, by appropriating elements from the referential world." But while Cheah predictably approves of this world-creating quality, he finds its understanding of creativity too constrained: "Although this approach suggests that literature, especially realist literature, has the power of creating a world, the literary world's status is one of virtuality," and thus in this model, "although literature does not just reflect the actual world, its creativity is not a causal power in the actual world" (4). Saussy, however, embraces a possible world model for literature, even seeing power in it for battling many of the same problems with world literature that Cheah cites. In "The Dimensionality of World Literature," he likewise takes issue with spatially reductive concepts of the world, and particularly with their impoverished flatness, "the supposition that literature can be mapped in two dimensions, or that nothing more than a plane surface is required to capture what matters most about literature" (289). Advocating plurality, Saussy asserts, "there is no such thing as a single World Literature, but rather always different local appropriations of the literature of the world, each instance being framed and energized by the particular conditions, possibilities, desires and fears of its place and time" (291). It is this advocacy that leads him to the bolder assertion, "literary experience negates determinate time and space," and as evidence, he catalogues the most fantastic examples:

> Literary worlds are out of this world, or at least often contain a door leading away from it. These imaginary worlds, the domain of the fantastic, are as regular a property of Chinese fiction and drama (think of the *Handan meng*, or any number of fables from the *Zhuangzi*) as of the *Odyssey*, the Jataka tales, Potocki's *Manuscript Found at Zaragoza* or Grimm's fairy stories: the combination of frame story with extraordinary event. These are the wormholes or portals whereby literary discourse marks its contest with ordinary discourse: the transition into another world which seems exactly like the world one gradually becomes aware of having left at the moment when the fish begin to talk, the ants form an empire and the looking-glass dissolves. Any attempt to map this inventory of alternate worlds onto the regular schemes of chronology and geography would end in frustration: there would be too many incompatible realities for the available space and time coordinates.
>
> 292

But far from restricting himself to fantastic possible worlds and merely the virtual, Saussy concludes, "There may be only one physical world, but there are a great many imaginative projections of possible and conceivable worlds; and people spend most of their lives in those latter worlds" (293). Saussy's catalogue of world portals is dimensionally suggestive and his sense of where most of us spend most of our lives suggests that while the physical world may be one for him, our lived worlds are endless alternatives that are not as completely sealed off as Cheah might contend.

In an even more recent and radical appeal to multidimensionality, Ryan Johnson builds on the work of Saussy as well as Eric Hayot and Alexander Beecroft to push possible worlds literary theory toward greater logical accountability and socio-historical awareness. Among possible worlds literary theorists problems of world relations persist in questions of how different possible worlds relate to the totality of world literature, to a single actual world they might inhabit, and to one another. For Johnson, all his examined theorists, while arguing for more pluralism and relativism than strict world-systems core–periphery models afford, still accept the need for "a common ground that allows for mutual intelligibility" and for all of them this is thought of as "shared physical space" (363). Saussy may be a particularly strong critic of flat models of world literature, but for Johnson, his "literary worlds still exist in a single dimension." That is to say, he still uses spatial metaphors to describe cross-literary world understanding between critics and authors. This assumption of shared physical space that Saussy's spatial metaphors betray means that for Johnson, Saussy's "literary worlds may be out of this world, but they are never out of this multiverse" (364). Johnson raises several examples that he believes current theories of literary worlds are insufficient for addressing. If, in one case, some Buddhist logic accepts that something can be neither true nor false or else both true and false, do we not take seriously Buddhism's stated goal of liberating all sentient beings from suffering if we treat this different logical system as merely a possible literary world (362–3)? If, in another example, we wish to compare French Romantic poetry with Tang dynasty Chinese poetry, what will we have to do to argue for a basis of comparison? Or, if Tibetan author Jamyang Norbu reprises the character of Sherlock Holmes in a recent novel, how do we confront the problems posed by a character who was defined by inhabiting one possible world but who then moves into another formed by a new author's very different socio-historical considerations? As Johnson puts it, in one way, we assume Norbu's Holmes is the character we know from Doyle, but we also "understand that Norbu, writing from a postcolonial perspective, has described neither Holmes nor Tibet as would have Doyle" (365). Given our own socio-historical circumstances, we are bound to interact differently with these two not entirely separate literary worlds. While not completely abandoning literary worlds theory to solve such problems, Johnson offers it a multidimensional upgrade as a "refinement rather than a replacement" (366).

Although Johnson's engagement with analytic philosophy, both Western and Asian, is too richly detailed to capture in a brief discussion here, still, his desire for a model that retains recognition of difference while allowing for greater fluidity is notably in keeping with Cheah's guiding principles. Drawing on the historian G. E. R. Lloyd, Johnson argues for a multidimensional model of comparison in which rather than having to demonstrate an ontological basis for comparing two texts, a proven meta-language, we demonstrate their "mutual intelligibility" in the very act of comparing them. Johnson admits this argument's circularity, claiming the ground of comparison is so rough or "primitive" as to be impossible to argue for in other ways. While the appeal is similar, he says, to Saussy's "one physical world," Lloyd would instead term this "reality," and "reality here is not synonymous with nature" (366). Nature is apprehended differently according to different cultural ontologies, and so, following Lloyd, Johnson proposes to speak rather of reality as "the brute physical world, or the world of sense data, that each human being encounters" and thus as multidimensional. And further:

> Between different dimensions of world literature, the boundaries are fuzzy. That is not to say that there are no boundaries. There is an intuitive difference between, say, Romantic French literature and Tang poetry; aside from the obvious linguistic and temporal differences, there are stylistic and thematic differences, not to mention differences in the ontologies that structured Tang China and nineteenth century France. Yet we will always be able to make analogies, as Lloyd tells us, between the two. It is best, then, to think of two literary worlds, not as possible worlds that access (or do not access) one another, but as composed of different domains that have different correspondences with different worlds. Each "dimension" of a literary space is made up of multiple domains: stylistic, formal, historical, ontological.
>
> 367

In some ways a dizzying argumentative appeal to circularly established primitive ground, a brute physical world of sense data, fuzzy boundaries where literary dimensions are concerned, and differently corresponding domains in different worlds, Johnson's multidimensional model is aesthetically intriguing for its desire to retain the multifarious magic of Saussy's catalogue, but with even more flexible borders. Perhaps Johnson is distinctive in objecting especially strongly to a model asserting a strict singular actual world set against a multitude of incommunicable possible ones. Yet despite their individual differences, many in the current wave of world literature theory want to move beyond static scenarios and circulations. In Cheah's case, too, the sealed-off quality of possible literary worlds from an actual world is a crucial problem. And for all three, Cheah, Saussy, and Johnson, appeals to multiplicity and an enactive creative process, whether worlding, wormholing, or comparing are the answers. That this ever-expanding campaign now plays out on dimensional grounds is significant for literary theory, but it's dazzling in the global anglophone novel.

The Global and the Animal

Call Me Zebra both further focuses and expands the core questions at play in literary worlds theory. While critics such as Saussy, Johnson, Hayot, and Beecroft often develop their theories out of considerations of the Asian world, Cheah merges Asia-aware world literature theory, considering, as we saw for example in Chapter 1, Eka Kurniawan in his Indonesian context, with postcolonial concerns and readings of such anglophone authors as Michelle Cliff, Nuruddin Farah, and Amitav Ghosh, a selection that covers the traditional three areas of postcolonial criticism: the Caribbean, Africa, and South Asia. Likewise, Van der Vliet Oloomi writes a strikingly hybrid form of cosmopolitan fiction. As a US-based Iranian diaspora author who then sets *Call Me Zebra* largely in New York, Barcelona, and Girona before heading towards Florence, she might seem well poised to contemplate philosophical conceptions of the world from the vantage point of select world cities. But Zebra's thoughts frequently take sharp postcolonial political turns as well, as she considers exile a form of subalternity and US power a form of neoimperialism. I will interpret *Call Me Zebra* as a global anglophone text, highlighting both its ways of worlding and its critiques of what Amitav Ghosh has called the "anglophone empire."[1] While Cheah mostly eschews the word "global" as he advocates attention to "world" against "globe," I will retain the word "global" for two reasons. First, I prefer to pit "globe" against "globalization," as Cheah himself does when, as we've seen, he glosses Marx and argues, "the capitalist world-system also radically undermines the achievement of a human community of *global* reach, that is, a genuine unity of the world. For Marx, the world is a normative category that exceeds the *global* market" (*What* 2, emphasis mine). Here I understand Cheah as observing a difference between global reach and global market, and it is just this reach and the idea of a community that might span it that I seek to retrieve. Following from this, I propose as a second justification the idea that in multidimensional thought, recourse to imagining a latticed sphere or even a stretched-out plane need not be viewed negatively. These mappings, while admittedly tools of global capitalism and artifacts in colonial history, are also elements of the human spatial imagination, an extension of what Jakob von Uexküll, whose theories will allow us to conceptually enrich Dimensionism, would call our perceptual world or *umwelt*. A mainstay of postcolonial literature—and Ghosh is especially known for this—is a scene in which a character rescripts an atlas or map, interpreting its information from a counter-hegemonic perspective, a moment in which we might say the erstwhile empire maps back. These scenes, such as Ghosh's famous one from *The Shadow Lines* that I discuss in the Introduction, are so effective because in these moments a flat plane is so illustrative. Ghosh even repurposes this recourse to two dimensions to an eco-cosmopolitan end in *The Hungry Tide* when he has dolphin researcher Piya abandon gesturing to her GPS monitor to instead sketch a line drawing for her fisherman guide Fokir to follow. "Just as she had thought, the reduction to two dimensions made all the difference," we're told as they then set their course (116). Using a postcolonial logic, we could argue that it is because of the existence of a historically dominating "anglophone empire" that crucial anglophone texts continue to stake claims in global terms, comparing quantities along flat planes or gridded lines, rather than absolutely shifting ground to argue exclusively in the name of the planetary or worldly. At the same time, however, it may be granting the anglophone empire too much power to give it such full dominion over the second dimension, to see the imagination of an atlas or even a globe's grids as merely a strategic rescripting. Rather than limiting the possibilities of new dimensionisms in global fiction by seeing them as moving only unilaterally, ever upscaling to plus one's, when we read *Call Me Zebra*, we will need to imagine them more dynamically, able to not just expand, but condense to whatever lines and planes are needed. It's worth recalling when we come to contemplate, for example, Zebra's imagined "Matrix of Literature," that a matrix has not only the etymological sense of being a womb, a biological sense as cellular tissue, a geological sense as an element containing embedded objects, but also the mathematical sense of being a rectangular array, with its rows and columns yielding various dimensions.

In addition to voicing postcolonial critiques of US imperialism and thus participating in the contemporary global anglophone novel's specific engagement with world literature, *Call Me Zebra* also speaks in the name of the animal, and this consideration of nonhuman animal worlds also calls for dimensional flexibility. In forcing us to extend our theories of the multiverse beyond the human, the novel's interest in the animal asks us to take up invitations both Saussy and Cheah offer. Significantly, Saussy's description of literature as a portal to a possible world is marked by the presence of the animal, albeit a magical one. He speaks tellingly, as we saw, of "the transition into another world which seems exactly like the world one gradually becomes aware of having left at the moment when the fish begin to talk" (292). Likewise Cheah in revisiting the normative and once spiritualist character of world literature, but updating it to become worlding literature, does so en route to analyzing Eka Kurniawan's novel of Indonesian tiger spirits, *Man Tiger*. For Cheah, such a postcolonial novel calls for particular attention to the nonhuman and to spirits because "the emergence of postcolonial peoples requires the constellation of Euro-American secular modernity with ways of living in the postcolonial South where spirits play an important role and non-human life forms are not merely raw materials to be subjugated by humanity" ("Worlding" 92). The animal becomes a clear impetus for conceiving of other worlds, other forms of world-making, and specifically realms not fully dominated by humans, in short, a ready emblem for multidimensionality beyond the human. Van der Vliet Oloomi's novel may not offer us the premise of speaking fish or a specific Indigenous context, however postcolonial, for spirit belief. But it gives us a heroine who allies herself with the animal and who perceives a spirit realm communicating through animals, all while she nonetheless persists in the world of contemporary geopolitics. It would be easy to type Zebra's narration as "unreliable," and thus to dismiss her animalized self-perception and her somewhat fantastic perception of animals, specifically the bird companion Taüt she inherits midway through the novel and that becomes, she believes, a vessel for a departed loved one's communications. Yet not only would this dismissal leave unanalyzed the novel's creaturely dimensions, but it would also make us miss the opportunity to consider the role of the nonhuman in multidimensionality. In theorizing this distinctively multiplicitous creaturely dimensionality, Uexküll's theories become essential.

In fact, not only does Lloyd's theory of reality, as Johnson cites it, bear an important resemblance to Uexküll's multiverse of animal perceptual worlds, but Uexküll's theory also influences Martin Heidegger's conception of world, Cheah's prototype for worlding. Citing Heidegger, Cheah sees worlding as a radically open ontological condition prior to subjects, objects, and reason, "a stance of sheer being-with other modes of life" that is "the ontological condition of possibility of world literature" and that "enables us to tell stories to each other, to translate languages, and engage in cosmopolitan literary intercourse" ("Worlding" 98). For Cheah, "we are part of the same world," but the word "worlding" is meant to get at an ontologically capacious ur-worldliness, one obscured by banal ideas of world literature and globalization. It's important to note, too, that unlike Lloyd who eschews nature as an underlying ontologically common element, Cheah retains it, albeit in a specifically Heideggerian sense. Worlding is tied to nature for Cheah in a way it is not for Johnson because of Heidegger's commitment to "the Greek idea of *physis* to develop an account of creative, generous nature as the original ground of all beings" ("Worlding" 94). This sense of a shared world and an ontologically radical view of nature as not simply organic phenomena but rather as "the very being of beings" ("Worlding" 95) is what allows Cheah to explore not only postcolonial literature, but postcolonial literature concerned with nonhuman animal spirits within a world literature frame, an investigation he claims "explores another dimension of the worlding force of postcolonial literature" ("Worlding" 97). Heidegger's formulations of world and nature are crucial to Cheah's attempts to conceive of a more robust and inclusive vision of world literature, one that can entail this other dimension. But Heidegger's anthropocentrism, Nazism, and ever more publicized anti-Semitism require Cheah to distance himself, qualifying his version of Heidegger as a "bastardization" ("Worlding" 99). While Heidegger's contemporary, key influence, and the founder of ethology, Uexküll also held anti-Semitic views as well as had early ties to National Socialism, his vision of human and nonhuman perceptual worlds offers an important alternative way to think of worlding, one more compatible with Lloyd's sense of reality and Johnson's of dimensions.

In the recently published English translation of Uexküll's 1934 text *A Foray into the Worlds of Animals and Humans*, we can see an animal-based multiverse beautifully illustrated. Undertaking this foray, Uexküll sets aside the approach of the physiologist for whom "every living thing is an object that is located in his human world" from that of the biologist, who "on the other hand, takes into account that each and every living thing is a subject that lives in its own world, of which it is the center" (45). As he invites his readers on a textual and pictorial tour through these multiple animal worlds that are "unknown" and "invisible" for such physiologists (41), Uexküll gives specific imaginative instructions:

> We begin such a stroll on a sunny day before a flowering meadow in which insects buzz and butterflies flutter, and we make a bubble around each of the animals living in the meadow. The bubble represents each animal's environment and contains all the features accessible to the subject. As soon as we enter such a bubble, the previous surroundings of the subject are completely reconfigured. Many of the qualities of the colorful meadow vanish completely, others lose their coherence with one another, and new connections are created. A new world arises in each bubble.
>
> 43

All animals have worlds that are bubble worlds, circuits in which perception organs take in specific features of the animal's surroundings and the animal is stimulated towards particular effects and actions, thus bringing a world into being for that animal. The bubble world might be seen as one in which the animal, like the Dimensionist art viewer, is both "the center and subject of creation." Such worlds can vary from simple to complex, depending upon the number of perceived stimuli that will elicit effects and actions, but nonetheless, the same principle is at work across the board: "All animal subjects, from the simplest to the most complex, are inserted into their environments to the same degree of perfection" (50). Just as Cheah is drawn to the way that in Heidegger's account we are beings thrown into a world, Uexküll draws attention to the way we are inserted into our specific cycles of perception, stimulation, and action—our bubble worlds. And just as Cheah, following Heidegger, objects to jumping to a conception of the world as a vast spatial container within which there are different subjects and objects, effacing worlding's grounds of possibility or "the very being of beings," Uexküll opposes our simply taking the human bubble for granted as the whole world:

> We comfort ourselves all too easily with the illusion that the relations of another kind of subject to things of its environment play out in the same space and time as the relations that link us to the things of our human environment. This illusion is fed by the belief in the existence of one and only one world, in which all living beings are encased. From this arises the widely held conviction that there must be one and only one space and time for all living beings. Only recently have physicists raised doubts as to the existence of one universe with one space valid for all beings. That there can be no such space comes already from the fact that every human being lives in three spaces [i.e., three dimensions], which interpenetrate and complete but also partly contradict each other.
>
> 54

Writing, as Sirató was, in the 1930s, Uexküll likewise rejects static past conceptions of the world, draws on recent theories in physics (however much he prefers biology), and proposes a dynamic alternative view which turns not only toward the myriad bubbles of living species but also to the instability of dimensions. If we see Uexküll's ethology as having proposed its own dimensionism, one in which animal worlds can subtract as well as add dimensions from an anthropocentric notion of N, then the turn to the animal in current world literature that engages the idea of multidimensionality shouldn't be surprising. The consideration of nonhuman animals and their worlds becomes concomitant with attempts to move toward the most radical, lively, and pluralistic forms of relativity.

Just as Cheah comes to Heidegger with provisos, however, it bears noting that Uexküll himself was not an unproblematic interpreter of perceptual worlds' significance in the human realm. His rejection of one shared spatial world in favor of many bubble worlds within which there might be an uneasy harmony of dimensions would seem compatible with Johnson's account of a rough reality of sense data that will be individually and multidimensionally interpreted. Yet Uexküll himself believed that bubble worlds interlocked according to a divine but unknowable plan of Nature. He closes the *Foray* with the words: "all these different environments are fostered and borne along by the One that is inaccessible to all environments forever. Forever unknowable behind all of the worlds it produces, the subject—Nature—conceals itself" (133). While, as Anne Harrington details, he opposed racist hierarchies and came to contest Nazi science's fixation on race as well as Nazi interference in universities' autonomy, nevertheless, throughout the post-Second World War period, he wrote texts analyzing the state and the German people or *Volk* in disturbingly organic terms (70–1; 56–62). As Harrington quotes his wife observing, when he turned to politics, Uexküll "searched in vain for the 'Plan' that he saw everywhere at work in Nature" (qtd. in Harrington 57). On the one hand, Uexküll saw equal "perfection" in animals' insertions into their bubble worlds. But on the other, he saw a natural hierarchical division of labor amongst organs within an animal. When he applied his theory of bubble worlds to the state and the Volk in what Harrington calls "an early venture into bio-politics," he arrived at arguments for monarchy's brainlike administrative necessity (as opposed to mass movements' demands for revolution or democracy) and individuals' needing to take up professions in keeping with their particular perceptual worlds, i.e., a class system. On a more macro level, he saw Germany's vitality threatened by parasites both external (England) and internal ("certain 'alien races' within Germany"), implicitly targeting Jewish people with the barely coded language of the day, a decorum he dropped in personal correspondence (59–60). The meadow through which Uexküll invites his readers to stroll in the *Foray* seems a perfect example of a ground on which to observe in multidimensional terms Cheah's "sheer being-with other modes of life." Yet when he applied ethology to politics, Uexküll interpreted his potentially pluralistic model in a way that would deny minority populations the very thing that Van der Vliet Oloomi's heroine bemoans lacking: belonging. *Call Me Zebra*, by contrast, pushes the multiverse of perceptual worlds theory to contemporary biopolitical limits as it asks us to contemplate the multidimensional imagination of the dramatically deracinated. And this imagination knows few bounds.

2. To the Znth Degree

Zebra's Worlds

Wasting no space or time, *Call Me Zebra* assumes our induction into its expansive world with its very frame, beginning with immediate metatextual and multidimensional conceits. Its dedication issues not from the author, but rather her protagonist: *For all my dead relatives—Zebra*. This sense of having profound debts and extended ties further expands, both cosmically and karmically, with the Buddhist epigraph that follows:

> However many beings there are in whatever realms of being might exist, whether they are born from an egg or born from a womb, born from the water or born from the air, whether they have form or no form, whether they have perception or no perception or neither perception nor no perception, in whatever conceivable realm of being one might conceive of beings, in the realm of complete nirvana I shall liberate them all. And though I thus liberate countless beings, not a single being is liberated.
>
> THE DIAMOND SUTRA

We are presented not only with an indeterminate number of realms in which beings might exist; in the case of having perception and of being liberated, we also get the expansion beyond the West's accepted logical principles that Johnson notes in Buddhism. Cheah's "stance of sheer being-with other modes of life" and sense of "the very being of beings" must stretch to something like the being-with of however many conceivable realms and countless beings of not a single being—riddles for even bastardizing readers of Heidegger. These barely extratextual elements of the novel signal the scope of the "Matrix of Literature" its heroine will envision.

As befits a matrix-themed text, we open the novel with its heroine's birth and the world into which she is thrown. The novel's first section, a prologue entitled "The Story of My Ill-Fated Origins," reviews the tragedies of Iran's history—particularly the failure of its Constitutional Revolution, the oppressive power of the Shahs, the Islamic Revolution, and the Iran–Iraq war—through a familial lens, as we watch Zebra's forebears and then Zebra and her parents get forced from the nation. But exile is also a seemingly originary state for Zebra's family line. Born Bibi Abbas Abbas Hosseini to a family of artists and intellectuals, Zebra claims that their exile is predetermined, the consequence of "a kind of superintellect" that renders them "ill-fated, destined to wander in perpetual exile across a world hostile to our intelligence." A Manichean tension emerges throughout the prologue between the forces of what we have recently come to call "fake news" and this specifically literary intelligence, deemed almost a biological fact in Zebra's family, as she remarks, "We are convinced that ink runs through our veins instead of blood" (3). Similarly corporeally rendered is the family line's distinctive relation to death. In the wake of the failed Constitutional Revolution of the first decade of the twentieth century, Zebra's great-great-grandfather feels incipient danger, paints what becomes a family heirloom, "a still life of a mallard hung from a noose," and announces, "Death is coming." Thereafter, as Zebra says,

> This seemingly futile moment marked the beginning of our long journey toward nothingness, into the craggy pits of this measly universe. Generation after generation, our bodies have been coated with the dust of death. Our hearts have been extinguished, our lives leveled. We are weary, as thin as rakes, hacked into pieces. But we believe our duty is to persevere against a world hell-bent on eliminating the few who dare to sprout in the collective manure of degenerate humans. That's where I come into the picture. I—astonished and amazed at the magnitude of the darkness that surrounds us—am the last in a long line of valiant thinkers.
>
> 4

Representing the force of new birth in dark times, Zebra is charged with upholding the family's tradition of having "pursued the life of the mind" (3). This mission that is almost a collective allusion to the signature themes of Hannah Arendt—her appeals to natality, new birth as the basis of politics; her admiration of those who struggle to create in dark times; and her exalting of the mind's life—is, however, surrounded on all sides by death. Trying to envision an affirmative Arendtian necropolitics in effect, this family of self-declared "Autodidacts, Anarchists, Atheists" passes down the motto: "*In this false world, we guard our lives with our deaths*" (4). Along with transmitting this motto, her father repeats in Zebra's ear when she is just born a monologue she memorizes, a manifesto that in the midst of detailing national and familial history has a key thesis: "the point of this notable monologue, is to expose the artful manipulation of historical time through the creation of false narratives rendered as truth and exercised by the world's rulers with expert precision for hundreds of years" (6). As a country whose history has a founding empire but also a series of tumultuous modern regime changes, Iran for its intelligentsia becomes the site of a struggle between triumphalist historical narratives, whether spun from inside or outside the nation, and more nuanced, that is, literary, understandings of narrative, ones that would lead to more complex and truthful interpretations of history.

In addition to outlining the Hosseini family's traditional role as keepers of literary complexity and Zebra's part as the family's last inheritor, the prologue gives the specific fate-sealing circumstances of her birth and her family's successive flights from home. Cursed with being constant dissidents, the Hosseinis suffer under several regimes. With the rise of the Ayatollah Khomeini, the failing Shah's violence increases, and Zebra's 89-year-old great-grandfather is executed, causing her grandfather to die of a heart attack. Less than zealous about a revolution he believes will be co-opted, Zebra's father finds he and his wife (then pregnant with Zebra) must leave Tehran as Islamic leaders seize more and more power and war breaks out with Iraq. Fleeing to a family outpost in Nowshahr, Zebra's father casts a tearful look back at Tehran and proclaims prophetically, "That pig-headed Saddam is going to level our city." This occurs, but by that point, Zebra's parents have made it to the family haven, a beautiful stone house near the Caspian Sea that has long been a refuge beyond the capital's political turmoil. Named the "Censorship Recovery Center" and the "Oasis of Books" by Zebra's great-great-grandfather, the house contains at its core a "library, which was designed in the shape of an egg and built around a date palm that shot to the sky through an opening in the roof." It is here that Zebra is born: "My mother leaned against the trunk of the tree and pushed. I—a gray-faced, black-eyed baby—slipped out of her loins into a room lined with dusty tomes, into a country seized by war," recounts Zebra, adding, "I immediately popped a date in my mouth to sweeten the blow" (10). Zebra's infancy in this library-dominated house becomes a time of intense education, as her father, a multilingual literary translator, reads aloud to her and makes her memorize a vast array of world literature. Repeating his words, Zebra utters what for world literature theorists would be a credo: "Literature, as my father would say, is a nation without boundaries. It is infinite. There are no stations, no castes, no checkpoints" (11). Zebra then becomes a living testament to this credo.

Zebra's world comes to seem organized by flat surfaces, lacunae, and distortions, as she increasingly metamorphoses into a kind of mobile living text. She refers, as we've seen, to her "weary" and "thin" family as having "our lives leveled," and we see the constant Iraqi attacks in particular leave Zebra and her father ever more attenuated and flattened. Tearfully beholding the Tehran he knows Saddam will level, her father, according to Zebra, "wept until the skin around his eyes was paper-thin" (10). Then when even Nowshahr becomes unsafe in the war and the family leaves for Turkey, Zebra's mother dies as an abandoned house she is exploring collapses on and buries her. Zebra feels, "Her death flattened my heart into a sheet of paper. It leveled my mind" (9). Not only are these traumas explicitly flattening, but they seal Zebra and her father into their fates as preservers of literature, transforming them into sheets of paper or even moving chalkboards. Zigzagging their way through the war-torn landscape, Zebra and her father come upon a demolished school and they salvage the blackboards to wear as protection. Never missing an opportunity for literary transmission, even as they grow increasingly exhausted and emaciated, Zebra's father continues his nighttime lessons and Zebra's recitations, writing verses from memory on their blackboards, which Zebra reviews in the day until they make it on foot to Kurdish Turkey. At the border, her father disguises himself as a Kurd, but because, despite the many languages he has taught Zebra, he has neglected to teach her Kurdish, he blindfolds Zebra and claims he is seeking medical treatment for his deaf-mute daughter who, without a specialist's attention, is about to also go blind. Zebra leaves Iran deprived of a usually dominant sense, but more aware than ever of "the immense magnitude of the darkness that surrounds us," the scent of "the eternal return of the residue of history," the "ringing void of the long exile that lay ahead of us, first in Turkey, then in Spain, and finally in the New World," and lastly, "the white noise of death ... booming in the margins of the universe." By the prologue's end, she commits to "drag the stench of death out with me," and "to exhume the buried corpse of our deadly collective history—our truth" (20).

While the hyper-literary and textualized refugee's recourse to figures of flatness may seem to parody the objectionably two-dimensional world Cheah and Saussy find to be the basic premise of theories of globalization and world literature, it's important to note that Zebra's closing metaphors speak not just to flatness, but to interiority, to a meaningful void within. In addition to the two-dimensional textual motifs that have governed her life since her birth in the library and taken on added importance in her flight, there is a force of interiority and depth represented by her mother and by Zebra's need for nourishment. Just as she is born amidst tomes, she is also born into an egg-shaped room where she immediately pops a date in her mouth. Before their flight into exile, Zebra's mother worried about her one-sided education and its gendered implications, having told her husband, "Abbas, you are raising this child to be a boy! How will she survive in the world? Who will marry her?" And when Zebra's father reproached his wife for worrying about marriage amidst wartime, her objection was, "And who do you suppose will feed her once we are dead?" In even stronger physiological terms, her mother had declared, "A mother has to worry about her child's stomach!" But, recounting this episode, Zebra tells us she can no longer remember her mother concretely or the end of that argument because "the void left by her death would push me and my father over the edge. He would fill the lacunae of our lives with literature. Over time, my mind, filled to the brim with sentences, would forsake her" (12). Zebra's recurrent references, however, to lacunae and to a death within that needs to be drawn out belie this claim to have forsaken her mother. Even her descriptions of her reaction to her mother's death are telling. Although she feels leveled, it is with a figurative cooking implement, and the feeling leaves a stomach-centered void: "I felt as though someone had taken a rolling pin to my heart, razing it and extinguishing its warmth. I felt a gaping hole bloom in my gut" (13). When they retrieve her mother's body from the collapsed house in which she was searching for food and prepare to give her a proper burial, the counterintuitive perception of flatness in her mother's face causes a traumatic ripple in Zebra's world:

> Her face was flat and gray. It was covered in dust. It could have been anyone's. Once I had seen it, I couldn't unsee it. Her face had introduced a distortion in my visual field. The world, all of its parts, which, when summed up, still refused to make a whole, seemed unstable at the edges.
>
> 14

Moments of intense unworlding, her mother's death, exhuming, and burial are formative for Zebra while also setting the terms for the novel's development of its core concepts. Before feeling as though a rolling pin has flattened her heart, Zebra declares, "The world seemed nebulous, unnavigable." But after feeling the void in her gut, she hears a family motto: "Then those crucial four words of the first Hosseini Commandment, which my father had whispered to me upon my birth, trumpeted through my void: *Love nothing except literature*" (13). There is the singularity of the literary word, and there is a multidimensional matrix that belies it. The sight of her mother's death mask resembles the sight of an eclipse: a nourishing source of warmth is effaced, and space around this shadowed face warps. In the spacetime of this altered vision, the world of world literature doesn't add up.

Zebra's Dimensions

The full solar eclipse has a special revelatory significance for art in Einstein's age, and while no such eclipse occurs in *Call Me Zebra*, Zebra composes a manifesto inspired by bursts of light amid darkness, apprehensions of rippled or looping space, and the overlapping of planes. Curved and warped space fascinated early twentieth-century visual artists, as Vanja Malloy explains, at the same time that photographs of the era's eclipses made Einstein's relativity real for popular audiences:

> Einstein's general theory of relativity became more than just an abstract concept in the popular photographs of the 1919 and 1925 total solar eclipse, which proved an important postulate in Einstein's theory by documenting the bending of starlight [visible around the sun when its own light is shadowed] as it traveled through space. Einstein's abstract theory introduced this new perception of the cosmos, in which the mass of a cosmic body exerts an immense gravitational pull that makes the celestial landscape curved, irregular, or otherwise non-Euclidean.
>
> "Introduction" 14

It's not surprising, as Malloy details, that some important signees of the Dimensionist manifesto such as Duchamp and Calder referred to the eclipse in their artwork ("From Macrocosm" 82). Likewise, Zebra's mournful description upon the loss of her mother of the "distortion in [her] visual field" and her sense of a gap that warps everything around it resonate with the surrealist period's artistic renderings and scientific understandings of the total solar eclipse. Zebra seems repeatedly fascinated by spatial distortions and strange glimpses of light in darkness, and when she comes to write her own literary manifesto, it's notable that her creativity often shines in moments when the moon ascends.

If the novel's prologue offers its protagonist's origin story, its first chapter operates as her manifesto, both telling of its creation and setting forth its core credos. Zebra takes up the manifesto's composition in one of the global capitals of surrealism, New York City, site of an important total solar eclipse viewing by Calder among many others in January 1925 and site of an important 1945 exhibition of Duchamp's work, one in which he featured innovative forms of a shape that also comes to fascinate Zebra, the circle. Repeated in double-sided spinning discs, the many moving circles of Duchamp's *Rotoreliefs* powerfully suggested further dimensions and evoked non-Euclidean space (Malloy "From Macrocosm" 71; 82). Likewise, in the first chapter Zebra, now twenty-two, circles back on her past, telling of her life with her enfeebled father in New York, where they had arrived after years in Europe spent "moving across the surface of the earth" and feeling like "the refuse of the world" (23). Zebra describes their dispossessed and wandering European years in typically cosmic terms, retracing their steps through a space that appears far more Einsteinian than Euclidean:

> We would move across huge chunks of this uneven universe at the speed of light, then, suddenly, breathless and exhausted, we'd be unable to proceed and would move backward again. The path we had taken would fold over itself, looping

> backward as if it were leading us toward some information we had been too impatient to discover the first time. We would scurry back in a panic only to discover that there was nothing there. This sense that we had forgotten something—the haunting aftereffect of an indigestible loss—had turned both of us into entirely unintelligible beings.
>
> 23–4

As Hosseinis who not only guard their lives with their deaths but also place a premium on literature, transmitted and received with a special super-intelligence, Zebra and her father push their mission's principles to new limits as they pursue a hollow, unintelligible quest for "some information" in the midst of "indigestible loss." While the literary refugee's movement across borders seems to suggest an endless tracing of a flat plane, the recursive looping around some indigestible fact suggests a traumatic loss that is rendered analogous to spacetime's conceptual disruption of space/time. In the particular physiological allotment of functions for the Hosseini family line, this new sense of dimensionality also becomes analogous to the growth of a mind pushed toward taking on the functions of a stomach or womb.

Knowing her father's death is near, Zebra feels pushed to a further existential limit in New York until she seeks out a new mentor, the Chilean exile and NYU professor José Emilio Morales, and decides to write a manifesto. A radical communist, Morales takes Zebra on as an unofficial independent student after she, having seen him several times walking the city while reading his copy of Pablo Neruda's *Tercera Residencia*, follows him to his campus office. Hearing her life story and giving her the test of identifying random lines of poetry that she correctly declares are Neruda's, Morales agrees to meet with Zebra weekly. In the first of these meetings, she tells him of her urge to write a manifesto "to honor [her] father, Abbas Abbas Hosseini, a man whose mind was as vast as the library of Babel," adding that she will call it "A Philosophy of Totality: The Matrix of Literature." When quizzed on its intended methodology, Zebra answers it will be memorization and boldly expands on her theme:

> I informed Morales that I wanted my mind to become so elastic it would be capable of containing all of literature; once internalized, the maxims, diatribes, and verses written by the Great Writers of the Past, my ingenious forebears, would begin to mingle spontaneously with one another in the decimated fields of my consciousness and produce unexpected but truthful associations that I planned to record in the manifesto for the good of my fellow vermin. Memorization, I declared, is the Hosseini way.
>
> 30

Not only does Zebra's method aim to encompass all literature, to, as she says a moment later "metabolize texts" (31), but following it, she herself will become via her especially well-trained memory a living mental womb spawning new hybrid literary insights. Moreover, she proclaims to Morales that she is particularly suited for this mission because she is a survivor of brutal regimes and war:

> I told him that we [the Hosseinis] have combated the potential loss of will to power, a natural consequence of war and our lifelong ill-fatedness, by reciting lines from the vast web of literature. Memorization, I insisted, is how we have kept our minds engaged, decolonized; it is how we have kept ourselves from giving in.
>
> 30

Beyond putting a new, even postcolonial, spin on rote learning, Zebra's program moves across traumatic terrain to become explicitly multidimensional in several senses.

Just as Zebra's sight of her dead mother is an epicenter for traumatic ripples in her visual field, at the center of Zebra's intellectual epiphanies is her father's death, both as she intuits its approach and as she confronts its aftereffects. This death pushes Zebra further into new realms, sharpening her critique of the United States, which she will rename "the Unanimous Station of Apathy" (44), and even US academe. As she reports telling two unfortunate poetry MFAs who try to engage her in casual conversation:

> "I have no time for small talk! While you two expose yourselves to the detrimental effects of a formal education—reduced self-knowledge, submission to authority, covert institutional indoctrination in linear time—I am employing unorthodox methods of learning in order to facilitate grand associative leaps, heightened cognition, and transcendental intellectualism, because with my father's death fast approaching"—I bore into them with my eyes—"it is my duty, as the last remaining member of the Autodidacts, Anarchists, and Atheists to make a major philosophical intervention aimed at correcting the skewed and pitifully narrow perception of the world's pseudo intellectuals and heretics, your erroneous brethren!"
>
> 34

Ever battling linear temporality and perceived neoimperial obliviousness, Zebra finds this outburst helps her crystallize key phrases for her manifesto—"grand associative leaps, heightened cognition, and transcendental intellectualism"—but beneath the big talk also lies her sense of doom and even caregiver burnout.

As she watches her father's eyesight and overall health fail and his mood deteriorate, Zebra copes with his frustrated outbursts by reading to him from his favorite texts, reciting as she circles him "like an old peripatetic Greek" or "Better yet, like an old Sufi mystic, the way I had walked in that oval library as a child" (26). In his last days, Zebra's father, too, mentally retraces his steps, as though "working his way backward across his life," and observing him, Zebra feels "a sharp pain in my chest" that she senses comes from "the sudden and unexpected loosening of the screws that kept the lid on my past tightly shut." Contemplating having to reopen this mournful interior space that already holds her mother and all their various traumas, Zebra is "sure those forgotten fragments of memory, sharpened into spears on the jagged cliffs of time, would inevitably slip out and stab me in the gut," and envisioning a space that is a negative counterpart to the Matrix of Literature, she adds, "I had no doubt that upon my father's death I would enter a labyrinth of grief so complex that I may never find the exit" (37).

On the heels of this revelation, Zebra recounts finding her father dead in his armchair upon her return from her weekly meeting with Morales, and her subsequent impressions again mix flattened textual, planetary, and cosmic imagery in ways that play inventively with dimensions. She finds a leather-bound notebook her father has left her with the inscription "Ill-fated child of the Hosseinis! Add to history's pile of ruins the uselessness of our suffering." And as she casts her mind back, she sees "the wrinkled surface of the Mediterranean, how it shone like treated leather" (38), imagining it as "like a photograph, a surface without depth" and imagining of her father that "He has gone back to the beginning, to the space before his birth. His mind is in the process of being reabsorbed into the mind of the universe" (39). These events and fragments of feeling come together in an epiphany after Zebra has called 911 and the paramedics and police leave, and this epiphany resembles a multidimensional work of art that calls for a concomitant form of action. Repeating their ritual, Zebra circles her now dead father while reading and whispering to him throughout the night, and in the morning catches her own distraught image reflected in the window. Just as she sees herself, she catches also "the half-moon, which had risen in the night" as it then fades and is "turned a translucent white." With dawn, the streetlights then also fade, and Zebra watches as "Instantly, my image vanished from the window's reflective surface" (42). This enigmatic moment seems to lay a foundation for her subsequent formulation of a plan. Finding a burial plot on eBay, taking her father's body there herself (in an enormous suitcase along with his favorite books), and then waiting with a mortician as burial preparations are made, Zebra suddenly articulates her next steps: "I found myself saying that I intended to reverse our exile," and this by "retracing our jerky, incoherent journey across the Mediterranean, street by street, in a backward manner" (43). She realizes, too, that this is a plan she has long been forming. In the slow but increasingly crystallized formation of this reverse exile plan, a trajectory Zebra will come to call in another early hour moment of inspiration the "GRAND TOUR OF EXILE" (48), her creative process comes to light.

Zebra's death ritual for her father is, like the Dimensionist program for all art, dimensionally expansionist, and the epiphanic moment in which it culminates can be seen, as can an eclipse, as a superimposition of planes. Reading out loud lines of text as she walks in circles, she makes the textual line the plane of the well-trod floor; embodying the texts herself as their live reader, she makes the plane three-dimensional; and moving as she reads, she makes three-dimensional space kinetic, a movement through time. Moreover, moving in circles, she suggests a space that can loop back on itself, fold over. Such doubling is further suggested both by the idea of reverse exile and by her beholding her reflection. The space of this doubling then becomes cosmic as she glimpses the partly shadowed moon, and then both the darkness's scattered light and the plane that reflects her image vanish with the reemergence of the sun. Zebra has become "the center and subject of creation," advancing her ritual towards dimensionally expansionist art's vanishing point, Sirató's proposed stage of "vaporization" and the dissolution of boundaries. This proto-epiphany plays out in miniature the desired course for her reverse exile tour as well as indicates an important template for the epiphanies that follow. Not surprisingly, much later in the novel when Zebra travels to the grave of the famous critic of linear temporality and progressivist history, Walter Benjamin, the photo she takes of the memorial's glass panel records an obscure overlapping of images: "In the picture, my shadow was superimposed both on the glass surface, which is inscribed with a German verse I couldn't read, and on the sapphire waves churning in the background: my death, my ghostly pewter-colored double, my shadow, superimposed on that impossible future." When her traveling companion insists she retake the photo "without the shadow" and then sits back to light a pipe as evening falls, Zebra describes its smoke, cosmically and extra-dimensionally, as "a ghostly thread eclipsing, like a secondary ethereal world, the falling darkness" (263).

Among the first chapter's closing epiphanies, Zebra will have two others that are crucial to her manifesto and her mission: she will rename herself Zebra as her father is interred, and she will realize the true multidimensional nature of the Matrix of Literature with its special relation to exile as she absorbs her father's spirit. Zebra conceives of her mission to retrace and record the history of her flight with her father as not only a looping back through space, but also a plunge into a central void, proclaiming, "I intend to dive into the lacunae of exile. In other words, just like my father and my mother, I am going to become nothingness, fade into the white noise of death," but crucial to her is that she will do this by "physically retracing [their] ill-fated steps," that is, via a corporeal reenactment (43). The epitaph Zebra offers the funeral director, drawn from the Arab-Israeli writer Emile Habiby, likewise speaks to the body and to animality: "*Like the desert camels of thirst dying while on their backs water bearing.*" Hoping for a textual rendering of embattled life, one that resignifies the italics in which the novel has just reproduced Habiby, Zebra asks for "the words to be lopsided, as if they were written hastily and upside down during times of war, between bouts of carnage, detonations, and bombings." The image of the emaciated and burdened camels seems to merge in Zebra's mind with her memory of the blackboards and their chalked writing. As she stands over the newly dug-up burial plot, "a moist black hole," and sees her father placed there, she experiences a sense of vertigo: "I was at the point of delirium, until I felt myself double, triple quadruple." As her self-perception divides and expands, she has a luminous moment of realization: "It occurred to me that I would need a new name for my journey of exile, one that referred to my multiple selves," a "scattered collective of selves ... composed of literary fragments systematically organized into a vast matrix, with each portion reflecting a disparate self" (45). A sudden light through the trees casts stripes on her father's coffin, so that Zebra claims, "for a brief moment, my inner and outer worlds were in perfect alignment." This "chiaroscuro" of "shadowy, inky bands laced with contrasting stripes as white as paper" suggests a message, the new name *zebra*, which, as she contemplates it, represents "an animal striped black-and-white like a prisoner of war; an animal that rejects all binaries, that represents ink on paper." In an eponymous utterance that bewilders the funeral director, she proclaims, "Call me Zebra!" and as if textually locking the name in between bars, adds epanaleptically to the reader that while the director mistakenly looked for an animal in their midst, in fact, "I was the zebra; the zebra was I" (46). While the intertextual nature of her utterance clearly recalls Melville's Ishmael, it also fittingly affiliates Van der Vliet Oloomi with Melville's multifarious inheritors, from Rhoda Lehman's 1973 feminist romp *Call Me Ishtar* to Agha Shahid Ali's 2003 poignant and posthumous poetry volume *Call Me Ishmael Tonight* to Amitav Ghosh's 2008 maritime adventure novel *Sea of Poppies*. At the same time, the figure of the zebra as name and as title condenses so many of the novel's and its protagonist's key tendencies. Both white noise and black hole, both camel-like beast of burden and borne blackboard text, both two-dimensional striped plane and three and four-dimensional mobile embodied life, *zebra* is a name for the retraceable patterns of a multiple self, one defined by a matrix that can expand or shrink its arrays. Linking it to exile, Zebra makes this name speak specifically and hyperbolically to the multidimensional umwelt of the deterritorialized and animalized human.

After this epiphany, Zebra begins to mentally draft her manifesto, and the beliefs she formulates turn toward not only the cosmically multidimensional but toward the mystically so. She first returns to the empty apartment and spends a grief-stricken night circling the space in "ever-expanding concentric circles" because the "circle—prehistoric, divine, natural god of geometry [is] responsible for the ever-increasing speed of human travel" and is, in addition to being for "the Greeks, the smoothest, most perfect of forms," also "Innate. Embedded in the earth, manifest like death in the body" (47). In due course, as the sun rises, Zebra realizes her intended reverse exile journey is actually a tour, a grand literary one comparable to Don Quixote's and Dante's, but one that requires material resources—that is, ten thousand dollars. When Morales offers to redirect funds her way if she composes her manifesto, she becomes newly inspired, so much so that she moves her particular brand of dimensionism (as did some artists of the surrealist era) toward spiritualism, latching onto a theory of transmigration. If, as her family maintains, the soul is the mind and if her father's mind was absorbed by her as it hovered immediately after death and before it could be absorbed back into the mind of the universe, then, Zebra reasons, perhaps she contains it. Following from this premise, Zebra pursues a train of thought that begins with adding one mind to another, hers and her father's (M+1), and proceeds to become a vision of literary multidimensionality comparable to Ryan Johnson's:

> As a result [of mental absorption], I was thinking with the brain capacity of two minds, each of them multilingual, extremely literary, and shattered by their shared and perpetual exile; which is to say that each mind contained multiple minds inside of it, many of which, by virtue of having come into existence under different cultural and linguistic parameters, had different intentions, objectives, and patterns of thought.
>
> 49–50

Concepts of transmigration, superimposition, duplication, and distortion run together in Zebra's mind as she considers her newly discovered mental multiplicity comparable to "the many-headed country of [her] birth and origin: Persia, Pars,

Iran," but also, as with Johnson's example of Sherlock Holmes, comparable to a literary entity that moves across different writers' texts, in this case, *Don Quixote* as engaged by Jorge Luis Borges and by Kathy Acker. This view of literature's self-aware and self-perpetuating intertextuality sparks a practice of reading "concomitantly by going back and forth between them [Borges and Acker] with my many minds, metaphysically superimposing the texts and blurring the lines between them" and a comparison to her family line: "we, the Hosseinis, have been operating like literature for centuries. In other words, each of us is a distorted duplicate of the others" (50). Zebra's literary matrix becomes transgenerational to the point of becoming also transincarnational. As she watches "the moon's blue light glide" (52), she considers that texts appear to be "closed systems capable of operating independently of one another, when in fact, they secretly reside in a mutable and ghostly environment, a dynamic matrix where they disappear inside one another, mirror each other in a series of replicas" (51). Similar to the novel's Buddhist epigraph, with its invocation of "whatever conceivable realm of being one might conceive of beings," literature in this model is the possible mind that can conceive of all possible minds, and this reflective network of mental possibility sets up a mesmerizing ontology.[2]

After her last long day at the library, Zebra crystallizes these ideas, arriving at not only the formula "*Literature, with its cunning and duplicitous nature, aware of itself, in possession of a supraconsciousness, is the only true thing in the world; it exposes man's denial of reality's shattering pluralism*," but also the role of the exile as the one "whose identity is shattered with each progressive displacement from her homeland" and so "unmasks reality's dizzying multiplicity." Contemplating the others who will not have this multiplicity unmasked for them, Zebra walks through the night, punches a rose, watches its petals fall amidst "a sinister beam of light coming off the moon," and claims she "had never felt more awake" (53). She verbally delivers her manifesto to Morales the next day, setting out to prove that "literature is an incarnated phenomenon" and that she as "an exile and a Hosseini [is] the embodiment of literature," and so her tour and its record will be a collecting, revealing, and birthing of multiple truthful selves spawned by exile (53–4). Moving from the aesthetic to the philosophical to the political to the natural and to the cosmic, Zebra's thought is never settled, rooted in one realm. Likewise, her intended matrix is multidimensional in its ability to contain and create conversational passageways amongst possible literary worlds; physiological in its use of her living mind as a vast mental metabolism and womb; and geopolitical in its relation to the dark times that have fostered this radical survival technique. Not only this, but in an attempted feat of auto-dimensionism,

Zebra herself becomes the further dimension the totality of the world's literature must unfold in and her journey becomes an embodied testament to this lived dimensionist aesthetic.

But here we reach a pivotal critical question. We can read *Call Me Zebra* as a text that takes issue with the impoverishing models of space and time—smooth two-dimensionality and progressive linearity—that exploitative geopolitics and triumphalist historical narratives propound. Instead, we follow the refugee and exile's looping trajectories across leveled territories. As Zebra tells the police officers who respond to her 911 call when she finds her dead father, "Keep on bombing Iraq and invading Afghanistan, strangling the region, and there will be more of us here!" (41). But if the text wishes to advocate instead for multidimensionality, taking problematically flat planes and straight lines and making them into superimposed images, alternating bands, or rotating circles, why does it forbear advocating in earnest? In making Zebra herself the vehicle and vessel for its proposed dimensionism, the novel charts both a cosmic and comic course, often deflating rather than expanding its heroine's persona and shifting several genre codes along the way. While one might never expect *Call Me Zebra* to become a book club favorite on par with Yangsze Choo's *The Night Tiger*, it nonetheless works to blunt its protagonist's political critiques with textual mockery and soften its survivor tale opening as it develops into a bizarre love story. As a contemporary global anglophone novel, then, just what kind of animal is *Call Me Zebra*?

Zebra's Animals

In her satiric essay, "We Refugees," Arendt links what we've come to think of as the animalized human to the cosmic one, suggesting, as we saw in Chapter 1, that those who feel disinherited by earthly polities will try instead to lay claim to the stars. Invoking a form of posthumanism *avant la lettre*, she speaks of "a new kind of human beings" that "contemporary history has created"—those liable to become camp dwellers, or more specifically, "the kind that are put in concentration camps by their foes and in internment camps by their friends." If these new human beings make it to countries such as the United States, they, having future aspirations like anyone else, will "try to clear up the future more scientifically" and will "leave the earth with all its uncertainties behind" to "cast [their] eyes up to the skies." As members of an imagined spiritual community based more on prophecies than print culture, these beings claim, "The stars will tell us—rather than the newspapers—when Hitler will be defeated and we shall become American citizens" (265). Far from offering astrology as a science in any manner other than an ironic one, Arendt nonetheless charts in cosmic terms a geopolitically disenfranchised community's turn from the earth to the heavens. She shows how the uncitizen becomes a satirically celestial subject, as the "We the people" of the nation-state becomes we the star-crossed of the planet. In this way, "We Refugees" might be seen as an ur-text of ironic autobiography for a geopolitical era in which the very terms defining "human" life are at stake, that is, in an era of global biopolitics. Her essay performs and encapsulates textual strategies for those who might find it impossible to look back on their lives' journeys as testaments to planetary progress.

Zebra, however, is never a camp dweller, is grateful for her passport, and favors the term "exile" rather than "refugee" to describe herself. And although this is also the preference, according to Arendt's opening lines, of even her essay's subjects—"In the first place, we don't like to be called 'refugees'" (264)—still, Zebra takes note of her privileges when she slots herself in the middle rather than bottom tier of an imagined "Pyramid of Exile" (72). Nevertheless, her spiritualist turn and transcendent frame of reference—sources of much of the novel's humor—are, as we've seen, directly tied to her experience of a violently leveled earth, one she's unable to take root in and instead continually crosses, burying her dead along the way. To this degree, Zebra is an Arendtian animal. About this animal, in Arendt's prototype the Jewish pariah, Arendt writes in her essay's rousing conclusion:

> Those few refugees who insist upon telling the truth, even to the point of "indecency," get in exchange for their unpopularity one priceless advantage: history is no longer a closed book to them and politics no longer the privilege of the gentiles. They know that the outlawing of the Jewish people in Europe has been followed by the outlawing of most European nations. Refugees driven from country to country represent the vanguard of their people—if they keep their identity. For the first time Jewish history is not separate but tied up with that of all other nations. The comity of European peoples went to pieces when, and because, it allowed its weakest member to be excluded and persecuted.
>
> 274

Here we see Zebra's trademark themes: the insistence on truth telling to the point of indecency, the steadfast clinging to identity (however imperiled), and the sense of embodying a leading-edge analysis of world politics—all points Giorgio Agamben notes as well in Arendt, giving them a contemporary biopolitical treatment. Because it is Agamben who has recently placed Arendt's "new human beings" into a long history of conceptualizations of the difference between the human and the animal, it shouldn't be surprising that he calls one of his early essays "We Refugees" and there takes up Arendt, opening with her essay's conclusion. In the English translation of Agamben's essay, however, Arendt's words are rendered differently, with the line, "Refugees driven from country to country represent the vanguard of their people" becoming "Refugees *expelled* from one country to the next represent the *avant-garde* of their people" (114, emphasis mine). This rendering serves to bring Arendt's formulation closer not only to the language of science, with the less agentive and more clinical reference to expulsion, but also to the language of art, as refugees become part of a global avant-garde, implying that the refugee or exile can suggest links between biopolitics and art at its most experimental.

What links such art to biopolitics, and Zebra makes this especially clear, is the multidimensionality of animal worlds evoked by the figure of the nonhuman animal. But in the problematic world of nation-states, this animal-inflected multidimensionality must often appear as a kind of living death or "bare life." Agamben credits Arendt for the observation that in the case of refugees, in her words, rights "that were based on the supposed existence of a human being as such collapsed in ruins as soon as those who professed it found themselves for the first time before men who had truly lost every other specific quality and connection except for the mere fact of being humans" (qtd. in Agamben, "We Refugees" 116). As he does at greater length in *Means Without End* and *Homo Sacer*, Agamben proposes that this "mere fact of being humans" is a "bare natural life" that "the legal-political order of the nation-state" inscribes as "the Rights of Man" but that is meant to vanish from view, just as "in the classical world" such "bare life (the human creature) ... was clearly distinct (as *zoé*) from political life (*bios*)" but "now takes center stage in the state's concerns and becomes, so to speak, its terrestrial foundation" (116). In the tying of so-called human rights to citizenship, that is, to birth, nativity, and nation, "Rights ... are attributable to *man* only in the degree to which he is the immediately vanishing presupposition (indeed, he must never appear simply as man) of the *citizen*" (117). In his later text *The Open, Man and Animal*, Agamben will outline an analogous mechanism's role in conceptualizations of the human, calling it "the anthropological machine" (*The Open* 33–8). In looking for humankind's evolution of a distinctive trait (language) that would separate it from the nonhuman animal, but at the same time, looking for proto-humans, pivotal species that seemed en route to developing this faculty and becoming human, nineteenth-century paleontology likewise inscribed a designed to vanish animality at the foundation of the human. This questionable move also left open a core uncertainty, a "zone of indifference

... within which—like a 'missing link' which is always lacking because it is already virtually present—the articulation between human and animal, man and non-man, speaking being and living being, must take place." In this ambiguous empty zone, no-man's-land where borders must be constantly redrawn, we get "neither an animal life nor a human life, but only a life that is separated and excluded from itself—only a *bare life*" (38). We can see the name "Zebra" as alluding to *zoé* and to the bare life of "the prisoner of war" she mentions. But the utterance, "Call me Zebra!," suggests a paradoxical ability by which a pivotal vanished animality can speak, and speak its new name, an impossibility within the historical dimensions of biopolitics' that Agamben outlines, and so an avant-garde or novel experiment.

Because Zebra's biopolitics is, as we've seen, frequently a necropolitics, her novel engagements with animals, while sometimes magical, are often also sepulchral and spectral. But the novel is also most absurdly humorous when it is at its most morose and macabre, setting up intriguing interpretive paradoxes. While one might expect literary animals to participate in a vital zoopoetics, marking off a territory of lively nonhuman alterity, Zebra's animals are often caught up in her family line's special relation to death, beginning, as we saw, with her great-great-grandfather's still life painted on the brink of Iran's failed Constitutional Revolution, the bird in the noose known ever after as *The Hung Mallard* and meant as a reminder for future Hosseinis to guard their lives with their deaths. We get another ghostly bird, Taüt (Catalan for "coffin"), when in the third section Zebra arrives in Barcelona and sublets the apartment of a vacationing former literature professor and Dadaist, Quim Monzó, who is not to be confused with the famous writer of the same name. Along with the sublet comes the care of his strange pet cockatoo, Taüt, and in this chapter as well as the ones that follow, readers may feel that the novel does not entirely inhabit the realm of realism. In one way, the premises set by the prologue and first chapter are, by contrast, given more reality, yet in another, they are pilloried. Following the logic of many Borges stories in which alternative theories of reality are chanced upon within the text only to dictate the course of the plot thereafter, upon arriving in Spain, Zebra seems to move in the world of the matrix she has theorized in the book's preceding sections. Accordingly, we might feel, as with Borges's text "Borges and I," that Quim Monzó is and is not Quim Monzó and that Taüt is and is not real. Both seem part of a fabric of associations that Zebra weaves around her. Not simply following chains of association, but actively trying to become a channel for information, Zebra describes her matrix as though it were a spirit realm beyond the veil of death that sends her messages and signals. These come sometimes in the voice of her father, sometimes in the voices of the writers he translated and in whose works he educated her. As the medium of her matrix, Zebra becomes an ever more textual being, speaking frequently in epigraphs, aphorisms, and quotations, but stumbling and bumbling as she moves through the physical and social world. Tellingly, at this point as she becomes ever more attuned to signs and voices, she has a vision of her "body, due to exile, [as] undergoing a steady process of erasure" and concentrates this perception in a way that will continually haunt her on her dominant hand: "My writing hand, I thought, looking down at it and thinking again of Blanchot, is a *sick hand*" (76). Just at the period when she begins to estrange her highly human writing hand as sick, she gains an unusual animal companion in Taüt. Ever uncanny, the bird fails to appear at all until after she has spent a week in the apartment and then disappears and resurfaces at odd moments throughout the text. It is as though the novel, when it makes it back to Europe, turns a corner, and all its inspired philosophical insights work to its protagonist's detriment as she struggles to make her matrix identity work in the human world.

At odds with Taüt is the human companion Zebra finds in Barcelona, her lover Ludo Bembo, an Italian expatriate teaching philology in Spain, and, according to Zebra's research, "a descendant of none other than Pietro Bembo, the famous sixteenth-century literary scholar, poet, Petrarch connoisseur, and member of the Knights Hospitaller" (66). As the student of a mentor who owes Morales a favor, Ludo picks Zebra up at the airport, and the two begin an affair not long after their first meeting. The novel sets up a fairly straightforward tension between death and eros, the timeless life of the mind and the here-and-now life of the body, as Zebra and Ludo are drawn into an intensely sexual but argumentative relationship, one in which Ludo feels his love repeatedly spurned and Zebra feels unseen in all her dimensions. Somewhat predictably, she takes aim at his lack of literary complexity and he complains of her inability to be happy. At this point, the novel seems to tip towards psychology, while still, in this meeting of a figure of Western proto-modernity with one of non-Western postmodernity, retaining potential for allegory. While the "absorption" of her father's mind, and via him, her mother's that Zebra describes in spiritualist, intertextual, and multidimensional terms is also easily read psychoanalytically as a sign of unresolved mourning or melancholic incorporation, it's worth noting that there is nothing cryptic about this significance, as Zebra makes no secret of her constant state of grief as well as her straightforward desire to memorialize her parents and country of origin.[3] And she makes no secret of her feelings of disloyalty to her matrix and memorializing efforts when she enjoys Ludo's company. Zebra even reports strange feelings of pain and electrical energy in her "sick hand" in her encounters with Ludo (99; 122). As with everything else in the novel, its allegorical tendencies included, the character arc by which Zebra must come to embrace love after taking memorialization to its breaking point is played out hyperbolically.

Fittingly, the nonhuman animal Taüt is often at the center of this hyperbole, bringing together the novel's strands of strange spirituality, global morbidity, and bizarre comedy—all offering perspectives from which we might look askance at mundane human life. Indeed, this hand-me-down animal companion becomes almost Zebra's familiar, all too present when she and Ludo are not getting along and strangely vanishing when they renew their passion. Introduced, moreover, as a millennial animal, Taüt is charged not only with a deathly aura, but also with an apocalyptic energy that alludes to the era of the Great War and encompasses that of the War on Terror. Recalling his "wickedly aware" look at the camera in the photo Monzó had sent her, Zebra muses:

> I had never seen anything like it. Then I remembered the bird's date of birth: January 1, 2000. So that bird, wherever he was, had been born the same day that the odd parade of the twenty-first century began, which so far had been a century of haphazard bombings, of revenge killings, of undeserved misery, of terror without reprieve, of death. It wasn't the Great War, but it was the end of the world as we know it all over again.
>
> 81

As she contemplates a world endlessly at war, Zebra imagines a constant and endlessly looping apocalypse. She sees Taüt, with his distinctive look at the camera, as, like her, a knowing animal of this umwelt. Already associated, as the apocalyptic pet of a Dadaist, with the expansive forces of art that draw attention to the absurdity of human life and that transcend human death, Taüt sees her, she speculates, as likely "reduced to nothing more than a sick hand" (90), and he later becomes in Zebra's eyes a vessel for the spirit of her mother.

Taüt's significance intensifies as Zebra trails Ludo and releases parts of her reverse exile travel plan. After several arguments in Barcelona, Ludo returns to his home in Girona, only to have Zebra and Taüt eventually follow him there, but her stay in Girona entails her facing several losses, even briefly Taüt's. While the bird poses no problem for Ludo's apartment mates, the sculptor Fernando, his partner and model Agatha, and the dog Petita, Ludo and Taüt are always at odds, seeming rivals for Zebra's affections. When Zebra and Ludo effect a temporary rapprochement, Taüt disappears, and Ludo alone refuses to help look for him.

Bereft of Taüt's companionship and quarreling anew with Ludo, Zebra's sense of exile deepens. After time spent contemplating Benjamin's exile and eventual suicide in Spain, she comes to a realization about her own reverse exile ambitions: "My plan to retrace the path of my exile was impossible. I could make it all the way to Van and salute the Iranian craggy border, but I could go no further." As she imagines disastrous outcomes, including the possibility that she "would be killed instantly for being a woman traveling alone or for being a Western spy" (224), Zebra renounces her original plan, replacing it with a series of local group pilgrimages to honor places and figures she admires, Josep Pla, Salvador Dalí, Benjamin, and Jacint Verdaguer among them. Bringing her worship of the dead and her deathless matrix to a crisis point, these tours undertaken with Ludo, his apartment mates, and the odd characters of their neighborhood seem to necessitate the presence also of Taüt. Sure enough, just as the new "Pilgrimages of Exile" begin, he reappears, hidden in a cupboard and having bathed himself generously in Ludo's prized olive oil. During this low point in her grand journey, and perhaps related to her new awareness of her limitations as a lone female traveler, Zebra's thoughts have repeatedly turned to her mother, the loss readers know to be so key to the Matrix. When she beholds the newly anointed Taüt, Zebra concludes that his reappearance's coinciding with her recent recovery of memories of her mother is significant. "She must have reincarnated into this bird, and Quim Monzó had been keeping her for me without even realizing," she decides, or else Taüt has magically absorbed through the "fumes" around her and "through the power of metempsychosis" the spirit of her mother (228). In this way, Taüt crystallizes a convergence of the novel's comedy and spiritualist melancholy.

Although Taüt might seem a livelier vehicle than *The Hung Mallard* for Zebra's familial necropolitics and poetics, at times on the Pilgrimages of Exile, the two share space, and this also to comic effect. Having traveled with the suitcase that once carried her father's body, Zebra refits it with art objects, some stolen from Monzó's apartment, to become a "miniature museum" that she calls the "Mobile Art Gallery" (169). As much mausoleum as museum, this suitcase still carries the odor of her dead father as well as *The Hung Mallard*. Using it to sometimes also carry Taüt, Zebra has breathing holes drilled in it, ones from which he emits unsettling noises. When the pilgrims commence their tour in homage to Josep Pla at his favorite bar, the Centre Fraternal, Zebra finds Taüt making "macabre screams" from inside the suitcase. When she then yells at it, "Taüt! ... Taüt!," strangers, no doubt registering this as the Catalan word "coffin," glare "wide-eyed, jaws dropped, newspapers in their laps, cigars hanging from the rafters of their mouths" (240–1). In more than one way, Taüt, like the new pilgrimages, brings death to life, making it more embodied and real, but also ridiculous. In fact, the Pilgrimages of Exile will also end on a woefully absurd note when during the final one, Zebra nearly gets everyone lost on a stormy mountain, and she, despite Ludo's warnings, insists on taking refuge in an about-to-collapse ruined house. She sinks to her lowest point as she announces she will relive the memory of her mother's death and eats clumps of mud in the downpour. As if this weren't already pushing Ludo past his limits, when they make it out of the storm, he watches as his car, carrying the mobile museum but not Taüt, slides from the mud into the river where it sinks. While this nadir marks a catharsis of sorts for Zebra, who has never been able to fully mourn her mother or release the mausoleumlike aspect of her matrix, it is too much for Ludo. Once home, he resolves to leave Zebra to return to Italy and his ailing father. Through the novel's dimensionally enhanced, mobile, and finally overburdened vehicles—the evanescent bird, the suitcase museum, and Ludo's sinking car—it conjures its particularly morbid humor, a humor so pathetic it's sad.

Indeed, these middle chapters of the novel work as trials to be undergone en route to its explicitly apostrophic and elegiac end. Perhaps as part of this contemporary novel's gesture to Dante, it sets up a comic purgatory, one in which the Arendtian irony surrounding the refugee's spiritualism intensifies and its heroine's signature principles are upended. In keeping with its surrealist heritage, however, it cites Dalí as well as Dante for its technique. In the middle of her second pilgrimage, in homage to Dalí, Zebra gives a mini-lecture exalting him for a method of sublime inversion that could apply in reverse to the novel at large:

> "After reading Nietzsche," [she] continued, "Dalí decided he would be the one to outdo the inventor of the overman, otherwise known as Zarathustra, Nietzsche's most transcendent, mystical, and lofty creation, by developing a Dalínian cosmogony, a cosmogony littered with anuses. In other words, Dalí flipped Zarathustra on his head by ascending to sublime heights through the grotesque."
>
> 258

While Zebra's chosen name can also be read as an animalized play on "Zarathustra," her pilgrimages' progress runs the opposite of this Dalínian course, descending from questionable heights into the grotesque, a path that literary theorists might more commonly associate with the carnivalesque of Bakhtin. Indeed, Bakhtin's description of "the parodic-travestying forms of the Middle Ages, and of the ancient world as well, [that] modeled themselves on folk and holiday merrymaking, [and] which throughout the Middle Ages bore the character of carnival and still retained in itself ineradicable traces of Saturnalia" (*Dialogic* 79) fits with the bizarre feast in which a mud-gulping Zebra takes a death she has held sacred and brings it absurdly low with a dramatic reenactment. But perhaps Zebra never cites Bakhtin because one of his crucial elements is missing: laughter.

Musing on Benjamin, however, Zebra admits having a predilection for thinkers "like Barthes, Borges, Blanchot, and Beckett—the writers of the *B*" (207), having once in despair over Ludo Bembo practiced her habitual bibliomancy by browsing for signs from the universe in the "B" section of Monzó's library. Appropriately, and despite her omission of one theorist of the "B," we can see her personal brand of animalized identity as taking Borges to the point of Bakhtin. Indeed in her epiphanic moment of taking on the identity of an "animal that rejects all binaries" and is "like a prisoner of war," Zebra might recall not only Borges's bestiary *The Book of Imaginary Beings* but also his story "The God's Script." As this story's protagonist does, she engages with a form of fantastic animality that must appear within confines it will never escape. When Zebra declares at her father's grave, "the word appeared in my head: *zebra*," the text begins to converge with Borges's story, and the resemblance grows stronger as Zebra recounts her revelation's details:

> I watched the undertakers—three men dressed in black, all of them strangers—sow my father into the earth, thinking, as I did, that the juxtaposing stripes of light and darkness were sending a message to me, a message that consisted of that very word, *zebra*, which had spontaneously manifested itself much as the truth does.
>
> 46

These words look past their setting to Borges's fictional Aztec priest. Imprisoned next to an animal he refers to as a jaguar and a tiger and sees for only a flash each day when a slot opens, light briefly shines, and food is delivered, this priest replays his memories of his teachings. He recalls learning of a magical sentence written long ago by a god and meant to save future generations from destruction. Searching his mind for places that might host this empowering writing and imagining it could take form in nature, the priest realizes it would need to take a consistent form. He then conceives the possibility of his "god confiding his message to the living skin of the jaguars, who would love and produce without end" and envisions "that net of tigers, that teeming labyrinth of tigers inflicting horror upon pastures and flocks in order to perpetuate a design" ("God's" 171). Although the imprisoned priest will correctly glean the magical sentence from his limited sights of the beast in the cell beside him, he will not use its power to free himself and defeat his captors because the transcendent ecstasy the script gives him makes his old sense of self meaningless. As the story conjures for readers the idea of a living message that also somehow can't get out, vital significance and corporeal containment coincide. And as with *The Night Tiger*, with *Call Me Zebra* we have the moment in which an animal epiphany comes to a protagonist open an intertextual pathway back to Borges's otherworldly dreamtigers, as though they offer the most concentrated embodiment of a vital novel experiment. Portals in lived warped space, these striped animals perpetuate not only a design, but the idea of interdimensional access.

In its most exalted version in *Call Me Zebra*, the experimental chiaroscuro animal, with its alternating bands, gives added form to the two-dimensional. In this way, it works well to suggest a lived dimensionism in which geopolitical flattening yields an unforeseen matrix. The fantastic premise of a zebra that can call itself by name by demanding others do so can be linked to new dimensionisms—auto, bio, and dialogical—as opposed to the strictly Einsteinian ones inspired by physics. Such an exceptional bio-dimensionism would be based not simply on the premise of an expanding universe, but on a multiverse of bubble worlds that can reduce or expand in relation to N as well as address each other. The self-proclaiming zebra would make such a multiverse her umwelt.

By contrast, in its most bathetic form, the animal that pleases itself by forever citing its possession of multiple selves becomes impossible to take seriously. In this regard, a peculiar but also telling moment occurs two-thirds of the way through the novel when Zebra recounts Ludo's introduction of her, along with Taüt, to his apartment mates in Girona:

> "Everyone, this is Zebra and her bird, Taüt."
> "Zebra?" they asked in unison, emitting a pleasant hum.
> "Yes, Zebra."
> He sounded like himself again: strong, unfazed, those dreamy eyes limpid and alert. I, too, had recovered, content to have a roof over my head.
> "Thank you, Ludo," I said. "It pleases me to hear my name echoed so many times because, as you know, I stand in possession of multiple selves."
> He rolled his eyes.
>
> 183–4

Although Zebra's original moment of self-naming supposedly occurs before the funeral director at her father's burial, the name lives such a largely interior life in the text that it becomes hard to imagine anyone referring to her by it and a little startling when someone does. When "Zebra" appears in someone else's direct discourse, it seems to have to appear three times, and when Zebra herself interprets this repetition, Ludo's previously limpid eyes roll, flipping the moment's significance. (Taüt's name, however, uttered in Ludo's and not Zebra's voice, passes here without comment.) A word that cannot perceive itself straightforwardly, on its own terms, but comes as though always perceived through a filter is Bakhtin's word "with a sideways glance." His historical example is Roman literature, the idea that, as he claims, "From its very first steps, the Latin literary word viewed itself in the light of the Greek word, *through the eyes* of the Greek word; it was from the beginning a word 'with a sideways glance,' a stylized word enclosing itself, as it were, in its own piously stylized quotation marks" (*Dialogic* 61). The "word with a sideways glance" might represent incipient polyglossia for Bakhtin, the beginnings of a self-aware "interanimation of languages," perhaps a matrix, that creates the conditions needed for the emergence of that distinctively dialogical form, the novel (82). But it's less clear in which direction the ironies surrounding the spoken emergence of Zebra's name tend. While the Pen/Faulkner prize judges described *Call Me Zebra* as a Borgesian "library within a library," we might think of it instead as giving form to a reciprocal relation between Borges and Bakhtin whereby the expansive animal of one is always found within the ironic enclosure of the other. Indeed, Bakhtin's favored revolutionary forces—the powers of the low earth, the lived body, the live message, and the other's look—are always pulsing throughout the novel but fail to be fully liberating when they are constant frames of reference, as they are for Zebra in her exiled state. Not only this, but she is paradoxically always sublimating her state of being brought low as she views it from the perspective of a dynamically multidimensional supraconsciousness, but this heightened awareness fails to bring about a sense of worldly communion. The gut-wrenching tensions of Zebra's all-metabolizing mental Matrix, marked out from birth, hounding her in early life, explicitly theorized in young adulthood, and trailing her throughout her pilgrimages, define the strange realm that the text externalizes in its epilogue. It's as though only at the end can the true language through which Zebra's words have always viewed themselves begin to be given expanded space.

Zebra's States

If Zebra is laughable without the text letting anyone laugh about it, the final chapter is about her becoming lovable without anyone seeing it. Here Zebra admits to herself the defense-mechanism-ridden nature of her matrix, and although she still rages against the "bloodthirsty, disordered universe," she discovers the "greatest revenge ... the simplest revenge of all: to love against all odds, to prevail, to persist in a world that fought tooth and nail to eliminate me" (284). After lost days in Girona brooding on her life and on Ludo's absence, Zebra determines to go find him in Florence and books passage on a ship that will cross the Mediterranean, or "The Liquid Continent." Traversing this body of water that Zebra will also call "The Sea of Sunken Hopes, the sea of refugees" forms the last leg of what was to be her reverse exile journey (289), and it also gives external living form to the Matrix of Literature. Even before formulating her plan, she had already imaginatively transformed the Matrix into water. Lying on the bed in Ludo's old room, Zebra describes contemplating this substratum: "I sank into the swampy Matrix of Literature. In my mind's eye, I navigated its dark waters until I felt time collapse into a single surface, indicating that everything had both already happened and was about to happen" (282). We return to the flat plane, this time of time, and far from establishing a globe that effaces a sense of world, it enables an omnipresence of moments that becomes a world. In this regard, this moment recalls Zebra's contemplation of one of the objects she pilfered from Monzó for her mobile museum, an object that must have drowned with Ludo's car, "the ghost globe."

When she first encounters Monzó's old effaced desk globe, it is at another one of her low moments, just prior to her taking a random selection of pills from the medicine cabinet and temporarily passing out in the bathtub. Zebra courts suicide in alarming ways at more than one point in the novel, and these moments are ones of intense unworlding, however much she also espouses a Nietzschean belief in eternal return. While she says of the globe, "I concluded it was a sign of my unbecoming," before heading to the bathroom, her fascinated description of it just prior makes it represent a spacetime of expansive importance, one she reclaims in the novel's final brief chapter. The old globe, with "its surface wiped clear" and "devoid of land and water masses," appears as if "the representation of the world had either eroded or been scraped off, leaving a pure white surface, as though the universal clock had been set back to the beginning of the beginning." Zebra revises this first interpretation, deciding "the desk globe represented a nonplace where time did not exist, or it if it did, its fabric was undifferentiated—the past, present, and future had folded over one another, rendering their boundaries indivisible, unclear" (158). At this time in her life, this spacetime is "the event horizon of a black hole" that makes the void call to her, "to begin the process of unbuilding, of becoming residue, the nothingness that is everything" (158–9). While we can certainly see in the globe the nonplace of globalization that Cheah and others object to, interpretation shouldn't stop there. The ghost globe also suggests postnational fantasies, the current and politically controversial idea of an open-borders planet. In yet another way, the globe's evidence of a world effaced or eroded conjures thoughts of the Anthropocene, of humanity's geological agency taken to an endpoint of human-made planetary catastrophe. But in yet a further way, the ghost globe opens up, as does Zebra's tumultuous cross-Mediterranean voyage, an extra-human realm.

In an era of rising sea levels, it's no small matter to think of a body of water as "The Liquid Continent," and as the ship navigates a dramatic storm that makes everyone sick, Zebra sleeps, dreaming of a realm underwater. She fantasizes a rendezvous there with Ludo in which they finally understand each other, all walls and arguments dissolved, "getting," as she says, "along swimmingly." Still, in the dream Ludo pushes her, asking when she will say *"the great and coherent yes to life,"* and "Why this obstinate perseverance to live a life you are not committed to?" Zebra then thinks, "We can only conquer life a little at a time," and that "There will always be a remainder out of reach." But this line of thought makes Zebra also realize that what she calls "the cruel facts of my life" only exacerbated a quality that was there to begin with: her disincarnateness, that though she descended the birth canal as all humans do and "arrived physically," still, she says, "there was a part of me that lingered behind. My descent was incomplete" (289). When she then comforts Ludo by boldly declaring herself "an irregular genius who is in the process of synchronizing her multiple minds in order to acquire the privilege to arise in the morning and say *a great and coherent yes to life,*" the narrative finally lets Ludo—dream Ludo—laugh (289–90). The storm at sea then reaches its height and an awakened Zebra throws up along with everyone else, filling the ship with "the stench of death," before returning to sleep and one final dream before the storm abates (290). In this dream she wanders an apocalyptic Florence, where, further contemplating Nietzsche's concept of *amor fati*, she tries, imperfectly, to attain a state of love and acceptance for her fate. Thinking of Ludo, Zebra claims, "As soon as I thought of him, Ludo manifested," and she is finally able to confess to him her former belief that if she had said she loved him, she "knew that he, too, would inevitably disappear" (291). After this last encounter and admission, the storm ends and Italy comes into view. She finds the "sooty, industrial, sinister" coast of Genoa "perfectly lovable," even though she also describes its mountains as "the bones of the sea, the fangs of the earth" (292). The pleasures of this epilogue are largely poetic, as Zebra addresses a Ludo who isn't there, claiming that through their dream encounters, she and Ludo have "been transformed by our own narrative" (291).

She looks on her own life and the earth from an altered perspective, reviewing all her signature concepts: "I stood there staring at the land. I thought of the Matrix of Literature. I thought of all the black holes and crevices. I thought of the Pyramid of Exile. I thought of my sick hand. I thought of the mind of the universe." It's notable too that Zebra takes Taüt with her on the voyage and closes the novel in italics, the lopsided letters she might associate with camels, blackboards, and an epitaph. As she sifts through her "eschewed" and newly "awakened" memories, she listens to this "mind of the universe," hears "the voices of the writers of the void speak to [her] in a calm susurrus," and she declares, "*The air*, I thought, remembering, *is full of noises*" (292). All this evinces the persistence of the Matrix and her creaturely state. If Zebra continues to speak, even to herself, with the sentences of others, then her word is always mediated. But in her role as the channel for others' interanimating words, she has finally made room for mockery, for someone to laugh and the Matrix to turn. The novel opens up a vast disincarnate space where in fact its heroine has always been residing and looks at it not just as an expanse enclosed in self-containing quotation marks, but also as a realm that can be looked at askance. And before Zebra leaves the water that has made this vision possible, we leave her, as though amidst the sea's ripples, she's seen a script that has finally made extraneous any question of flight or escape.

Part Two

Portals

3

Provincializing Dimensionism: The Paranormal Ontario of André Alexis's *Days by Moonlight*

1. Revisiting the Spatial Fourth Dimension

The Fifth Dot: Hypercubism

Imagine a transparent cube and at its core you can see another, interior cube. Now imagine this internal cube pushing its way out through the middle of the outer cube, and as it does so, turning the outer cube outside-in to become the inner cube and begin the cycle all over again. This weird visualization is something like the scene that plays out before you if you watch the animated video of a tesseract, or more precisely of the "3D projection of a tesseract performing a single rotation about two orthogonal planes" found on Wikipedia's "Tesseract" page ("Tesseract"). The ever-looping rotation of the hypercube becomes hypnotizing.

It's strange to think of a hypercube as retro-chic, but it's a geometric representation of the fourth dimension that had to make a comeback. According to Linda Dalrymple Henderson, temporal rather than spatial definitions of the fourth dimension held sway from roughly the 1920s until at least the late 1950s, the decades immediately following the popularization of Einstein's relativity, and this meant that earlier geometric models of a fourth dimension lost cultural traction (7–8). It's ironic to think we might have outer space to blame. Many have wanted to imagine Einstein's cultural influence acting immediately, for instance, on the early twentieth-century Picasso and the development of cubism, thus furthering what Henderson calls "the Cubism-Relativity myth" (13). But she stresses the debunking of such speculation and marks the ascent of relativity's popularity instead with a celestial event: "Further research quickly established how implausible was a supposed artistic interest in Einstein in pre-World War I France: with minor exceptions in Germany and Russia, the general public heard of Einstein only after a 1919 eclipse expedition confirmed one of the predictions of his General Theory of Relativity" (2). As we saw in Chapter 2, public viewings of eclipses helped popularize Einstein, as they afforded observers of the darkened sky visions of gravitational force bending starlight. Non-Euclidean geometry, curved space, and a notion of the fourth dimension of space as time became conceptually inspirational, shifting emphasis away from previous geometric imaginings of higher dimensions. Yet, as my opening example suggests, late twentieth-century advances in not only physics, with its much-discussed multidimensional superstring theory, but also in computer technology and digital images, enabled, as Henderson points out, the spatial fourth dimension's return (9). And among the culturally compelling features of a spatial fourth dimension has been its amenability to spiritual interpretations. Henderson notes that Mary Baker Eddy, founder of Christian Science, referred to a "fourth dimension of Spirit" (qtd. in Henderson 8) and that pre-Einstein interest in higher dimensions took place in the context of Victorian "ether physics" (14) as well as furthered Theosophical mysticism's blending of "Neoplatonic philosophy and Indian thought, to argue for the attainment of 'cosmic consciousness'" (5). Underscoring the many ways the late twentieth century was a good match for the late nineteenth and early twentieth, Henderson pinpoints its desire for expanded awareness as key: "the widespread goal of revealing invisible higher dimensions in the early years of the century found its counterpart in the quest for expanded perception and consciousness in the 1960s and 1970s" (15). An older generation's forays into higher dimensions, ones often cast as realms of spirit, were recovered not just by later decades' technological advances, but also by their spirituality movements.

Now imagine another cube, this one opaque, so that if it holds an interior cube, you can't see it. Mark on one of its sides the point at the center behind which the interior cube would reside. Now mark the square face's corners. You have a square plane with five dots like the side of one of a pair of dice. André Alexis, winner of numerous prestigious Canadian literary awards, in 2019 published the fifth novel, *Days by Moonlight*, in a series of five he calls a quincunx, but what's especially intriguing is his reason for delaying to publish the third, which finally appeared in the fall of 2021. As the *Globe and Mail* reported after the publication of the fourth novel, "Alexis explains it like this: Imagine the project like the number five on a dice [sic]—a dot in each corner, and one in the middle, but it must include elements of the other four, so it must be written last" (Medley). Alexis's quincunx model means that the third is really the fifth, the fifth is really the third, and/or the third is not entirely of the same order as the other members of the series. It's this core instability and mobility of the center dot—its double duty as the series' end and the middle as well as its special microcosmic role—that recalls the animated movement of the inner cube of the Wikipedia tesseract.

As with many pre-Einstein imaginations of further dimensions, Alexis's spatial model for his five novels' relationship has a spiritual underpinning. All the dots are attempts to get at something that eluded a single novel, and that may even elude the completed series, something inordinate. In *Quill and Quire* he describes the series as "the result of a failure," claiming, "For years, I tried unsuccessfully to rewrite (or re-imagine) a work by Pier Paolo Pasolini called *Teorema* [Theorem]." He summarizes this film (which Pasolini had also created, nearly simultaneously, as a novel): "In *Teorema*, a god comes to earth and interacts with the members of a well-to-do family. This interaction leads to madness, despair, grace, and the miraculous." Impressed with this tale, Alexis says he tried, abortively, to retell it, but faltered and "ended up writing inept versions of Pasolini." A deconstructive, essentially fracturing epiphany then liberated him, as he "finally stripped the story down to its essence—divine visitation—and thought about the ways in which that essential story could be told." At that point, he says, "Five approaches came to me at once." The five approaches play with common aesthetic modes, specific historical or popular genres, and broad themes: pastoral, apologue (which he defines as "a moral tale involving animals"), quest narrative, ghost story, and, in the final third volume, "a kind of Harlequin romance" ("Last Word"). And the *Toronto Star* reports of the series that Alexis, in a further recursive, looping gesture, has "plans to rewrite all five after its completion" (Carter). Derived from a divinely confounding "theorem," Alexis's quincunx of novels resembles pre-Einstein dimensionisms: as with two-dimensional geometrical sketches that then form the basis for the animation of higher-dimensional objects, it uses available generic means to suggest a view of earthly life—human, nonhuman animal, and vegetal—from beyond their customary bounds. But Alexis's dimensionism is also distinctive and he puts it to distinctive social and political use.

In his quincunx's fourth/fifth volume *Days by Moonlight*, Alexis offers readers a radically provincialized dimensionism, one that conjures a sense of ambivalent belonging by working in paradoxically expansive and localized terms. On the one hand, Alexis's text gestures to a macro-dimensionism by retrieving key features of pre-Einstein geometric imaginings of higher dimensions and blending them with post-Einstein modes. The novel also, while engaging with the nonhuman via plants and animals, insists on an extra-human realm of spirit. In addition, as Van der Vliet Oloomi's *Call Me Zebra* does, *Days by Moonlight* situates itself in a capacious matrix of literary influences. On the other hand, the text is repeatedly drawn to the land itself, to rendering the regional, and to scrutinizing politics at not only the lofty level of the nation but also at a municipal level involving the pettiest of quarrels. This flexibly eclectic mode allows Alexis a vehicle for voicing poignant forms of longing and belonging, ones we could associate with not only his literary protagonists but also his own standing in the Canadian literary world and understanding of the role of the artist in the unusual polity of Canada.

A highly prized and multiply awarded author, Alexis has also been caught up in debates and controversies, notably to do with race. Having written a critical review of David Gilmour's novel *A Perfect Night to Go to China*, Alexis found himself caricatured—and this according to authorial admission—in Gilmour's subsequent work *The Perfect Order of Things*. Alexis called out the racist tropes in Gilmour's caricature and expressed disappointment that so few in the Canadian literary community joined him. In his essay, "Of a Smallness in the Soul," Alexis describes Gilmour's caricature and his reaction to it:

> "The Pigeon," a short chapter in *The Perfect Order of Things*, concerns the revenge exacted upon a reviewer by a novelist who has received a bad review. The reviewer is black and is named "René Goblin." (He is a spook, you see.) Mr. Goblin is described as a "deposed African tyrant" with greying dreadlocks, pink gums flashing when he smiles, who wears thick, dark glasses. The narrator asks "why are all those men so ugly?" (Flirting aggressively with "They all look alike.")

Alexis claims he answered Gilmour by parodying him in his novella *A* with the character Gilbert Davidoff, "a mediocre novelist and compulsive womanizer." Yet this response dissatisfied him. "I began to feel," Alexis recounts, "that I had given a literary answer to a question that should have been answered by my *social* self, by the self that is black, lives in Canada, and has to figure out his society's workings in order to feel at home." But some have found problematic this distinction between a social self that writes essays on unsettling events and an artistic self that has, in Alexis's words, "longed for a place where my aesthetic concerns might be given precedence" and declared, "For the sake of the art I practice, I would almost prefer to have no race at all."

Publisher Scott Fraser, for example, in an essay entitled "The Complicated Place of André Alexis in Black CanLit," remarks, "The fact is that André Alexis is a brilliantly talented writer and also the subject of substantial debate within Canada's Black literary community and the main reason for this is that he tends to avoid the subject of race altogether." Fraser describes the perception of Alexis as part of a "second generation" of post-1967 Caribbean Canadian immigrants, ones supposedly less tied to any Caribbean roots and more influenced by the socializing forces of White Canada. Fraser notes that fellow Caribbean Canadian writer David Chariandy accuses Alexis, when he does engage with race, of "do[ing] so in a way that flirts with self-disgust over his Blackness while the elements of his Caribbean culture are depicted as something menacing." And in a 1999 interview with Michael Redhill, Alexis himself discusses his seemingly indirect strategies for confronting race on his own terms in his f iction. If in his first novel *Childhood* (1998) it is revealed relatively late that the character Thomas is Black, Alexis says this is because, "I think it should be a shock within the narrative because it should be a shock to the reader, in the same way that it is a shock to Thomas, to be told 'you are other' and how that feels." And his following words about that early novel ring true for *Days by Moonlight*: "it's a book about origin, and origin includes a wide sub-set of categories, one of which is race, another of which could be religion, the land, the experience of the land—all of these things have to do with where you come from" (52). It's this multifaceted quality that Fraser also celebrates when he concludes that Alexis "whether he likes it or not, remains a part of and apart from Afro-CanLit," and that in avoiding commodifying Blackness for a White audience, for example, with the trauma narrative, he is "an avant-garde voice within Afro-CanLit and a hopeful figure, despite his infrequent and unpopular interventions on questions of race."

Without reducing Alexis's multidimensional aesthetic to a diasporic allegory on race, it's worth seeing the way his negotiation of multiple social desires, demands, and debates resonates with a complexly layered artistic practice. As a later work, *Days by Moonlight* seems consciously crafted to inhabit the caesura between what Alexis has in the past called his social and artistic selves, his essayistic and novelistic modes. It's a narrative of what Fraser terms a "Complicated Place" where the artist is "a part of and apart from" various communities, a supposedly overarching polity, and the animacy of the land itself. The political and aesthetic theories of Giorgio Agamben and Mikhail Bakhtin, reexamined in dimensionist terms, can illuminate Alexis's complicated position and help us appreciate the way his core tropes of the road trip and local festival are rendered with exceptional affection and upending energy. But before arriving at these admittedly enshrined theorists, we need to track the distinctive way Alexis himself addresses his literary intertexts as well as his literary avoidances.

The order of Alexis's quincunx of novels suggests a complex geometry, but a multidimensional textuality inheres in each volume as well. While the cycle's five novels—*Pastoral* (2014), *Fifteen Dogs* (2015), *The Hidden Keys* (2016), *Days by Moonlight* (2019), and *Ring* (2021)—form a matrix themselves, each novel comes with its own matrix, an author's note on the text at the end, sometimes paginated and other times not, detailing inspirational sources, influences, and intertexts, as well as liberties taken. In the case of *Days by Moonlight*, the note opens with an important aesthetic declaration, one that echoes Pasolini and that might also be compared to schematic sketches of higher-dimensional objects:

> *Days by Moonlight* is not a work of realism. It's not a work that uses the imagination to show the real, but one that uses the real to show the imagination. For instance, though most of the place names in the novel exist, the cities and towns they refer to are distortedly, exaggeratedly, or (even) perversely portrayed.

Pasolini's commanding narrative voice makes similar paradoxical assertions at the outset of the novel *Teorema*, or in its English translation, *Theorem*:

> As the reader will already have noticed, this, rather than being a story, is what in the sciences is called 'a report': so it is full of information; therefore, technically, its shape rather than being that of 'a message', is that of 'a code'. Moreover it is not realistic but, on the contrary, is emblematic—enigmatic—so that any preliminary information about the identity of the characters has a purely indicative value—it serves the concreteness not the substance of things.
>
> 9

Or, a little further: "We repeat, this is not a realistic story, it is a parable; and moreover we have not yet penetrated to the heart of events, we are still at the stage of statements" (11). Not a story, not a message, not realistic, but rather a parable, emblem, enigma, a cryptic shape that can be made concrete if not substantial—Pasolini's *Theorem* can be analogized to a series of imaginative propositions, "statements," that suggest another realm's forms. Indeed, Stefania Benini draws on both Umberto Galimberti and Mircea Eliade to describe Pasolini's notion of the sacred, the divine that disruptively visits the bourgeois realm in *Teorema*, and in both cases, she refers to another "dimension." For Galimberti, Benini notes, "the sacred is a quality that pertains to the relationship and contact with superior powers, an 'other' dimension that is above the human, apart from it, and cannot be controlled by human forces. It is a dimension that powerfully attracts humankind, inspiring fascination and awe, and repels us, arousing horror and fear" (18). Benini adds that for Eliade, a key influence for Pasolini, "manifestations of the sacred [*hierophanies*] appear in the realm of the profane and through a profane object that is itself but also becomes something else, something that transcends its dimension" (20). In a sense, the profane object is to the hierophanic as the cube is to the hypercube, just as Alexis's novels, taken singly, likewise become vehicles for complex geometries of textual convergence.

Equally important in Alexis's author's note are the textual traditions he reframes and repurposes, seen in the other influential works listed along with *Teorema: Lazarillo de Tormes,* Dante's *Paradiso,* Cervantes' *Don Quixote,* and Swift's *Gulliver's Travels*—picaresque, pilgrimage, quest, and travel texts that might easily overlap with Zebra's literary matrix—but also Nikolai Gogol's *Dead Souls,* E. T. A. Hoffman's *The Golden Flower Pot,* and Kazuo Ishiguro's *The Unconsoled.* Included are irrealist works, but eschewed are obviously magical realist ones. As we saw in Chapter 1 with Eka Kurniawan, magical realism is a sticking point for authors, especially those with ties to a "Global South," who want to make their own matrices. The "About the Author" notes that follow Alexis's authorial ones all begin with the same sentence: "André Alexis was born in Trinidad and grew up in Canada." And the *Star* reports that Alexis relates his qualms about magical realism to others' images and assumptions of Trinidad:

> Alexis's work has been categorized as magic realism but it's a label he rejects. "People tend to associate that with the climes you come from," he says. "They say, 'Oh, he's from Trinidad. He must be a magic realist because he's southern." But Alexis connects more with northern fantasists and thinkers such as Franz Kafka and E. T. A. Hoffman. It was his father, who took a classical literature course during medical school, who originally taught young André European mythology, a counterpoint to the traditional Trinidadian folklore he read as a child.
>
> Carter

Far from talismanic, invocations of realism's blending with globally legible forms of regional magic can come to do unwanted work for authors. In Alexis's case, with *Days by Moonlight,* he finds he must claim to reject realism altogether. His closing author's note points to an imagination that must use hyperbolic vehicles, taking what exists and treating it perversely, as though projecting its angles just beyond habitual points of reference and politically benighted categories for fiction.

In moving beyond habitual reference points, Alexis's quincunx must also expand beyond human-centered perception's traditional confines. As we saw in Chapter 2, *Call Me Zebra* took the geopolitical experience of compelled exile and pushed the multidimensional literary matrix of its protagonist not only towards an auto-dimensionist realm of supposed life writing, but also towards a bio-dimensionist realm of the animal, all while maintaining a constant sense of parody and with it an implied dialogical address to a skeptical reading other. Alexis's quincunx also entertains animal worlds, particularly with its second novel, *Fifteen Dogs*, in which the gods Apollo and Hermes grant the title's trial canine sample human intelligence in order to bet on whether endowed with it they can die happy. Dogs appear also in *Days by Moonlight*, but the text gives even greater space to the land itself as well as botany, even including illustrations of key (often fanciful) plants. These depictions are implied to be the work of protagonist Alfred Homer, a lab scientist who loves to sketch nature and who justifies going on the novel's key road trip partly to search for the legendary medicinal *Oniaten grandiflora*. When the text does engage with animals, however, it is often with spirit animals, whether totemic, demonic, or strangely hybrid. As with Eka Kurniawan's and Yangsze Choo's novels, such animals often act as portals. Every small town in Southern Ontario seems to host guests in an animal-named tavern; an encounter with a demonically possessed pig becomes pivotal for one key character, sending him on a pilgrimage Homer will then repeat; and Homer himself undergoes an intimate trial with a werewolf, or, in this case, a fantastical human-wolf that defies the masculine prefix "were" by appearing in female form. In several senses, Alexis's Quincunx Cycle is an ordered pushing of order, a geometrically schematic cube that elides its designated core and uses perverse exaggeration to insist on the expansively imagined.

It would be wrong, however, to see Alexis's rejection of the label "magical realism" as indicating an apolitical interest in spiritualism and the tradition of "northern fantasists." Alexis's multidimensional sense of perceptual worlds and of diverse genres informs his novel's eccentric lines of critique. Indeed, *Days by Moonlight*'s multidimensionality allows for a layered critical appreciation of a new world nation from the perspective of a culturally eccentric yet centrally administrative province. As with *The Night Tiger* and *Call Me Zebra*, a literary foray into extra-human dimensions arises concomitantly with philosophical and political explorations of questions of belonging. Choo's novel depicts a crisis in a seemingly fixed Confucian conception of the human amidst a Malaya of diverse animal spirits, diasporic populations, and colonial interlopers. And this crisis is subtly compared to the unsettling Einsteinian awareness of warped and expanding non-Euclidian space. In Van der Vliet Oloomi's novel, the protagonist is an uprooted exile compelled to roam the earth as if moving through such space, all the while looking to transcendent orders for answers. Like Choo's Ren and Van der Vliet Oloomi's Zebra, Alexis's Alfred Homer is also a lonely orphan who undertakes a quest. But his relatively contained travels and understated narrative speak to questions of belonging in an elliptical way, as the text addresses shifting models of majoritarian or more diversely inclusive cultural identity in a (post)colonial nation that officially espouses multiculturalism. The complex forms of hospitality and othering in such a nation find intriguing and appropriate structural analogues not only in Einsteinian dimensionisms that revise familiar conceptions of space and time, but also in earlier geometric dimensionisms and the fractal complexity of an animated tesseract. Yet however otherworldly the geometry of such higher-dimensional forms can seem, the ever-revolving and self-involuting nature of the animated tesseract as an aesthetic political metaphor suggests the relevance of one of the most earthly of political literary theorists.

Bakhtin in Ontario

Alexis's acknowledgment of Gogol's *Dead Souls*, a recurrently cited text for Russian theorist Bakhtin, points up an unexpected intersection of northern fantasists with Caribbean culture: carnival, a festival maintained in Toronto, Alexis's city of residence. As with *Call Me Zebra*, *Days by Moonlight* takes inspiration from the inversions of a moonlit world and merges the tradition of the travel narrative—however paradisiacal, purgatorial, or quite literally provincial in the case of this Southern Ontario road trip—with parodic reversal. Homer's journey through small Ontario towns becomes a tour of meant-to-be culturally respectful festivals gone wrong and would-be edifying institutions turned injurious or unsettling. Indeed, even Alexis's emblematic cube can be associated with carnival in three ways: with reference to the fields of mathematics, literary theory, and biopolitics.

Among the sources Henderson cites as renewing interest in the spatial fourth dimension in the later half of the twentieth century is Martin Gardner, who, she says, "was beginning to refer to the geometrical fourth dimension and its history in his 'Mathematical Games' column in *Scientific American*" (10). Gardner reissued his columns in a series of anthologies, and intriguingly, the 1975 volume containing a 1966 column as a chapter (fittingly the fourth) called "Hypercubes" is entitled *Mathematical Carnival*. Justifying his title and general approach, Gardner invokes "a spirit of play" as uniquely powerful in inspiring educational interest (xi). "Surely the best way to wake up a student is to present him with an intriguing mathematical game, puzzle, magic trick, joke, paradox model, limerick, or any score of other things that dull teachers tend to avoid because they seem frivolous," he exhorts, declaring of his book, "The topics covered are as varied as the shows, rides, and concessions of a traveling carnival" (xii). For Gardner, the down-to-earth strategies of roadside attractions help move mathematics out of a lofty realm of removed contemplation into a space of common, playful appreciation.

Not only is the carnival an apt metaphorical venue for exhibiting the hypercube, but according to Bakhtin, playful cubes are emblematic of the energy of carnival. In his early formulation of literature's carnivalization in *Problems of Dostoevsky's Poetics*, Bakhtin states not only that reversals of fortune are key to carnivalistic energy, but that "Gambling (with dice, cards, roulette, etc.) is by nature carnivalistic," and hence since "antiquity, the Middle Ages and the Renaissance ... Symbols of gambling were always part of the image system of carnival symbols" (171). Also characteristic of carnivalistic energy, which Bakhtin describes not only as a vital force, but as the force of "'life turned inside out,' 'the reverse side of the world'" (122), is "*profanation*: carnivalistic blasphemies, a whole system of carnivalistic debasings and bringings down to earth, carnivalistic obscenities linked with the reproductive power of the earth and the body, carnivalistic parodies on sacred texts and sayings, etc." (123). Bakhtin's discussion of carnival as a time when "the laws, prohibitions, and restrictions that determine the structure and order of ordinary, that is noncarnival, life are suspended" (122) and his emphasis on the profaning of the sacred find echoes, not only playfully in Gardner, but philosophically in Agamben's biopolitical theories of the state of exception and of profanation. And here Agamben too has recourse to games of chance, as though the force of fortune is prime among the powers of profanation. More than seeing an important step on the way to Agamben in Bakhtin, however, we might usefully revisit Bakhtin's theories from a biopolitical perspective, seeing them as always having been theories of life's politicization.

In *State of Exception*, Agamben looks to ancient Roman law's institution of the *iustitium*, the suspension of the law, as a paradigm for the paradoxical presence of anomie within law. Two key examples culminate his discussion: public mourning for the sovereign and festivals of license such as carnival. Sovereigns concentrate the law in their living presence, and so their deaths, if not seemingly regulated in public mourning rituals, might unleash anarchy. But the period of ritual mourning for the sovereign is nonetheless considered a time of suspension of the city's normal life, hence making the forces of "anomie and *nomos* coincide in [the sovereign's] person" (70). Law and anomie also coincide in a manner that is "symmetrical and in some ways inverse ... to the imperial *iustitium*" in "periodic feasts" such as carnival. Agamben notes, as Bakhtin did before him, that such feasts are marked by inversions of order, "the suspension and overturning of normal legal and social hierarchies" (71). Agamben concludes not only that the licentious feast "brings to light in a parodic form the anomie within the law," but also that it indicates "a zone in which life's maximum subjection to the law is reversed into freedom and license," while suggesting, "the real state of exception as the threshold of indifference between anomie and law" (72–3). Both Agamben's anomie and Bakhtin's carnival, while erupting only sporadically, resist containment in some way nonetheless. For Agamben, anomie is intertwined with the law not merely in isolated instances, but in a longstanding and integral way. Likewise, Bakhtin sees the reality of carnival as capacious and even all encompassing. For him, carnival is not a clearly demarcated pageant, but a form, for however long, of total communal life subjected to carnival laws:

> Carnival is a pageant without footlights and without a division into performers and spectators. In carnival everyone is an active participant, everyone communes in the carnival act. Carnival is not contemplated and, strictly speaking, not even performed; its participants *live* in it, they live by its laws as long as those laws are in effect; that is, they live a *carnivalistic life*.
>
> 122

For both Bakhtin and Agamben, carnival is a mode of life for the polis, but while Bakhtin's conception of it is more than capacious, Agamben's discussion of carnival remains *textually* localized and contained; it functions as a delimited example. Agamben is then left to contemplate the political force of play through other means.

In *State of Exception* Agamben finds hope instead in a concept of highly absorbing, "studious play," an activity he describes elsewhere as profanation. Rather than standing down from states of exception, returning from anomie to normalcy and again using normalcy to hide anomie within, an alternative path for humanity might be to look upon law from a renewed, playful perspective: "One day humanity will play with law just as children play with disused objects," writes Agamben, "not to restore them to their canonical use but to free them from it for good" (64). This movement of the law from canonical to emancipated use parallels a movement Agamben describes elsewhere of entities from the realm of the sacred to the profane. In pointing up a transit from the sacred to and through the profane, Agamben's discussion of profanation resembles not only Bakhin's carnival, but also Eliade's, and by descent Pasolini's and Alexis's, hierophanies. If, for Agamben, the sacred is, as it is for Eliade, a realm apart, then key to religion is the act of removing things from worldly circulation so that they may be given over to the gods. In "In Praise of Profanation," Agamben speaks of rites, prime among them sacrifice, that enact "the passage from the profane to the sacred, from the human sphere to the divine" (*Profanations* 74). Play, by contrast, offers a reverse or inverse route: "The passage from the sacred to the profane can, in fact, also come about by means of an entirely inappropriate use (or rather, reuse) of the sacred: namely play." In fact, games and rites, he says, are linked: "Most of the games with which we are familiar derive from ancient sacred ceremonies, from divinatory practices and rituals that once belonged, broadly speaking, to the religious sphere." Not only are these types of activities linked, but they are also linked in a literally revolutionary sense. Agamben claims, "games of chance derive from oracular practices; the spinning top and the chessboard were instruments of divination," and adds, citing Emile Benveniste, "play not only derives from the sphere of the sacred but also in some way represents its overturning" (75). Just as children can make a toy of nearly anything, play allows for the recirculation of what was once oppressively set apart, the repurposing of such items into "a new dimension of use, which children and philosophers give to humanity" (76). How appropriate that in the fifth novel of Alexis's Quincunx Cycle, the implied double of the third volume, an unusual force of carnivalization and profanation turns its conjured world inside out or outside in. Indeed, drawing on the geometrical, the oracular, the playful, and the political, the carnivalistic hypercube suggests an intriguing model for understanding Alexis. It might be seen as the singular die that rolls itself.

At the same time that *Days by Moonlight* might be multiply and uniquely carnivalistic, Alexis's persistent emphasis on setting, whether the land of rural Ontario in the cycle's first and fifth novels or his distinct sense of contemporary Toronto in the second, third, and fourth, suggests not only the relevance of Bakhtin's interest in the earthy, in the lofty brought low, but also a further important concept of his, one with an explicitly dimensionist aspect: the chronotope. Introducing this term for literary interweavings of time and space, Bakhtin describes the chronotope palpably as the way "spatial and temporal indicators are fused into one carefully thought-out, concrete whole," and, "Time, as it were, thickens, takes on flesh, becomes artistically visible," as "likewise space becomes charged and responsive to the movements of time, plot, and history." Even more significantly, Bakhtin directly, if briefly, acknowledges Einstein:

> We will give the name *chronotope* (literally, "time space") to the intrinsic connectedness of temporal and spatial relationships that are artistically expressed in literature. This term (space-time) is employed in mathematics, and was introduced as part of Einstein's Theory of Relativity. The special meaning it has in relativity theory is not important for our purposes; we are borrowing it for literary criticism almost as a metaphor (almost but not entirely). What counts for us is the fact that it expresses the inseparability of space and time (time as the fourth dimension of space). We understand the chronotope as a formally constitutive category of literature; we will not deal with the chronotope in other areas of culture.
> Dialogic 84

Writing in the 1930s, Bakhtin shows his awareness of Einstein even as he distances himself from other discussions and potential applications of him. Yet in "borrowing" from Einstein for literature, he nonetheless refuses to relegate his own relativity entirely to the realm of metaphor, leaving it in an intriguingly in-between space. Bakhtin's literary dimension of time-space is tied to his wide-ranging theory of genre, an interest Alexis, in his formally diverse quincunx, shares. En route to discussing the chronotope in such later works as, for example, Alexis's espoused intertext, Gogol's *Dead Souls*, Bakhtin examines its role in Greek romance and Rabelais. Even more relevant to Alexis, Bakhtin claims that from Apuleius through to Gogol, a crucial chronotope in the history of the novel is the road. And it is crucial for a reason similar to the one that gives such emblems of gambling as dice importance for a profane carnival world: "The road is especially (but not exclusively) appropriate for portraying events governed by chance" (*Dialogic* 244). Indeed, if the festival of carnival showcases the dynamic forces of inversion and subversion, the chronotope of the road is important for its powers of convergence:

> The road is a particularly good place for random encounters. On the road ("the high road"), the spatial and temporal paths of the most varied people—representatives of all social classes, estates, religions, nationalities, ages—intersect at one spatial and temporal point. People who are normally kept separated by social and spatial distance can accidentally meet; any contrast may crop up, the most various fates may collide and interweave with one another. On the road the spatial and temporal series defining human fates and lives combine with one another in distinctive ways, even as they become more complex and more concrete by the collapse of *social distances*. The chronotope of the road is both a point of new departures and a place for events to find their denouement. Time, as it were, fuses together with space and flows in it (forming the road); this is the source of the rich metaphorical expansion on the image of the road as a course: "the course of life," "to set out on a new course," "the course of history," and so on; varied and multi-leveled are the ways in which the road is turned into a metaphor, but its fundamental pivot is the flow of time.
>
> *Dialogic* 243–4

Bakhtin's interest in reversal and happenstance seems fitting with regard to his simultaneous awareness of Einstein yet recourse to analyses of literary space. He might be seen as repurposing a fourth dimension of spacetime to write a deep history of genre in which understandings of Einstein are turned around and we are asked not to see a dimension of space as time, but instead to perceive a series of literarily rendered times (adventure time, road trip time, etc.) as they take place in texts. Indeed, in contrast to the seeming primacy he gives handlings of time in outlining examples of the chronotope, Bakhtin shows his preoccupation with space when he discusses carnival and its tendency to sprawl: "The main area for carnival acts was the square and streets adjoining it. To be sure, carnival also invaded the home; in essence it was limited in time only and not in space; carnival knows neither stage nor footlights" (*Problems* 128). Temporal delimitation is noteworthy, one suspects, because it allows us to perceive distinctive renderings of space. In synthesizing this capacious sense of carnival and literature's carnivalization with the repurposed relativity of the textual chronotope, we begin to see the outlines of an Alexian dimensionism.

Alexis's multidimensional play with carnival is well poised to bring out potential not always recognized in Bakhtin. And the dimensionist Bakhtin that *Days by Moonlight* makes particularly visible and malleable is useful to a writer such as Alexis, as it allows not only for wide-ranging intertextualities, but for reclamations of space, an awareness of deep time, and channelings of aggression as well as spirit. Far from explicitly revolutionary, Alexis's novel whimsically critiques the complex dynamics of power and sovereignty in a provincial setting that is at once formally subject to an erstwhile empire's monarch, seat of a federal government, home to a capital city in which the White population's loss of majority status has been much discussed (with reports after the 2016 census hailing the city as "now majority visible minority," paradoxical terminology since discarded[1]), and in which multiculturalism has been part of national law since the 1980s. In one way, Ontario's officially exalted blend of (post)colonial diversity and inclusion, a version of Canada's proverbial mosaic, might seem a vast form of containment that obviates enlivening movements toward subversive revelry and profanation. Yet in another way, this conclusion fails to recognize Bakhtin's complexity, the many dimensions he attributes to ambivalence. As a concentrated site of eccentric sovereign power, Ontario lends itself to a literary form of carnival whose effects might be likened to a solar eclipse's. As with the event of an eclipse that both effaces the sun and reveals tellingly bent starlight, one of the centerpieces of carnival festivals, the coronation of the slave or fool, plays with doubling, crowning, and decrowning to the point that Bakhtin says in such mock ceremonies, "a decrowning glimmers through the crowning" (*Problems* 125). It's no surprise that protagonist-narrator Homer, the butt of so many cruel jokes throughout *Days by Moonlight*, should finally come into a strange spiritual power and be advised not simply to let it stealthily do its work, but to "do the work so the work eclipses you" (204). Far from fantastical or spiritual in an escapist sense, power in *Days by Moonlight* is channeled through a "spirit of play" yet is all the while stealthily overwhelming.

2. Touring Tests

Telling Details

Methodical on the surface, *Days by Moonlight* can read as a regional travelogue, full of quaint encounters and nods to natural beauty. As Homer's account of his tour through Southern Ontario with his deceased parents' friend Professor Morgan Bruno, the novel is premised on and structured by the pursuit of details. These details bespeak worlds in miniature and provide the text with a special imaginative idiom, yet they also have a vitality that takes death, loss, and disappearance as their backdrop.[2] Professor Bruno calls to invite him, Homer opens by reporting, on a research road trip just as he is eating an egg and watercress sandwich (implicitly explaining the novel's inclusion of an illustration of watercress just beneath the first chapter's number and title). This invitation also occurs on the anniversary of Homer's parents' death. Significantly, his parents, he says, died "in a terrible accident on the 401," the major and somewhat notoriously accident-prone highway that runs from east to west in Ontario (11–12). The plant watercress that reminds Homer of his mother's garden combines with the sandwich, the afternoon in August (also Homer's middle name, we later discover), the phone call from Professor Bruno, and the memory of his parents' death to form an assemblage full of meaning that Homer himself leaves understated. Although as a narrator Homer remains low-key throughout the novel, often fixating on small things, the text itself hints at epic significance in both humorous and melancholy ways: the name Homer, of course, but also the sandwich's contravention of Horace's much-cited advice not to begin an epic *ab ovo*, or with eggs. Horace famously disapproves of retelling the story of the Trojan War with Leda's twin eggs, one of which hatched Helen, who is then said to have launched the thousand-ship war effort. The idea of twin eggs textually transforming to become two sandwich ingredients might seem humorous, but the novel's humor cuts many ways. The movement towards the body and the earth implied by the sandwich and garden memory is combined with Homer's thought of his parents' fatal road trip. Beginning *ab ovo* isn't merely literalized with the eggs in the sandwich. Leda's two eggs also become the two deaths Homer is still grieving. And, even more ironically, these unforeseen deaths on the road would have occurred in exactly the way Horace prescribes for epics to begin, in the midst of things, *in medias res*.

Professor Bruno himself has both grand and tiny ambitions for his proposed trip. Finishing up a biography of the brilliant and mysteriously vanished Ontario poet John Skennen, Bruno wants to add telling real-life tidbits to his largely literary study. By "driving through the land on which the poet John Skennen had lived, the land about which Skennen had written, the land that had created the artist," he hopes to enliven his biography with "'touches': a few colourful details, any anecdotes he might glean from people who'd known Skennen at different stages of his life" (12). Homer grafts a minor quest of his own onto the trip, deciding to accompany Bruno as driver and note-taker because he can also pursue his interest in botany along the way, and in particular, seek out a special rarity, "a plant called five fingers (*Oniaten grandiflora*) that was said to have fantastic medicinal properties—the ability to cure jaundice, for instance" (13). This fanciful plant's name, "Oniaten," as Megan Kuklis points out and the text itself will later signal, recalls a legendary figure of Indigenous folklore, the spectrally disembodied and haunting "dry hand." The hand, as in *The Night Tiger* and *Call Me Zebra*, is a detail of manifold significance in *Days by Moonlight*. A key way that the hand relates to the details Homer most values is the implied conceit that the many botanical illustrations throughout the book represent Homer's hand-drawn pencil sketches. And the anecdotal "touches" with which Bruno wishes to embellish his biography are analogically linked to these botanical sketches that pepper the text. Both sketches and touches, while details, also exist in an exemplary relationship to the Canadian land. Bruno sees the art of poetry and the character of the land as existing in a mutually supportive circuit. He translates Goethe as saying something that, ironically, might resonate more with Area Studies proponents than with World Literature advocates: "If you want to understand the poet, then you've got to go to the poet's country." Affirming this, he goes on to add his own national perspective, however, one in keeping with the policies of a country with strong protections and support for its national arts:

> But I say if you want to understand a country, then you've got to go to the poets and artists, to the ones who refashion the world and make it live for their fellows. And where do these poets draw their inspiration? From earth, ground, stories, dreams, language, and history. That's what a place is, Alfie. It feeds off us while we feed off it. It's a bit of a paradox, you know, like context giving context to a context, but there you have it.
>
> 18

Bruno supports an imaginative symbiosis in which the Canadian land gives rise to Canadian art, which articulates a worldview through a Canadian context, lending others an understanding of the land. It makes sense that the idea of a road trip to collect oral history, verbal accounts of John Skennen's memorable moments, would work on his mind like an inspiring chronotope. A journey that stitches together anecdotal touches, short stopovers, and small towns works to sketch out a poetic Canada that is really an apotheosis of quirky, and not always hospitable, Ontario.

Likewise, Homer is drawn to the land in order to draw out in sketches its prized specimens, ones that have not just scientific but also talismanic value. And sometimes the legends or memories that lend this extra value are fraught. "The world doesn't exist until you draw it, Alfie!," he recalls his mother saying, and he agrees, remarking on all the memories that come back to him as he flips through his sketchbooks. Moving between the numbers five and four as both the text's motifs and imaginings of higher dimensions often do, Homer shifts from discussing the plant five fingers to the first one he ever sketched:

> My first drawing was of a four-leaf clover I saw in the schoolyard at Davisville. The clover, which I'd heard brought good luck, was a kind of 'mixed signal.' I found it just before John Smith punched me in the face and I punched him back. Then again, John and I have been close friends since Grade 6, a year after I drew the clover. I'm not a mystical person, but I think of it this way: I'm drawn to flowers, herbs, and weeds, some of which I draw over and over. I feel a connection to them, and, in drawing them, I allow them the place in my life they were meant to have.
>
> 15

The four-leaf clover Homer drew in Grade 5 inaugurates not only his sketching but also hand-to-hand combat, and yet a lifelong friendship later ensues. This detail condenses so much: the desire to cull meaning and fortune from the earth's plants, the human hostilities that take the foreground, and the friendship fostered nonetheless. Both Bruno's and Homer's considerations of the detail speak to strange circularities, paradoxes, "mixed signals," and struggles that inform a notion of place. But Homer's words go a step further than Bruno's. Bruno's frequent refrain "there you have it" that allows for as much befuddlement as possession differs from Homer's sense of allowance and destiny as he cedes plants a place "they were meant to have." His acknowledgment raises questions of rightness.

Just Rituals

If rituals of sacrifice are a key mechanism for moving worldly entities into realms of the sacred, and games of chance are often repurposed oracles that return what was once removed back into common use, what to make of the peculiar festivals and institutions that give the novel's small towns their character? At the core of these bizarre events and spaces lie questions of justice, and just as Bakhtin in *Problems of Dostoevsky's Poetics* lists two ancient "serio-comical" sources for literature's carnivalization, Socratic dialogue and Menippean Satire (109), we find characters debating the justness of their town's practices, and these practices are more than over the top. Exemplifying not only the anomie at the heart of laws and norms, but also the distancing tactics that thrive amongst people in close proximity, two neighboring towns, Nobleton and Coulson's Hill, each boast an absurd festival the other abhors. Passing through both towns at opportune moments, Bruno and Homer not only observe "Pioneer Days" and "The Indigenous Parade," but are also present in pubs as residents critique their festival's evolution, current state, and relative merits compared to the other town's event. Both festivals are meant to honor early inhabitants of the land in a respectful manner, and they have been successively altered to incorporate more inclusive respect and politically nuanced ideals. A strange standoff ensues when either an urge to enshrine the traumas of the past creates continual ethically questionable calamities in the present or attempts at all-encompassing inclusivity meet with an ever-overturning carnival force that exhausts itself. While both cases are seen as perverse, they are also presented as peculiarly emblematic of the nation.

Two houses, their building then burning, are at the center of Nobleton's "Pioneer Days," but in line with Bakhtin, the festival encompasses the whole community. Arriving just before the main events, Homer observes all the townspeople, whether they are dressed as pioneers or not, carrying pioneer era tools. In what might seem a hybridization of Shirley Jackson's "The Lottery" and Jorge Luis Borges's "The Lottery of Babylon," Homer recounts the destructive and potentially deadly festival's history as it has been conveyed to him. Supposedly begun in the 1950s, Pioneer Days was meant to "celebrate the 'pioneering spirit,' the current that had passed through the men and women—Europeans, mostly—who'd founded the town in the 1800s, carving it out of the scrub, shrub, and rock" (54). Originally, two teams, those living on either side of King Street, would compete for a trophy and thousands of dollars by seeing which could construct a home more swiftly. The newly constructed houses would stand for a year and be burned to the ground at the start of the next annual festival. Out of consideration for the county's impoverished families, the rules were amended in the 1960s to include a raffle with the winning poor families being allowed to occupy the new houses for a year until their ritually required burning. Then in the 1980s allowances were made for the families occupying the houses by permitting them to fight to save their dwellings. With the houses moved to a site on the outskirts of town and wells dug nearby, the competition reached a new stage of political and crowd appeal, and in the 1990s families began to train in fire dousing and townspeople started to wager on festival outcomes. An event with something for everyone, the festival includes on-site wells that appease those wishing to be generous to the poor, and, by contrast, "those who felt it was wrong to give unfortunate people homes they hadn't earned (Conservatives, mostly)" are placated by the difficulty and low success rate for families fighting to save their houses. Two ends of the town's political spectrum appeased, the ritual becomes a total communal form, a "spectacle" rendering "a close approximation of true pioneering distress," as well as "a living lesson in history, the past and present intimately touching" (55).

Yet the results of 2017's festival, as Homer and Bruno witness, leave everyone dissatisfied. When the town favorites and three-year home savers, the McGregors, have victory in sight, with a fourth straight win granting them by new provision their home permanently, they suddenly see their competitors' little girl run back into her family's rapidly burning house to retrieve her doll. "Now there was real alarm," Homer says, "the plight of children being of some concern to most Canadians" (59). When the strapping young McGregors run in after her, both families, McGregors and Ainsleys, must turn to extinguishing the fire consuming the Ainsleys' house. The valiant McGregors lose their home but save the girl as well as the Ainsleys' dwelling. Despite this double rescue, everyone boos. The town favorites have lost. Later in the Wolf and Pendulum tavern, "a place," remarks Homer, "that reminded me of taverns I've been in throughout the province," customers decry the house burning's outcome (61). One remarks, "People can't give the poor anything, without they burn it down, too," and another adds, "The fuckers giveth and they taketh away" (62). With a "general agreement that an injustice has been done," the customers turn to debating whether the festival's organizing committee, which refuses to take the McGregors' heroism into account or to honor the Ainsleys' offer to give them their home, acts without reason or reasons without a good purpose. In memorializing history, the organizers uphold a cruel working of fortune:

> It seemed, as far as the committee was concerned, that one had to remember the whole purpose of the house burning. The purpose was to celebrate the past through understanding. In the past, fate made no exceptions. Fire came. Houses burned. Lives went on, differently. Had their house burned two hundred years previously, the McGregors would have been left as they were now. That was the point. For the legions that had come from Europe and pushed the Indigenous off the land, calamity was irrevocable.

62–3

Far from a carnivalistic overturning of laws and fate, the festival's insistence on recurring calamity seems to repeat what Walter Benjamin in "On the Concept of History" has famously called history's "one single catastrophe" (392). Allowing for ritualistic alterations but no humane considerations, the festival partakes of the sacred more than the profane. If poor families' shelters are being sacrificed, that is, given over to gods, the gods are the pioneering Europeans and it is almost as though the families take the place of Indigenous peoples. Perhaps an uncomfortable intuitive feeling for this structure inspires everyone in Nobleton to say, "But at least we're not Coulson's Hill," and further, "You look up *stupid* in the dictionary, you'll see a picture of the Indigenous Parade" (62).

Yet before carrying on to Coulson's Hill in time for this pageant, Homer finds inspiration in the tavern debate's details for meditations on the nation and the land:

> Beneath these small impressions, there was something deeper. I could feel the flow of that particularly Canadian thing: passion brought on by outrage. Outrage seeped into the Wolf and Pendulum and permeated the place: an outrage that turned, at times, to aggression, an aggression that few of those in the pub would have permitted themselves unless prompted by their sense of political imbalance—the fate of the poor, petty rules running roughshod over good people, distant committees dictating to those who lived in Nobleton. In the Wolf and Pendulum, I recognized what you could call a 'Canadian instinct' or, if you were being unkind, a Canadian addiction: moral reproach.
>
> 63–4

An intriguing blend of consistent national sentiment and anomic anger licensed by a perceived imbalance in "petty rules," the tavern's outrage creates a sense of place on macro and micro levels. And these thoughts return Homer to figures of the human hand. Puzzled as usual by his "compatriots" in their compulsion for "moral superiority," Homer marvels that "No opportunity for finger-pointing goes untaken, while the finger-pointing itself leads nowhere but to more finger-pointing." Falling asleep reassured by the thought that he now sees these sentiments as "typical of Canadian life, of my life," Homer awakens the next day and sets out with Bruno for Coulson's Hill, along the way noticing a plant that is a variation of *Oniaten grandiflora* or five fingers (64). A specimen of *Monotropa cinqueflora* (illustration provided) or five flower pops up along Highway 27 where they've stopped while a hung-over Bruno throws up. Unexpectedly growing, as would a mushroom, from a fallen tree's stump, this specimen of five flower is actually four-headed, and although Homer searches vainly for a full version, he nonetheless feels gratitude for finally seeing this long heard of flower at all. Nationally normalized anomie becomes newly graspable to Homer, and encountering a relative of *Oniaten grandiflora*, though one not showing its full five flowers, spurs the same optimism he finds in the partly positive message of his Grade 5 four-leaf clover. It's as though a naturalization of nation occurs amidst an unruly and anarchically traditionalist town festival, but this apprehension of national nature, like Homer's sighting of a deficient relative of five finger, falls short of grasping fully something native to the land.

As with "Pioneer Days," "The Indigenous Parade" is "the product of a committee," but while Nobleton's committee pursues living memory to the point of injustice, the parade organizers of Coulson's Hill have justice uppermost in their minds. As Homer notes, "Like most Canadians, the people of Coulson's Hill sometimes noticed that the Indigenous populations of Canada had been mistreated in any number of ways and for quite some time," and as a result, "Most felt it was not enough to simply notice this. Justice demanded restitution, even if only a symbolic one" (70). Designed by a town councilor to be an "'amusing but serious'" event, almost an intentionally carnivalistic uprising, the parade stages Indigenous people throwing tomatoes or similar items at the nation's founders. Originally this involves some townspeople dressing up as the country's founding fathers and others, even some participants from out of town, dressing in supposedly Indigenous wear. A tourist success yet political mess, the festival draws regional participants and cultural outrage in equal measure:

> The use of sacred native symbols was roundly condemned by Indigenous people from around the country—or at least, by the few who actually heard about the parade. But so was the idea that Indigenous people should be the only ones allowed to throw tomatoes at the Fathers of Confederation. Where, for instance, was the restitution for the Chinese who'd died building the railroad across the country? Or the Japanese who'd been driven from their homes? And how could Coulson's Hill, the town, say they 'stood with the Indigenous' while enjoying the privileges that had come from Confederation? Then, too, there was the uncomfortable—and entirely unforeseen—fact that the French Fathers—George-Étienne Cartier, Jean-Charles Chapais, Hector Louis Langevin, Étienne-Paschal Taschéé—and their families were more vigorously pelted with tomatoes than were the English Fathers.
>
> 71

In response, the organizers both restrict and expand costume and vegetable rules, barring sacred Indigenous headwear but allowing for a category of "other grievances" that includes "blackface, there being so few Black people in the area" and cooked bok choy as a throwable item (72). French symbols are removed from the costumes for the French Fathers, and the consumption of alcohol is frowned upon. Still highly popular and highly offensive, the parade now draws Indigenous participants who feel no need to don costumes. But their zeal in tomato throwing inspires defensive feelings in a way that the dressed up Indigenous participants' efforts failed to: "As the attack was no longer altogether symbolic, it brought out passionate—not to say violent—argument and passionate defence of the underappreciated Caucasians who'd done so much to make the country what it is. The Fathers of Confederation, when you thought about it, had made their own (posthumous) humiliation possible. And that—the constitutional possibility of humiliation—was something worth defending" (72-3). The "largely Liberal" town council amends the festival with each wave of criticism, at first barring Indigenous people from dressing as anything other than founding fathers, sparking a protest in which the Indigenous elders occupy the trucks designated for the fathers while wearing full ceremonial dress only to be hesitantly pelted with tomatoes by townspeople trying to represent the Indigenous. A misguided attempt at historical redress founded on supposed respect for diversity, the festival's use of role play unravels into an entropy of aggression, fragility, and role reversal. The council believes it is then left with no option but to attempt a wholesale symbolic leveling of the festival's playing field.

By the time Homer and Bruno come to witness the parade in its eleventh version, everyone is frisked for Indigenous gear and uniformly given blue sheets to wear, "blue being a sacred colour" (73). The tomato pelting continues as before, but with a difficulty in distinguishing identities. Still, amongst the trucks of people meant to represent founders and their families, those groups with larger families are suspected to represent the French. This muted version of the parade completes itself and its success is praised at the Rebarbative Moose pub. While residents deem it the best parade of all and extol its "moral superiority" over Nobleton's "Pioneer Days," Homer finds, "Both events—the parade and the house burning—were founded on notions of justice, but both seemed perverse" (74). Their guide and recent interview subject, Mr. Henderson, who claims John Skennen hasn't died or disappeared at all, says Skennen would support Homer's views: "He calls both of them displays of power, not goodwill" (75). The mirroring festivals cast criticism on a town of mostly Conservatives and one of largely Liberals (a potentially two not three or more Canadian party critique), one with its unbending work ethic and exalting of the past, the other with its token and tokenizing gestures toward redress and inclusivity, gestures that barely hide

Eurocentric Anglo-French grudges. One festival essentially wants sacrifice but descends into tavern dissent, the other wants lively dissent, but only via a carefully curated uprising that undermines itself so many times its energy fizzles out as uniformly "sacred" sheets blanket everyone. As inverses of each other, both festivals reveal politics of the sacred and profane that provide neither hierophanic revelation nor carnivalistic revolution, but instead a kind of naturalized national stalemate.

Institutional Settings

On either side of Chapter 2's tale of two ill-conceived town fairs are two stressful institutional visits, first to a regional hospital where Homer's tonsils are almost unnecessarily removed and second to the thoroughly detailed dioramas of the Museum of Canadian Sexuality. Two powerful Bakhtinian forces, those of the earth and the body, are rendered questionable throughout the novel. Just as on-the-ground popular forms fail to adequately address or redress national history, injuries, therapies, and celebrations of the body lead to arbitrary arguments and alienating abstractions. Indeed, our narrator almost becomes voiceless in hospital. Having been attacked by dogs on a visit to Skennen's childhood friend, the farmer Brady, Homer overrides everyone else's apathetic reaction to his injuries and insists on going to a hospital. Brady and his son Dougal seem to take injuries casually, both displaying hands with missing fingers, and Brady explaining, "That's what it means to live on a farm. It's a lazy man who still has all his fingers, is what I say" (28). When Dougal and his father quarrel, over of all things poetry, Homer politely steps out the door only to be swarmed by Brady's three Argentine mastiffs before he can run to the car. Explicit about the danger the deep bites to his thighs might pose, Homer speculates, "had I been even slightly better endowed, I'd have lost part of my penis" (33). Homer and Bruno make it to Our Lady of Mercy Health Centre in East Gwillimbury where he awakens to find a nurse concerned over his loss of blood now that he is being prepped for a tonsillectomy. Insisting there's been a mistake, that he's there for dog bites not tonsillitis, Homer is told by the courteous but firm nurse, "Well, there you go ... the dogs probably made your tonsils worse. That's how trauma works sometimes" (37). After several rounds of this sort of debate, Homer describes feeling "engaged in a pitched battle of politeness, those kindly—but ferocious—skirmishes that are so common in our country: each side trying to polite the other into submission." Admitting he "prefer[s] these sorties to the open arguments that happen in the United States," he meekly confesses, "But I felt that, the battle being for my tonsils, it was important that I win." In fact, Homer's entreaties alone win nothing, and he is saved, he says, by "chance," as wheeled by Bruno before the planned surgery, he manages to yell for help and the two insist on the staff's rechecking the lists (38). Given a pomegranate by another nurse concerned at his lack of nourishment and told by Bruno that Brady's three dogs were like three-headed Cerberus guarding Hades, the hospital visit that ends Chapter 1 prepares us for what Bruno calls "travelling through the underworld" (39), a Hades he insists isn't Hell. To be sure, there is a carnivalesque force here that brings sanctified medical care low and reveals unseemly aggression lurking amidst consideration, but, again, in the pitched battle of civility itself, no one gives ground.

If the first chapter's hospital episode leaves us at a bureaucratic low point, the Museum of Canadian Sexuality in Chapter 3 provides an anxious and ambivalent apotheosis. At the heart of *Days by Moonlight* are interlocked tales of woe, loss of love, and failures in understanding. Coming off hearing and experiencing some of these, Bruno and Homer pick up a hitchhiker who tells them of New Tecumseth's special museum where he works as a ticket collector. He implores them to see it, even offering them his employee discount. Put off by the idea, Homer inwardly objects to the "'publicizing' of sex," and while claiming not to be "prudish," he recalls his father, a Doctor of Divinity, asking, "What's the point ... of surrendering the most wonderful thing humans have to businessmen and carnies?" and then declaring, "I just don't understand this need to abase the sacred" (121). It's not clear, though, that the Museum of Canadian Sexuality (its dioramas bound to recall for local readers the Royal Ontario Museum in Toronto) does commodify, carnivalize, or desecrate sexuality. Instead, it makes so-called Canadian sex a national religion.

Treating it at a well-meant remove, the museum offers an exalted taxonomy of sex that troubles Homer but arouses Bruno. Not only this, but the Museum of Canadian Sexuality provides an interlude that, however bizarrely institutional, most clearly coincides with, if also parodies, Alexis's original source of inspiration for the theme of visitation, *Teorema*. Just as in Pasolini's work each person, male or female, in an Italian household has sex with a strange visitor, and this encounter catalyzes upending life changes for each of them, Bruno and Homer's guide through the museum is the mysteriously compelling and gender nonbinary Michael. Clad in a royal blue pantsuit and evoking thoughts of Archangel Michael, this guide mystifies Bruno, who at first calls them "madam," while eliciting a cautious respect from Homer, who immediately refers to them with third-person plural pronouns. While Homer appears to remain neutral towards Michael, Bruno comes away admitting to feeling a surprising attraction. Uncanny angelic images emerge in two other moments as well: first in the exhibit of a lifelike, also gender-indeterminate and blue-clad, statue that's meant to represent "all Canadians," but that Michael, apologetically, tells Homer is for that day the "Caucasian model" (whereas the prior day's display was "the older Negro") and second in a poster Homer finds advertising a previous exhibit called "PIERRE TRUDEAU: ANGEL OF THE EROTIC" (123; 128). This use of Pierre Trudeau might seem particularly ironic to those who remember his famous utterance as a young Justice Minister: "There's no place for the state in the bedrooms of the nation" ("Trudeau"). In addition to the museum's parodic and Pasolinian angelic aura, one particular exhibit highlights theorems. Initially embarrassing yet absorbing for Bruno and completely off-putting for Homer is the first diorama to which Michael guides them: a display case featuring a hotel bed inside and countless algebraic notations etched on the outer glass surface. When Michael gives each of them a card with a legend for deciphering the symbols, Bruno blushes upon understanding the sexual positions indicated. But Homer reflects on the political desires behind the diorama: "This desire for completion—which was a desire for inclusion—accounted for the sheer number of 'notations' stenciled on the glass. Meanwhile, the penetrations and accommodations accounted for, the theatre of the Canadian sexual imagination could be given its due with the dioramas" (124). Much as Homer likes details and taxonomy in the realm of botany, a realm that might be romantically tied to the land, this particular exhibit and the museum's vision of the nation in general have an effect on him similar to that of Brady's dogs and the proposed tonsillectomy. He feels swarmed, overwhelmed by bureaucracy, and virtually unmanned. Not only is Homer still grieving his parents' death, but he begins the road trip on the heels of a breakup, reporting that his would-be life partner Anne has left him for someone else. The museum's rarified catalogue of potential couplings broadens Bruno's sense of possibilities, despite his forbearing to act on them, but robs Homer yet again of a sense of real belonging, and this loss is often cast in virile terms. Thinking of love as potentially yet another alphanumeric representation, he reports feeling "as if Anne had left me yet again" (130).

What Homer emphasizes as most embarrassing about the museum, however, is its targeted typing of others in its attempts at inclusion. Even before Michael apologizes to Homer for the racial representation, or lack thereof, in the hermaphroditic all-Canadian statue exhibit, they greet both Bruno and Homer in the museum's antechamber by asking pointed questions: "Is it just the two of you?"; "Are you heterosexual?"; and "Is your partner also heterosexual?" (122). Ever in fear of causing offense in the midst of causing it, as is the case with so many of the town festival organizers, Michael explains that although the questions are intrusive, the answers are good to know because the museum's content "includes any number of gratifications. So, if you think you're likely to be offended, you can get a full refund at this stage and we'll go no further" (122). Just as these opening forays put the onus on visitors to profess their potential narrowness and desire for no further progress, the final display Bruno describes, one Homer forgoes, puts visitors in control of creating their perfect partner. In this interactive exhibit called "The Canadian Construction," participants select "mouths, eyes, accents, vocabularies" to create their desired virtual "Canadian lover." Bruno admits the choices are "typically Canadian, based on the population we have," in other words, dominated by "European characteristics" and offering, for example, a "Malaysian accent," by special request only and only if enough Malaysian-accented visitors have appeared that week (133). A send-up of potentially state-sanctioned pansexualism, the portrait of the museum merges this critique with one of a misguided cultural mosaic that devolves into fetishism, tokenism, and endless taxonomy in its quest for all-encompassing inclusion. On the one hand, it's as though two national policies often associated with the years of Pierre Trudeau's prominence—the decriminalization of homosexual acts and the evolution from French–English biculturalism to multiculturalism—are parodied as forming the basis for an alienating national religion of inclusion. On the other, this enshrined urge toward inclusive representation that takes differing selves as objects rather than subjects and can objectify according to the perceived vagaries of popular demand is panned as particularly injurious to someone with Homer's longings and dilemmas.

Mixed Signals

Against this ambivalently multiculturalist backdrop, Homer has a wistful reminiscence of his romance with Anne that carries significant traces of an intriguing, perhaps residual Anglophilia:

> We'd been walking together along Kingston Road when she showed me the steps to Glen Stewart Park, not far from where she lived. It was summer, my first time in that green place, and I was enchanted by everything: the broad wooden steps, the plank railing, the steep decline into the ravine, the sound of the stream

running through it. We were happy then, and she turned to me, smiling, tucking a strand of light-brown hair behind her ear and then kissing me, for no reason but pleasure in the moment, knowing the pleasure was shared, taking pleasure in the knowing, before we walked through the park, past houses that were like modest mansions in some secret England.

130

Taking in this mix of imagery, suggestive of Andrew Marvell and Jane Austen as well as Jean Rhys, readers might wonder about the degree to which Anne signifies Anglo-Canada (Queen's Anne's Lace being one of the few non-fanciful plants illustrated in the novel) and its tenacious dominance in Ontario, or else the anglophone in its many literary and geographic manifestations. But the novel tends, as does Homer, toward extreme discretion and understatement in matters of identity. In fact, Homer's feelings about his own racial identity come to the fore most explicitly halfway through the novel in the account of the town he and Bruno visit just before New Tecumseth with its illustrious museum.

As though delaying in catching up with a John Skennen he's now been told is very much alive, Bruno suggests detouring for a lunchtime stopover at Schomberg's famous tavern The Scruffy Dog. It turns out that Homer is familiar with Schomberg's tavern but is ambivalent about being in the town:

> The Scruffy Dog was no different from taverns all around the province, except that it was in Schomberg. Of course, that, in itself, was noteworthy. Schomberg is different. I knew the town. I'd known it since I was a child, having spent summers there as a boy, between the ages of seven and fourteen. Even so, I find it an unsettling place. My unease has nothing to do with Schomberg's Black population. Being Black, I'm comforted by the thought of a town of Black people. My problem is more practical: when I'm in Schomberg, I'm often unsure of what's being said to me.

112

In Alexis's version Schomberg is a town populated in the nineteenth century first by abolitionists and then by the freed slaves who use the Underground Railroad to get there. Fueled by their ideals yet unprepared for actual Black people, the abolitionist residents of Schomberg tolerate everything except Black speech, since "It was disconcerting for Schombergians to hear their town become foreign." Outlawing Black speech in public during the day, these Schombergians force Black residents into new communicative modes: "They kept quiet but developed a culture of silence, communicating with each other by hand signals and movements of the head" (113). This mode of "day speak" becomes a point of pride for the Black community over time, and as the White population drifts away, the current residents keep the speech laws, "arguing that their ancestors had put racism to good use, creating a unique language and culture" (114), a phrase that ironically echoes rhetoric used to support bilingualism as well as multiculturalism with its principled preservation of diverse heritages. While Homer mostly gets by in day speak, his imperfect command leads Bruno into trouble, notably when he sends him to The Scruffy Dog's bartender to order tea. Interestingly, Bruno is all too enthusiastic about being in Schomberg. While Homer usually takes some "pleasure at the sight of so many Black people" and experiences "an immediate connection to the place, a sense of belonging," Bruno's companionship and fascination with the town throws him off (114). "He knew, or was familiar with, the idea that there are places in Ontario where he, though white, would be in the minority," reflects Homer, but adds, "an idea is not a thing. It's the thing behind the thing and it's always a little odd (or exhilarating) to feel an idea come into the world, like a phantom become solid" (115). Instructed by Homer to keep his hands down on the street, Bruno inadvertently raises them when confronted by a woman, only to be roundly slapped for sexual indiscretion. Later at the bar when Homer feels he's safely taught Bruno the gestures for herbal tea, Bruno mishandles his fingers and signals a need to vomit. Homer himself is embarrassed to find his own cues a little off when he attempts the order and gestures for water not tea. These mishaps, while awkward for Bruno, are humiliating for Homer, who feels thrown into confusion about who he is.

Homer becomes aware not only of "the gulf between blood and culture" but of "a kind of doubt in me that I was myself Black," and further, he questions whether his ideas of Blackness in relation to Canadianness will withstand his own scrutiny:

> I brooded on the idea that the remaining white people of Schomberg who knew 'day speak' were, in some way, more 'Black' than I was. Was I, then, more Canadian than Black? This was an even stranger thought, since Schomberg and its inhabitants were all proudly Canadian. It was proof that I unconsciously excluded the people of Schomberg from 'the Canadian.' Which is to say that, to some extent, I excluded myself, too. In Schomberg, I ended up feeling inadequate, shamed, cancelled out, as if I only precariously belonged anywhere.
>
> 118

If Homer's memory of Anne is one in which a shared knowledge of shared pleasure creates a perfect sense of belonging, his negative counterpart occurs, even before the state-sponsored pansexual bedroom exhibit, in his experience of the body in language in Schomberg. As a child what he finds confusing is that despite knowing "people 'spoke' with their whole bodies ... there were also times when heads and hands moved without signifiying." And this inability to distinguish instances of meaning and non-meaning in moving bodies causes the child Homer "bad dreams in which trembling willows or billowing drapes said nasty things to me," or, in other words, moments when animated plants and even inanimate objects rebuff him (114). As with *The Night Tiger* in which the human hand is seen as disturbing when each finger embodies its own disconnected intelligence, an expansive and unsettling animacy is figured here in heads, hands, trees, and even objects. Homer's journey through Ontario and through memory offers so many instances of dispossession, as though languages of the hand, the body, the land and its houses that all seem to beckon to him also fail him.

Nation and Profanation

A wandering mock-epic hero, Homer is repeatedly brought low, but also humble from the start. While the town fairs and taverns he visits all boast their special and supposedly preservation-worthy traditions, he sees uniformity, constantly remarking on their equally perverse interpretations of justice and the interchangeability of their gathering spots. Ever tolerant, he withstands others' awkward efforts at inclusion, but often leaves feeling, if not explicitly injured or threatened, not quite recognized yet all too interpellated. Among models of the profane, Agamben's, Pasolini's, and Bakhtin's, it's difficult to say which might sketch a way out of the impasse that is Homer's Ontario. If we look for a return to common use, a disruptively manifest divinity, or a force of radical familiarization alone, we will probably be frustrated. In a sense, carnivalizing comedy arises yet neutralizes itself, as public spaces, the commons are already set apart as sacred and they set ever more distinctively defined individuals apart as well, with even disquieting images of divinity pressed into this service. Amidst this fractal model of difference and inclusion that seems to play out in ever increasing dimensions, where, the novel seems to ask, is there left for an earthly, sensuous, familiarizing energy to go?

At the same time, however, this outlining of an interpretative predicament underrates the central role ambivalence plays in Bakhtin's carnival. It's crucial to carnival's energy that it not remain one-sided, its critiques ideologically monological or obviously consistent (*Problems* 126). A key, longstanding festival act that embodies this core two-sidedness is the crowning and decrowning of the mock king. Here the prime values of the carnival world—fortuitous change, death, and renewal—are typified:

> Crowning/decrowning is a dualistic ambivalent ritual, expressing the inevitability and at the same time the creative power of the shift-and-renewal, the *joyful relativity* of all structure and order, of all authority and all (hierarchical) position. Crowning already contains the idea of immanent decrowning: it is ambivalent from the very start. And he who is crowned is the antipode of a real king, a slave or a jester; this act, as it were, opens and sanctifies the inside-out world of carnival.
>
> *Problems* 124

Although Bakhtin refers to a sanctifying of carnival's inverted world, we shouldn't take this gesture as straightforwardly sacred. Ever dualistic, Bakhtin's carnivalization makes for messy mixtures, especially of the sacred and profane: "All things that were once self-enclosed, disunified, distanced from one another by a noncarnivalistic hierarchical worldview are drawn into carnivalistic contacts and combinations. Carnival brings together, unifies, weds, and combines the sacred with the profane, the lofty with the low, the great with the insignificant, the wise with the stupid" (124). Nonetheless, such urges toward non-hierarchical combination and dualistic ambivalence play out in unexpected ways in a multicultural liberal democracy that is the successor to two settler colonialisms. A novel of parodic yet truly wistful longing, *Days by Moonlight* uses its eccentric fantasism partly to engage with an indigeneity it seems unable to address in any other way. Ever presenting its key ideas through interanimating doubles, the novel outlines two fantastic approaches to the Indigenous: a colonial explorer's queer orgy and a national poet's pilgrimage. The second diorama in the Museum of Canadian Sexuality depicts a field of the plant fire-lions (the word seemingly a mischievous pun on fire-loins). Although explorer accounts from the 1500s are vague, Michael explains, "It's here ... that Jacques Cartier and a handful of his men are rumoured to have engaged in a spontaneous orgy amongst themselves, under the influence of what we now know to be the aphrodisiac contained in fire-lions." Underscoring the Indigenous element, or what two-spirit writer Joshua Whitehead would critique as a settler colonialist "Indigiqueer idyll,"[3] Michael adds, "One of Cartier's own men wrote that the Iroquois had warned them about the field and told them in the plainest way what would happen" (125). This rehabilitated colonial queer history preemptively mocks the more romanticized story of Skennen, carving out an in-between path for Homer's own quest narrative.

If Homer is a mock Odysseus or Orpheus journeying through Hades with a chatty Hermetic Professor Bruno, Skennen (his adopted last name coming, we're told, from an Ojibwe word for "peace") is a mock sovereign double for Homer, an absent poet-king of the land. All his poems express longing—for ecstatic union with the land or for his lost love object, the enigmatic Carson Michaels. When Skennen first meets her, she is said to be "the most beautiful woman in Southern Ontario," a poet, and "a lovely twenty-one-year-old, dark-skinned, of Antiguan descent." Michaels is a native of Schomberg who has moved to Coulson's Hill, and because of her numerous suitors, she's also thought of "as a Penelope waiting to meet Odysseus" (84). But before she'll date anyone, she demands they answer a riddle and tell her what thing it is that makes her cry. Falling, as many have, in love with her at first sight, Skennen goes on a quest for the answer. Failed suitors from all over the region compile a list of rejected answers, but even luckier for Skennen, he happens onto the one man who can help him. Having been seduced in France and then cursed by a witch he abandons, Glenn Baillie is then doomed to love Michaels yet help another win Michaels' love. Fated to repeat his tale of woe until it helps someone win over Michaels, Baillie unfolds his story to Skennen in The Pig's Ear tavern in Peterborough. Fittingly, it's a detail in the story that suffices. Baillie mentions a painting, Pieter Balten's *La Kermesse*, that hung on the witch Madame Madeg's wall, and Skennen, familiar with it, has an immediate image of a porcelain jug a woman carries on the right side of the scene depicted. He has no idea why, but he knows a white porcelain jug makes Michaels cry. The porcelain jug answer wins Michaels' love, but the actual jug comes to be at the center of that love's loss, moving this vessel from eccentric detail to central object in a mysterious parable.

Mistakenly believing that anyone who knew her most significant object would know her, Michaels is shocked when one day Skennen smashes the jug she cares about so much. Skennen himself believes the white porcelain jug is at the heart of a trauma because when he, not wanting to admit his complete ignorance, guardedly questions Michaels about its significance, she claims it reminds her of her father, a potter: "How strong he'd been. Handsome and tall, gentle and loving, but terrifying, too. He'd once put her mother in the hospital with a single, backhanded blow" (105). Not understanding until it's too late that Michaels' mother was an abusive alcoholic and her father acted to defend her brother who was being whipped with a telephone cord, Skennen endeavors to steal the jug from her brother's house and smash it, retaining a fragment he later shows Michaels. When she realizes that her lover has shattered her father's first piece of pottery, an heirloom that serves the family as "the last true memento . . . of a man they'd all adored," Michaels has a revelation: "And so it finally came to her that she'd fallen in love with a man who'd known nothing about her, the very thing she'd tried to avoid!" The text then poses the question, partly in focalized free indirect discourse, partly at large: "But don't we usually fall in love with strangers?" (107). Thereafter, Skennen, bereft of Michaels' love, wanders the province in a drunken haze, eventually disappearing from view as others spread rumors of his death. Undoubtedly profaned, brought low, and shattered, the exalted white porcelain jug is at the heart of a series of misrecognitions: of the nature of love, of liberation, of past trauma. A side detail that takes center stage, it is something made and destroyed by hand. Stupidly casting himself out of his lovers' paradise, Skennen then becomes a central—provincialized, nationalized, naturalized, and, as we'll see, spiritualized—figure of grief in the novel, a vessel for Homer's working through of his own feelings of melancholia, mourning, and unbelonging.

Homer learns of Skennen's trials when, upon leaving the Museum of Canadian Sexuality, Bruno again detours the trip, mentioning the guide Michael has invited them to dinner at their home in Marsville. An engaging dinner party ensues as Michael's housemate, a photographer named Judith, is present, along with her doting father John Stephens, who, it turns out, is John Skennen. Skennen, now reverting to his birth name Stephens, unfolds his tale of lovelorn wandering that eventually led him, after being saved from a seemingly possessed pig's attack on a moonlit road, to Feversham, a haven boasting "the highest percentage in the world of priests and holy people living in it," not to mention, "foods to accommodate Jews, Hindus, Buddhists, Muslims, Shintoists, Neo-Pagans, Wiccans, and so on" (148). Said to be a place where God reposes, Stephens is encouraged to resolve his woe there, since, "Those in distress, those teetering between life and death who manage to stay with God as God sleeps, those who manage to share God's dreams, are granted grace if they choose it" (149). Not sure what to believe, but suddenly curious, Stephens comes to Feversham, and although it is ostensibly "as he remembered it: bland and unremarkable," its houses "identical to small houses all over the province," they now seem "falsely normal," as though strategically "hiding" their secret sacredness. In a Bakhtinian epiphany that turns Borgesian, Stephens confronts this appearance of the sacred amid the ordinary as a conundrum:

> Stephens accepted that Feversham might be sacred to him because he could no longer see it as profane. But he couldn't tell if profane Feversham was real or if sacred Feversham was. Which Feversham was the illusion, which the real? Or, to put it another way: between illusion and reality, which was least untrue?

For the novel's sovereign bard, the sacredness of his destination is, like Bakhtin's ritual of crowning and decrowning, "ambivalent from the very start."

At the core of Feversham's legendary closeness to God is a sacred grove referred to, with a seeming nod to Heidegger, as "the clearing." Yet while many pilgrims journey there, only some surrender to dream visions. Stephens tells of his reverie in which a female deity of love offers him the choice of magically coercing Michaels to love him again for one day, with the price being the loss of his gift of poetry ever after and his agreement to become a custodian of the clearing for four hours daily over twenty-four years. At first he is ready to have Michaels' love him however truly unwillingly. But upon reflection, Stephens finds the specified costs shocking. He then realizes that although he had thought of himself as a poet of love, poetry is too high a price to pay for it. Detecting falsity now in his love for Michaels, he releases it and goes onto love and marry another, settling down in nearby Barrow. He keeps his poetic craft, writing the poetry that makes him famous under the penname John Skennen, but then feels poetry slowly leaving him and takes up daily custodianship of the clearing by choice. Hearing Stephens's story effectively completes Bruno's quest but adds a crucial step for Homer's. In describing the clearing, Stephens mentions seeing at the edge of a pond at the end of the grove "a patch" growing "of what looked like human hands—greyish, severed from bodies, some lying palms up, some fingers down" (155). This detail seals Homer's desire to visit the clearing.

As a way to approach the *Oniaten grandiflora* at last, Homer takes up the pilgrimage, although he's told not everyone has visions let alone finds this plant there. Luckily, Homer spots them right away, and a woman walking beside him explains they make a wonderful salad. Finding himself at her cottage, Homer notices that all her wall paintings show men attacked by wolves. But his hostess, Clare, claims to she's drawn to the paintings' colors and compositions, not their violent content. They then share the salad, Homer finding the leaves' flavor "somewhere between a mild coriander and the taste of clover," and the fingerlike parts delicious, if somewhat crunchy and crackly. When Clare invites Homer to stay the night, she claims it's not for sex, but rather to set her free from a curse. "I'm a lycanthrope, but I turn into a wolf only when men desire me," she explains (166). Despite her belief that Homer is kind and must be her liberator, Homer declines upon hearing that were he to feel desire, she'd have to attack him. His attempt to leave fails, however, when he steps out the door to howls and a sense of shadowy creatures closing in on him. Quickly returning to the cottage and jumping under the bed's covers, Homer finds, unfortunately, that Clare sleeps in the nude and he's unable to suppress feelings of desire. Hearing growls from the other side of the bed, even as his thoughts turn to Anne, he feels a wolf stand briefly on his chest before leaping off and prowling around. The room seems full of wolves but Homer reports, "none of them attacked me. I assume this is because my longing had nothing to do with Clare. All my desire was for Anne. In my imagination I was with her and happy to face death in her arms" (169). The night over and ordeal survived, Homer awakens within the dream, finding himself in the clearing in the spot where the *Oniaten* used to be. Overcome with a sense of redemption and "love for creation itself," Homer feels "accounted for and taken in, taken in so completely that there was no longer any need for me to be a self," and further that "The boundary between Alfred Homer and the world was erased" (171). He then truly wakes up, this time in the guest room of the Methodist Reverend Sara Crosbie's cottage, and when he retells his vision, she and Bruno debate its meaning.

Bruno is clearly uncomfortable for the remainder of the novel with the idea that anything spiritual has happened in Feversham, and while he tends toward Freudian and Marxist modes of dream interpretation, his interpretative skills meet a challenge when Homer subsequently displays an uncanny ability for hands-on healing. Not only does Homer find, when he's mistaken for a healer at a Tim Hortons in Seaforth, that he can soothe the painfully arthritic hands of an elderly customer, but, after word spreads ahead of them en route to Barrow, he cures two seriously injured dogs at a local Greek diner. Bruno is forced to explain these incidents as forms of auto-hypnotic suggestion, and, not wanting to disturb or disappoint him, Homer agrees. In the last stop on their journey, they accept an invitation to see John Stephens at his home in Barrow, and there Stephens reveals to Homer alone a similar effect his experience in Feversham's clearing had on him. According to Stephens, a loose affiliation exists amongst those who receive in Feversham not only a vision but one of three hands-on abilities: fire-starting, object multiplying, and healing—even to the point of bringing dead animals back to life. Stephens himself discovered this second ability when on a bus trip, he kept reaching into his lunch bag to find more sandwiches. Later visited by a woman with the healing gift who was sent to him by Reverend Crosbie, Stephens learned that there were others like him and of their need for special discipline and discretion to live their lives peacefully, hence also his "disappearance." Relating a chilling story meant as a cautionary tale, Stephens tells Homer of the young Geraint Jordan who let everyone know of his healing power, only to be kidnapped by a violent gang who forced him to erase their fight wounds, eventually severing his hand in the mistaken belief it could work independently of its owner. It is Stephens who gives Homer some of the novel's most thematically resonant advice: "I think it's wrong *not* to do good when you can. But you've got to be stealthy with the irrational, stealthy the way artists and priests can be. You do the work so the work eclipses you. When Geraint Jordan let everyone know what he could do, it became about him, even though he didn't mean it to" (204). The self-professed silence, exile, and cunning of the modernist writer become the stay-at-home stealth of the willingly eclipsed practitioner. In this case, a crowning glimmers through the decrowning.

While the powerful profanation at work in the novel moves through a fantastically sacred plot, and in this sense, stays true to Bakhtin's sense of carnivalistic combination, the emphasis Bakhtin puts on ritualistic ambivalence as expressing an inevitable creative power of shift and renewal might seem reversed in Alexis's text. In fact, when it comes to the realm of the human, Homer leaves renewal a starkly open-ended question:

> But, of course, I didn't yet know what I was capable of doing. If I was simply a healer—and one who could bring small animals back to life—I would live accordingly. If I could bring people back from the dead, I would have to deal with that, too. But what a complex moral equation! Though I accepted that it was, in principle, a bad idea to bring those who'd found peace back to this uncertain world, I would have to awaken someone dead to know what I could do, wouldn't I?
>
> 218

Homer never resolves the questions of this final-page train of thought. Rather, returned to a Toronto he thinks of as his Eurydice, he looks out at Lake Ontario, recalls his parents, and, again mixing five and four-fold thoughts, beholds "a handful of clouds" as well as a passing "four-seat scull" (218).

Linda Dalrymple Henderson tells us that from the late 1950s into the 1960s and beyond, the spatial fourth dimension often had to fly under the banner of a supposed fifth one. She cites Madeleine L'Engle's 1962 novel *A Wrinkle in Time*, which "introduced thousands of young people to higher spatial dimensions and inter-dimensional travel," referring to such travel as "tessering" and naming a chapter "The Tesseract." Nonetheless, in probable awareness of the reigning Einsteinian understanding of the fourth dimension, L'Engle, Henderson points out, "identified the Tesseract not with the fourth dimension, but with the *fifth* dimension" (48). For contemporary writers who need extra dimensions to unfold their complex critiques as well as potential reclamations of problematic humanisms, the number five becomes suggestive. Played off the number four, it might recall a quincunx of novels in which the volume written fourth is meant to structurally come fifth. Or considered biologically, it might suggest a distinctively human hand contrasted with the animality of quadrupeds, whether tigers, zebras, pigs, or wolves. When the next dimension is blurry, not stably conceived as exactly a fourth or fifth, the human wavers. Alexis's innovation, what we might call his provincialized intra-dimensionism, is to bring this uncertainty home to the land and to figure it in the complex mimesis of plants, albeit ones temptingly offered by a changeable wolf-woman. Before its first chapter, his picture-book novel contains a legend, a diagram of the zigzag trajectory through the ten visited towns plus Toronto. The line connecting the dots makes five outer angles, their corners stretching out like digits or the points of a crown. The five-pointed crown of *Days by Moonlight* represents its peculiar chronotope, a road trip yielding vision in which the land itself has a stealthy sovereignty, one that comes through in odd detours and details. As with Homer's sketchbook, the novel's implied imagistic double, the illustrative touches testify to a longed-for connection between those drawn to details and the places where such drawn out details belong.

4

Foreseeable Futures: Avataric History in Amitav Ghosh's *Gun Island*

1. Incredulous Observers

Amid the COVID-19 pandemic outbreak of 2019–20, those looking for philosophical reflection from contemporary theorists might have happened onto the *European Journal of Psychoanalysis*'s thread "Coronavirus and Philosophers," which initially boasted postings from such European luminaries as Giorgio Agamben, Jean-Luc Nancy, and Roberto Esposito (Foucault et al.). What jumps out in the version of the conversation posted in March 2020 is the degree to which biopolitics, always controversial, became grounds for sharp, if extremely courteous, debate and the surprise from the intellectual community at Agamben's stance. Beginning on 26 February 2020, Agamben began to issue on the Italian Quodlibet website a series of brief essays decrying, as his first post was called "The Invention of an Epidemic." Certainly, Agamben wasn't the only one wondering what forms of freedom, expression, and community we were losing and might continue to give up long after the pandemic had passed. But his language in questioning Italy's response in light of statements from the National Research Council merged with the rhetoric of such far-right political leaders as Donald Trump in a way that was for many unexpected:

> The disproportionate reaction to what according to the CNR is something not too different from the normal flus that affect us every year is quite blatant. It is almost as if with terrorism exhausted as a cause for exceptional measures, the invention of an epidemic offered the ideal pretext for scaling them up beyond any limitation.
>
> "Invention"

Suggesting others might use a novel coronavirus as reason to deploy a model of exceptional measures previously made applicable by the War on Terror, Agamben risked appearing to be conceptually doing the same thing. Hence, perhaps,

Nancy's merging of the person and the paradigm in his own remarks on the thread. He declares that though Agamben may have given him unhelpful medical advice in the past, attempting to dissuade him from the heart transplant he credits with saving his life, "It is possible to make a mistake. Giorgio is nevertheless a spirit of such finesse and kindness that one may define him—without the slightest irony—as exceptional" ("Viral"). If Nancy embraces the exceptional in his memories of his decades-long friendship with Agamben, he still has harsh words for biopolitics in his posted email reply to Esposito, who claims that the interrelationship of politics and biology has become now more obvious than ever, but that he and Nancy have long differed in their views on this point. "Dear Robert," writes Nancy, "neither 'biology' nor 'politics' are precisely determined terms today. I would actually say the contrary. That's why I have no use for their assemblage" ("Riposte"). Perhaps it's predictable that faced with a confusing new virus, one hard to track because of its asymptomatic or merely mildly symptomatic carriers and because of the inadequacies in nations' testing abilities it revealed, a rarified intellectual debate would turn on issues of verification, either in the form of accusations of false faith (in biopolitics as a valid theoretical model) or denial (of medical reality). Agamben assumes the familiar maladies of the seasonal flu and a deleterious state of exception, Nancy doesn't see either "biology" or "politics" as specifically verifiable entities, while others such as Esposito implore us to look at what "anyone with eyes to see cannot deny" ("Cured"). If the philosophical debate over biopolitics that COVID-19 sparked seems not only to reenact arguments over disease control but also to resemble our current disputes over climate change, this is not by accident. For Esposito and, as we'll see, novelist Amitav Ghosh, these crises and controversies can be seen as aspects of a common larger problem.

Writing for the *Los Angeles Review of Books*, for which Michael Marder has also curated a series of philosophical reflections on COVID-19, Esposito expands on his claim that when it comes to believing in biopolitics or a contemporary "intertwining of politics and biological life," the "evidence [has] kept growing until it became astounding." And not only this, but "Now, the coronavirus outbreak and the geopolitical consequences that arose from it have brought the direct relationship between biological life and political interventions to its culmination." Notably, for Esposito this is a phenomenon of "three dimensions" ("Biopolitics"). The second and third of these are familiar points for longtime readers of Michel Foucault and Agamben: "the double process of the medicalization of politics and the politicization of medicine" and the "shift from ordinary democratic procedures to emergency measures." But the first dimension of biopolitics' newly astounding and undeniable prominence, while also conceptually familiar, is suggestively rich for the number of current developments it takes in and synthesizes as aspects of one paradigm:

> The first [dimension] is a shift of the political focus from individuals to certain segments of population. Whole sections of the population—considered at risk, but also bearers of contagion—are now affected by prophylactic practices with a twofold objective of securing their safety and keeping them at a distance. This is also the result of a veritable immunization syndrome that has long characterized the new biopolitical regime. What is feared even more than the disease itself is uncontrolled circulation in a social body already exposed to the general processes of contamination. Naturally, in a world where all internal borders are permeable, the dynamics of globalization have heightened this fear. The sovereignist parties' (*partiti sovranisti*) violent opposition to immigration should be interpreted in light of this immunization paradigm, rather than as a continuation of traditional nationalism.
>
> "Biopolitics"

The themes of globalization Esposito lists and links to a conceptual paradigm of immunization—concern at "uncontrolled circulation" and "permeable borders" as well as "violent opposition to immigration"—are all ones that Ghosh takes up throughout his oeuvre but addresses explicitly in reference to climate change in his 2016 book of essays, *The Great Derangement*, and in his novel of 2019, *Gun Island*. And indeed, Ghosh's third section on politics in *The Great Derangement* accords easily with Esposito's immunization paradigm. Ghosh notes that while mainstream politicians may express denial at global warming, their states' military wings have long been preparing for climate change, entertaining what he cites Christian Parenti as calling "the politics of the armed lifeboat," that is, suppression of uprisings, extreme defense of borders, and "aggressive anti-immigrant policing" (qtd. in *Great* 143). Ghosh sees this politics already at work in the Anglosphere's response to the waves of refugees fleeing Syria, and his contemplation of the politics of the armed lifeboat links borders, biopolitics, climate, and contagion just as Esposito's current reflections on COVID-19 do:

> The outlines of an "armed lifeboat" scenario can already be discerned in the response of the United States, United Kingdom, and Australia to the Syrian refugee crisis: they have accepted very few migrants even though the problem is partly of their own making. The adoption of this strategy might even represent the logical culmination of the biopolitical mission of the modern nation-state, since it is a strategy that conceives of the preservation of the "body of the nation" in the most literal sense: by a reinforcement of boundaries that are seen to be

under threat from the infiltration of the pathological "bare life" that is spilling over from other nations.

The trouble, however, is that the contagion has already occurred, everywhere: the ongoing changes in the climate, and the perturbations that they will cause *within* nations cannot be held at bay by reinforcing man-made boundaries.

Great 143–4

Whether we call it an immunity paradigm or armed lifeboat politics, the outlines are consistent, but what's additionally interesting as Ghosh shifts from issues of actual immigration to ones of metaphoric contagion is his imaginative casting of "bare life" as pathogen. A complex immunity paradigm pervades Ghosh's thinking, and his conception of pathogens and contagion cuts across categories as he analyzes not only politics but also aesthetics in the era of climate crisis.

For Ghosh the "body of the nation" bears an analogical relationship to the imagined identities of artistic forms, which likewise fend off perceived vital threats. Just as a robust military might make plans to keep bare life at bay, so the aesthetic conventions of the literary novel have worked to defend it, according to Ghosh, against thoughts of climate catastrophe. Ghosh's rebuke of the contemporary literary novel's unwillingness to recognize climate change resembles Esposito's alarm where European philosophical skepticism towards biopolitics is concerned: where Esposito sees denial of the stunningly obvious, Ghosh sees, as his title signals, a pervasive and consistent derangement. It is as though the prevailing conventions of literary fiction have struggled to immunize it from climate crisis. So inimical to the dominant imbalanced world systems in place and the arts and culture they underwrite, Ghosh argues, are thoughts of climate catastrophe that true considerations are left to inhabit marginalized spaces and modes:

> To introduce such happenings [such as seemingly improbable but actually occurring extreme weather events] into a novel is in fact to court eviction from the mansion in which serious fiction has long been in residence; it is to risk banishment to the humbler dwellings that surround the manor house—those generic outhouses that were once known by names such as "the Gothic," "the romance," or "the melodrama," and have now come to be called "fantasy," "horror," and "science fiction."

Great 24

Drawing on the work of Franco Moretti, Ghosh claims the modern novel is paradoxically set up to avoid allowing the improbable to take center stage, however much convenient coincidences and accidents may subtly and peripherally propel plots' progress. "Here, then, is the irony of the 'realist' novel," he concludes, "the very gestures with which it conjures up reality are actually a concealment of the real" (23). Where realism avoids the real and so becomes insufficient to address current realities and very real possibilities, modes that engage the unlikely gain advantage. Though Ghosh doesn't put it this way, we can say that in contrast to dominant denial-based fiction, a literature that explicitly and critically contemplates a great derangement is a literature that enacts great dimensional shifts. And this argument lends itself, perhaps unsurprisingly given his reflections on his own fiction in *The Great Derangement*, to an analysis of Ghosh's oeuvre.

Many of Ghosh's novels have occupied such relatively stable contemporary categories as realist or historical fiction however much their particular use of their genres and modes has been inflected by metalevel critiques of Empire and gentle touches of the fantastic. But his recent novel of both climate and immigration crises, *Gun Island*, can be thought of as completing a trio whose aesthetic experiments are more explicit. Focused on Calcutta/Kolkata and the Sundarbans region, *The Calcutta Chromosome*, *The Hungry Tide*, and *Gun Island* might be seen as an unofficial threesome we could call a Bay of Bengal trilogy. While *The Calcutta Chromosome* includes elements many would associate with science fiction (although Ghosh tells Shreya Ila Anasuya he doesn't think of it as such), *The Hungry Tide* merges poetry with fiction, and *Gun Island* delves into a realm of unlikely events and synchronicities that Ghosh likes to call "the uncanny" or, as he remarks to Harsimran Gill, "the preternatural." We see many contemporary writers' familiar fatigue with both magic and realism, as well as what Nancy might call their assemblage, in the genre arguments from *The Great Derangement* that Gill quotes back to Ghosh, asking him to measure his new novel by his essays' yardstick:

> You wrote in *The Great Derangement* that as a writer, to treat the "improbable" occurrences of nature as magical, surreal or allegorical would be to "rob them of precisely that quality that makes them to [sic] urgently compelling – which is that they are actually happening on this earth, at this time." How did that thought shape the writing of *Gun Island*? Because you do have very strong elements of the unreal, folklore and myth in the novel, while saying that this threat to the planet is actually very real ...
>
> Gill

Ghosh responds by eschewing a real vs. unreal opposition, arguing for the natural presence of the inexplicable in our quotidian lives:

> Yes, because it is. It's real to the point of uncanniness and I think that's where I would put it, not in terms of real and unreal but this idea of the uncanny. Rather than saying natural and supernatural, there's a term I prefer, born during the

Inquisition, which is preternatural. It was something that the inquisitors would say – "we can't explain this". And so much of life is that. You're thinking of someone and the phone rings and it's them. Those things happen all the time.

qtd. in Gill

If climate catastrophe is a very real possibility that goes against our sense of reality, a possibility that we continue to fortify ourselves concretely and conceptually against, then writing that gets at the real unreal, so to speak, instead of the unreal real might offer a cognitive shift as countermeasure. And in offering such a transformation, fiction that works against a dangerous immunization paradigm might be allied with a dimensionist artistic impulse.

It's no surprise then that an important forerunner to *Gun Island*, which sets itself up explicitly as a sequel to *The Hungry Tide*, is *The Calcutta Chromosome*, a book about disease, discovery, and dimensional shifts. Reading for the presence of *The Calcutta Chromosome* in *The Hungry Tide* but especially in *Gun Island* affords a way of bringing out their conjoint immunological and dimensional experiments. If the supposed pathogen of bare life triggers an aggressive immunological response that can itself become deleterious, the preternatural and uncanny seem to offer therapeutic promise. And just as Esposito underscores biopolitics' focus on populations, Ghosh conceives of his force of the preternatural as working through groups of people. Indeed, as his telephone example suggests, his preternatural is necessarily and radically communicable. Yet if Ghosh's preternatural is communicable, it's communicable along unpredictable lines. Just as the intuition of the phone call arrives ahead of the phone call, the form of community that Ghosh imagines in *The Calcutta Chromosome* and elaborates in *Gun Island* consists in intimations and presentiments, connections one wouldn't naturally have made and exchanges of information that parties shouldn't have been able to know. And just as telephones have evolved dramatically in our time, so from *The Calcutta Chromosome* to *Gun Island* increasingly advanced communication technology becomes the vehicle for such uncanny links. To understand fully the force of Ghosh's preternatural, it's important to see its unlikely connections play out in many dimensions, not only through newly formed communities and through technology, but also through realms of textuality, the nonhuman, and the extra-human.

The logic of Ghosh's loose communities of fortuitous connections is intriguingly repeated in his own work metatextually. We might see an analogy for his distinctive form of prescient community in the literary network manifested by a successor volume that then makes select previous novels appear as half-knowing prequels. It's important to note, though, that however evanescent or mystical his networks may seem, Ghosh persistently emphasizes manifestation and revelation: his diverse transformative communities are ones that *will* make themselves known. Other authors' analogous networks are far more restricted, singular, selective, or clandestine—and this with ambiguous consequences for the types of healing and resolution their novels seem to desire. Choo, for example, as we saw in Chapter 1, stages her novel *The Night Tiger* as a mystery in which characters look for the missing member in a small set—a lost twin, a lacking representative of five Confucian virtues, a central thief, a key serial murderer—with the sense that a rupture can be sutured and a community healed once the plot is resolved, a resolution achieved only partly. Gesturing back to her first work, she reveals a minor character, the house servant Ah Long, to be the nephew of an important house servant in her previous novel, *The Ghost Bride*. But despite this suggestion that her two novels dwell in a shared fictional universe, it's difficult to imagine the first novel's long allegorical sojourn in the ghost realm and youthful romance plot as inhabiting the same aesthetic world and market category as the literary medical mystery that is *The Night Tiger*. The bridge between the two must span not only a generation but also a seeming mismatch in genres. By contrast, Van der Vliet Oloomi's *Call Me Zebra*, as we saw in Chapter 2, insists on uniqueness. Zebra takes the depleted state of the geopolitically exiled being and uses it as impetus for the revelation of a multidimensional literary matrix that has all the characteristics of a spirit realm but is also the solitary inheritance of a lone survivor. Zebra, often unwell yet given to singular epiphanies, takes the burden of her own healing onto herself and herself takes on the duty of channeling a vast literary matrix. She becomes a multiverse unto herself, and, so far, the novel that is her vehicle is a stand-alone entity. Alexis, as Chapter 3 details, fractures a single source of inspiration, Pasolini's *Teorema*, into a plan for five tangentially related works that then claim to draw on a myriad of intertexts. It's as though he imagines a family whose members, while keeping loosely in touch, individually research genealogies along overlapping yet divergent lines. Alexis's characters may selectively drop in to make cameo appearances across novels, and the heroes of his chronologically fourth yet structurally fifth volume may tap into paranormal healing modalities they know select others have, but his characters overall and the subset of these new magically enabled ones form loose groups whose members, despite their metatextual and metaphysical links, do not all know each other. Throughout the novels of his Quincunx Cycle, the moments in which characters from one volume appear in another feel marked out as special, as cross-textual visitations.

In contrast to all three authors, Ghosh imagines, against backdrops of crisis and contagion, mass migrations that take spiritually dimensionist form, and to do this he conceives of character and novel intersections not as sparks of light here and there, but as glimmers of a strong network that keeps exerting its force.

Throughout his career Ghosh has advocated for the agency and intelligence of figures pushed to the periphery, but his most recent work moves this consideration beyond the realms of geopolitics and ecology towards ones of specters and spirits. Unfolding his concept of the uncanny in *The Great Derangement*, Ghosh moves easily and tellingly from considerations of the nonhuman to the extra-human. To illustrate the eerie yet familiar quality of confronting agency and intention in realms beyond the human, he consistently turns to metaphors and analogies involving forms of communication, seeking to broaden definitions of communication as he goes. Retracing in *The Great Derangement* steps he took in *The Hungry Tide*, Ghosh likens a growing ecological awareness of the planet's life as far from inert but rather interconnected and able to interrupt our systems' cataclysmically to the sensation tiger attack victims in the Sundarbans might feel, even before seeing the tiger, that they are being watched—a feeling that comes to a head the moment the tiger reveals itself:

> To look into the tiger's eyes is to recognize a presence of which you are already aware; and in that moment of contact you realize that this presence possesses a similar awareness of you, even though it is not human. The mute exchange of gazes is the only communication that is possible between you and this presence— yet communication it undoubtedly is.
>
> But what is it that you are communicating with, at this moment of extreme danger, when your mind is in a state unlike any you've ever known before? An analogy that is sometimes offered is that of seeing a ghost, a presence that is not of this world.
>
> 29–30

Arguing for a similar intimation of the uncanny when faced with freak weather incidents, ones likely to increase with climate change, Ghosh like Esposito arrives at a single paradigm that takes in many current developments:

> Yet now our gaze seems to be turning again; the uncanny and improbable events that are beating at our doors seem to have stirred a sense of recognition, an awareness that humans were never alone, that we have always been surrounded by beings of all sorts who share elements of that which we had thought to be most distinctively our own: the capacities of will, thought, and consciousness.

> How else do we account for the interest in the nonhuman that has been burgeoning in the humanities over the last decade and over a range of disciplines; how else do we account for the renewed attention to panpsychism and the metaphysics of Alfred North Whitehead; and the rise to prominence of object-oriented ontology, actor-network theory, the new animism, and so on?
>
> 30–1

Rhetorically asking whether natural forces or "entities in the world, like forests" might be interrupting our species' monological thought to assert their presence and proposing that the various intellectual trends he enumerates might not truly originate with us, Ghosh claims that "to be alerted to such interventions is also to become uncannily aware that conversations among ourselves have always had other participants: it is like finding out that one's telephone has been tapped for years, or that the neighbors have long been eavesdropping on family discussions" (31). Ghosh's conception of eavesdropping is far from mere passive listening, and extending his analogy, he suggests that "the neighbors'" presence has actually, if subtly, been driving the conversation for a while. Interestingly, the scenario he outlines here in which supposedly human pursuits are being directed by extra-human forces is part of the premise of his 1995 novel *The Calcutta Chromosome*. There an underground network of practitioners "eavesdrops" on colonial scientists, harnessing the forces of disease mutation and, eventually, human information technology to create a pathway to immortality, a way for human beings to repeatedly transfer their personalities to new hosts. And far from enabling the transmigration of a select few, this network achieves collective migrations, realizing the dream currently espoused by transhumanist political movements of extending human life beyond the present limitations of human embodiment. It's as though in *The Great Derangement* Ghosh merges the transhumanist impulse portrayed in *The Calcutta Chromosome* with the attention to nonhuman species and ecology we find in *The Hungry Tide*, and *Gun Island* then becomes the novel counterpart to this endeavor.[1] As such, *Gun Island*, far from isolate, must unfold in many dimensions, manifesting subtle networks amongst its characters and compatriot texts, as it seeks to convey a sense that we're part of a larger community we've long suspected and hoped was there, waiting to contact and include us. If bare life, the theorized excluded interior of modern states, has now become more pervasive than ever and pandemics as well as planet-wide climate catastrophes are the bearing out of this thesis, then the hypothesis of alternative states, of an inclusive ulterior community whose gaze we barely sense but move towards nonetheless, becomes extraordinarily apposite.

Such a hypothesis, however, if it's being used to both address and redress the course of human history, requires a careful handling of time as well as theology. As we'll see, Ghosh's recent work relies not only on capacious notions of language and communicability that we might compare with Walter Benjamin's, but also a version of Benjamin's messianic time that Ghosh has arguably been honing throughout his oeuvre. This Benjamin-amenable element distinguishes both Ghosh's climate-change-aware dimensionism and his literary-political messianism, diverging them from a simplistically understood expansionist imperative to move art forms ever beyond N to +1 as well as from a more subtractive messianic model seen in Derrida's oft-cited reference in *Specters of Marx* to a "a messianism without religion, even a messianic without messianism" (59). In line with Benjamin's recursive approach to history, Ghosh looks for aporias we've accrued along the way, the ulterior within us that's been biding its time, as if to say the extra dimension beyond the N of world history, rather than being simply an advance or add-on or, less simply, the arrival of an irreducible otherness, is a looming element to be beheld retrospectively with a holistic glance back.

To bring out Ghosh's subtle theoretical navigations, one might compare his sense of a latent beyond best seen holistically to the rhythm of the messianic Benjamin describes in his "Theological-Political Fragment." Both conceptions will differ from the Derridean messianic hope Pheng Cheah compellingly reads for in a range of postcolonial texts, including *The Hungry Tide*. In his highly condensed yet enigmatic fragment, Benjamin sharply distinguishes world history's goal from its end, assigning the messianic not to the former but strictly the latter and thus placing the messianic in another order, seemingly another dimension, apart from secular world history and politics. We might see in this sharply drawn line a caution against what Samuel Weber, in discussing Benjamin's theory of translatability, has cited as "the (quintessential modern, Christian) risk of confounding the theological with the profane, the infinite with the finite, the immortal with the mortal" (67), although Ghosh, as we'll see, may have fewer strictures about absolutely avoiding such commingling. And yet, even though Benjamin writes that "nothing that is historical can relate itself, from its own ground, to anything messianic," he also states that the "secular order should be erected on the idea of happiness" and that this dynamically contrary force through its very opposite nature "promotes the coming of the Messianic Kingdom." On the one hand, there is the earthly logic of the secular order: "For in happiness, all that is earthly seeks its downfall, and only in happiness is its downfall destined to find it" (305). On the other, there is a puzzlingly paradoxical, pivotal quality to the rhythm of this logic taken as a whole: "The spiritual *restitutio in integrum*, which introduces immortality, corresponds to a worldly restitution that leads to an eternity of downfall, and the rhythm of this eternally transient worldly existence, transient in its totality, in its spatial but also in its temporal totality, the rhythm of messianic nature, is happiness. For nature is messianic by reason of its eternal and total passing away" (305–6). It's a perhaps kindred vision that Ghosh seeks to evoke by moving his characters' arcs not only towards their goals but also to a particular end, with the sense that that end's true completion exceeds the frame of the novel. It's not that he necessarily prevents his characters from attaining goals or fulfilling explicitly expressed wishes. It's that a terminus is invoked beyond such character arcs, a latent possibility that lends an aura of fatefulness to the narrative's movement as a whole.

By contrast, analyzing *Gun Island*'s predecessor in *What Is a World?*, Cheah reads for a core emptiness. He notes *The Hungry Tide*'s emphasis on translation and communication, but, arguing for an integral impossibility of arrival, asserts, "the novel also problematizes its function as deep communication and puts into question the power of stories to mend and hold the world together by pointing to the impossibility of arriving at a condition of perfect meaningfulness." For Jay Rajiva, similar qualities—critical self-awareness of how far its Westernized Indian characters can go in apprehending local traumas and entangled lifeworlds—set clear limits, signifying the novel can merely "gesture to but not fully envision an animist ontology," one in which a more expanded sense of relationality might be healing (77). Yet Cheah elaborates on fateful plot points, the loss of crucial testimonial documents that then can be retrieved only through reconstructive memories and the novel's devastating cataclysmic storm, to support his further claim that "at [the novel's] heart, there is a blankness that is at once utterly meaningless and also the condition of possibility of the novel's complex layers of meaning." And indeed, as we'll see, this duality between what can't be readily explained and what elicits more complex contemplation will remain in Ghosh's later novel. Cheah underscores, too, that his reading for a heart of blankness in *The Hungry Tide* is reading "against its authorial grain" (272). And it's regarding the meaningless or meaningful quality of storms that an authorial grain becomes even more important in Ghosh's later work. In light of *The Great Derangement*, it becomes more difficult to say of the weather in *Gun Island* what Cheah says of both it and the lost documents in *The Hungry Tide*: "The novel figures these blanknesses—the lost diary and the storm that leads to its loss—as something meaningfully destined by divine forces. But they are utterly devoid of meaning, because there is no reason why the storm takes place" (273–4). With this argument, Cheah, admittedly against the author's grain, takes the fateful movement of the novel and gives it back to an otherness that cannot be reduced to the meanings we might make of it. He restores the text's messianic impetus to a realm without messianism because it is there that, following a Derridean line of thought, he finds openness and hence hope. His argument is compelling in light of the novel's questionable strategies for representing its non-metropolitan characters, ones who seem to stand for subalternity.[2] As Cheah remarks, in the midst of its representation, this "subaltern world risks being distorted," but "the blankness at the heart of *The Hungry Tide* also points to an inappropriable otherness that resists the desires of capitalist modernity because it cannot be appropriated by human rationality," and he adds that such "otherness opens a world and is the promise of a future because it is the condition of possibility of telling stories about the subaltern world, including Ghosh's novel" (277). Crucial for Cheah is this openness associated with non-appropriability, and in the case of *The Hungry Tide*, meaninglessness serves to hold open this promise. By contrast, taking on the force of a planetary preternatural and depicting, rather than subalterns unable to consistently have a voice within a novel's linguistic frame, migrants who can use global media to self-advocate, Ghosh in *Gun Island* makes it more difficult to read strictly for either Cheah's against the grain meaninglessness or Rajiva's Western-centric and animist-unfriendly autocritique. Instead, Ghosh moves his novel toward a point of arrival that invokes another dimension, but one that has been both implicit all along and that suggests a reconsideration of what has come before. In prompting this highly recursive perspectival shift, the novel's ending can be read, admittedly in a more with the grain sense, as invoking, and this toward animist-amenable ends, a particularly Benjaminian messianism and dimensionism.

Not only is Ghosh's invocation of other dimensions distinctive for its harkening to a Benjaminian rather than Derridean messianism, but his method is uniquely avataric in the sense that all his characters can act for each other as fortuitous channels for such other dimensions. And this porosity also distinguishes Ghosh's turn to the nonhuman and to the planetary. Ghosh's appeal to a non-additive but rather enfolded and gradually felt to have been looming +1 can be read as a desire for a politically, ecologically, and spiritually ethical approach to expansive dimensions, ones that are both extra-human and suggested in the rhythm of human history. His attempt to move narratives towards an ulterior point beyond the fulfillment of character arcs becomes notably concomitant in *Gun Island* with a desire to see stories as not the sole province or property of humans; the extra-human dimension that the novel appeals to, as we'll see, is one that requires us, as humans, to cede exceptional ownership of not only our story, but of the very impetus and ability to relate stories. Whether in the form of a snake, spider, eagle, or tiger, the best figures for this expansively reconceived impetus and ability are nonhuman animals—often storied ones or else formerly reliably tracked species that climate change has rendered eerily appearing creatures. At the same time, in considering the scale of the planetary, Ghosh turns in his nonfiction to Gaia, the Greek goddess of the earth whose name James Lovelock adopted for his theory that our planet's forms of life are part of a self-regulating and self-sustaining system. Yet in choosing the snake goddess Manasa Devi as his novel's avatar for Gaia, Ghosh again achieves a careful negotiation, one that can be seen via a comparison with the Systems Theory approach Bruce Clarke has outlined. In *Gaian Systems*, Clarke details Gaia theory's neocybernetic evolutions and supports a concept of Gaia as "metabiotic," a systemic coupling of living and nonliving (or biotic and abiotic) elements. This model would evade charges, such as the one Clarke quotes theorist of autopoiesis Francisco Varela making, that Gaia has been "parasitized" by "animistic notions" (qtd. in Clarke 152). Ghosh's Gaian thought, much like Clarke's, can be seen as advancing a "planetary imaginary" that seeks to surpass a deleteriously limited immunity paradigm. But Ghosh, as an anti-colonial and anthropologically attuned writer, takes the complementary but counterpoised route of engaging simultaneously with the gridded globe and with porous, potentially parasitizing belief systems, ones that can be highly mobile, syncretic, and indeed animist. In choosing Manasa Devi as focal point, Ghosh mobilizes a goddess that is, as Amrita Dasgupta details, fearsome, forest-based, animal-themed, amenable to hybrid forms of worship, and above all, hydrocultural. "Water assumes the omnipotent position of the gods and goddesses of the Sundarbans, manifesting the strong syncretism prevalent in the region," Dasgupta writes (177). And it is this elemental force of fluidity—one Sarah Nuttall sees at work in not only Ghosh but a recent wave of global anglophone fiction dedicated to "pluvial temporalities and wet forms" (458)—that *Gun Island*'s Manasa Devi brings to Gaia. Both of local importance to the Sundarbans yet not bound to any earthly territory, this watery goddess's power animates *Gun Island*, migrating across multiple milieus, media, and dimensions.

2. Approaching Futures

An End to Apocalypse

We can see in *Gun Island* the culmination of a career-long tension in Ghosh's writing, one in which a desire to move novels to foreseen points—staged especially explicitly, for example, with the last sentence of *The Glass Palace* in which the narrator reports of an image just described, "I knew that it was with this that it [this book] would end" (547)—meets with a principled avoidance of apocalypse.[3] In "Beyond the End of the World: Human and Non-Human After the Collapse of 'Civilization,'" his online keynote address for the Penn Program in Environmental Studies' digital event series, *Climate Sensing and Data Storytelling*, Ghosh remarks on the prevalence of end-of-the-world books in the India of his youth. Noting that these books were all written by Western authors, he reports making a pact with himself to never end one of his novels apocalyptically. Even though in writing certain novels the temptation to move towards an end-of-the-world scenario may have been great, Ghosh claims it's simply inimical to him to "blow everything up." He mentions, too, that he's paid a price for his pact, with *The Hungry Tide* sometimes criticized for its "happy ending." His remarks make sense as writerly reflections, yet they might nevertheless mislead those unfamiliar with his work about the note on which many of his novels end. Far from uniformly happy, the endings of *The Shadow Lines*, *The Hungry Tide*, and *Gun Island* (not to mention *River of Smoke* and *Flood of Fire* in his *Ibis Trilogy*), often leave readers with, if not despair, complex emotions surrounding significant deaths and defeats. On the one hand, Ghosh wants to address inequities and the underrecognized costs of misguided courses of history. But on the other, he wants to immunize his version of the novel from apocalypse, particularly a geopolitically slanted use of it in which the West calls the shots. This creative tension arguably intensifies the more Ghosh considers climate change and forms of systemic collapse. In what might seem a desperate compromise, *Gun Island* can be read as pitting catastrophe against apocalypse as though hopeful potential lay in their disambiguation.

Yet the novel's final page can be interpreted as equivocating even about hope. A high seas rescue mission succeeds but a key character dies, albeit peacefully, leaving a mixed sentiment in her wake. The novel's narrator-protagonist experiences a mixing also of times as he sorts through his memories of her, looking for the hints that they would arrive at this moment. And this means that the bittersweet hybrid time of the closing can be seen as the counterpart to the uncanny prescience Ghosh underscores in his discussions of the intelligence and agency of the nonhuman. If an aid in undoing dangerous anthropocentric beliefs is to imagine the planet itself as an intelligent interconnected form of life, one that watches our steps as a stalking tiger would, then endings as the fulfillments of such presentiments will likely also carry a charge of self-consciousness. The novel's final words, "'We came too late,' she said. "Cinta's gone'" (312), carry an undeniable tinge of desolation. But following the logic of Ghosh's uncanny, we might see them, as the citing of direct speech hints we should, as overheard. And such eavesdropping could imply the presence of other dimensions. Among the manifestations of intelligent life that eavesdrop on *Gun Island* are many of Ghosh's other novels. While it's true that *Gun Island* reprises characters from *The Hungry Tide* and resembles *The Calcutta Chromosome* by entertaining the idea of smart technology's fantastic possibilities, these aren't its only cross-textual resonances. Ghosh's return to first-person narration recalls *The Shadow Lines*, a novel in which he dramatically deploys the two-part structure we later find in both *The Hungry Tide* and *Gun Island*. The use of first-person narration also ties *Gun Island* to *In an Antique Land*, and both these works are concerned with the slaves, merchants, and trade routes of early eras. Indeed, just as *In an Antique Land* makes a case for pre-twentieth-century forms of globalization, *Gun Island*, with its characters' discussions of "The Little Ice Age," points up the existence of earlier times' climate catastrophes. Finally, the death at sea amidst a dramatic rogue rescue operation at the end of *Gun Island* undeniably recalls *Sea of Poppies*, and there too, in the final lines, a key protagonist regards a key female character in a way that loops back on the past, the book's beginning. These resonances and the idea that Ghosh's past novels come to pay their respects especially at the end of *Gun Island* suggest intriguing and alternative readings of the novel, particularly its poignant close.

Perhaps it's no surprise that a novel so self-consciously textual as to culminate in an implied convergence of its many predecessors would also be capaciously cosmopolitan. Wending its way from Bengal to Brooklyn to Venice (first California and then Italy), *Gun Island* is the story of former folklorist and rare bookseller Dinananth Dutta, his friendship with the famous Italian history professor Giacinta Schiavon, and his quest to understand the truth behind a mysterious tale of a "Gun Merchant" and his Sundarbans shrine. Dinananth, or Deen as most call him, is a cousin of *The Hungry Tide* protagonist Kanai, and as the novel begins in Kolkata, it's Kanai who urges Deen to visit the mysterious shrine before he returns to his home in Brooklyn and before, as we later learn, the shrine is washed away by rising Sundarbans tides. But not until Deen gets further encouragement over the phone from Giacinta, or Cinta, whom he considers his mentor, does he undertake the journey. It's this trip to the Sundarbans that puts Deen in contact with other key characters from *The Hungry Tide*, the charitable organization leader Nilima Bose, boatman Horen Naskar, and most importantly, the dolphin researcher Piyali Roy and her sometimes ward Tutul or Tipu. As the son of Fokir, the fisherman guide whose death while protecting Piya in a cataclysmic storm lends tragedy to the end of *The Hungry Tide*, Tipu carries a fateful aura about him. Indeed, out of a sense of guilt, Piya has provided him with every advantage she can, including educational opportunities, time in the US, and technological devices. But Tipu remains unruly, a restless spirit. Not only is Tipu bound to no place, but when we meet him, he is secretly working as a liaison to "connection men," dubious entities that help smuggle people across borders. The novel will track Tipu's disappearance from the Sundarbans as he himself attempts migration to Europe in tandem with tracking Deen's haunting by the legend of the Gun Merchant and the vengeful snake goddess the merchant offended, Manasa Devi. In many ways, as we'll see, Ghosh's use of Manasa Devi resonates with Donna Haraway's musings in *Staying with the Trouble* on the chthonic and, what might seem a particularly creaturely version of Deleuze and Guattari's celebrated rhizome, the "tentacular." Haraway also eschews apocalyptic thinking and, looking for alternative ways to figure our era's many entanglements, asks, "How can we think in times of urgencies without the self-indulgent and self-fulfilling myths of apocalypse, when every fiber of our being is interlaced, even complicit, in the webs of processes that must somehow be engaged and repatterned?" (35). Creations made of string, creatures who spin webs, and deities of insects and reptiles become apt for her, as she engages with such entanglements. Appropriately, Ghosh's Manasa Devi is not only an earthly goddess of spiders and snakes who can reach out across realms, but she also migrates across cultures just as Haraway's Potnia Theron, the animal-friendly Gorgon-faced deity she takes up as exemplary of the tentacular, does: "A kind of traveling Ur-Medusa, the Lady of Beasts is a potent link between Crete and India" (52). Ghosh will invoke a similar migration route for a holy maternal figure late in his novel. The traditions of Potnia Theron and Manasa Devi allow Haraway and Ghosh respectively to speculate in quite concrete terms on far reaching chthonic forces that cut across cultures and are figured as female. Likewise, linking an era of previous climate catastrophes with our contemporary one, the tale of the Gun Merchant comes to seem highly prescient. And in investigating the tale's words, symbols, and probable origins, Deen has many uncannily apt epiphanies in which animals and forces of nature seem like neighborly eavesdroppers announcing their presence in unsettling ways. In some instances, Ghosh provides scientific explanations for the novel's unusual animal appearances and freak weather events, but in others he resists resolving uncertainties, as if to suggest that his notions of the uncanny and preternatural cannot be reduced to the familiar dimensions of human geopolitics or ecological knowledge. In this way, we have to see Ghosh as engaging not simply the postcolonial or ecological uncanny others have rightly discerned but also an extra-human and multidimensional one.⁴ Yet while Ghosh's imagining of an uncanny that can unfold across many dimensions exceeds ecological and ethological interpretations, it importantly takes animal forms to convey its power. Just as the tiger in *The Hungry Tide* and *The Great Derangement* might be seen as an avatar of nonhuman elements we ignore at our peril, so the snake and other venomous creatures become mediators of extra-human significance in *Gun Island*. Understanding conjointly Ghosh's use of animal avatars and his sense of the points beyond the human and beyond the end of the world from which his latest novel anticipates being overheard allows us to understand also the complexity of the unlikely events and ambivalent ending that distinguish *Gun Island*.

A Legend for Later

As if lending progressive dimensions to the text's core legend, the novel includes many retellings of the Gun Merchant's story. From the outset, the story's goddess is described as reaching out beyond pages, and the story's cryptic lines are said to need future interpreters. Deen first receives the story from Nilima when he arrives in the Sundarbans. As Deen will later observe of the boatman Horen (59), Nilima marks time in the Sundarbans with storms. She recalls learning of the Gun Merchant and his shrine during a 1970 cyclone in which she and Horen found villagers sheltering there. Attributing their survival to the snake goddess Manasa Devi and the shrine the merchant built to honor her, the villagers claim it's the temple's roof, walls, and nearby well with clean water that has sustained them. Nilima asks to see the shrine and is surprised to learn that while it honors a Hindu goddess, its custodian is Muslim, with Muslims revering the site as "a place of jinns, protected by a Muslim *pir*, or saint, by the name of Ilyas" (16). Nilima is told a few seemingly nonsensical lines to the strictly orally transmitted poem that recounts the Gun Merchant's tale. Although she's also told that "it was impossible for most people to make sense of the legend," she manages to get its basic details: a wealthy merchant refuses to honor Manasa Devi; enraged, she plagues and pursues him with "snakes ... droughts, famines, storms, and other calamities" until he flees to a place supposedly free of snakes "called 'Gun Island'—Bonduk-dwip" (17), but even there is hounded, until he again flees, is caught by pirates who wish to sell him into slavery, until at last he relents and promises to build the goddess a temple if she frees him to return home, which she miraculously does, setting loose "all manner of creatures, of the sea and sky" against the pirates as their captives successfully rise up against them. Amassing wealth on his return journey, the goddess's new devotee becomes known as

"Bonduki Sadagar—the Gun Merchant" and the shrine becomes known for him (18). As if setting the terms for Ghosh's novel early on, the goddess who haunts the merchant is said to have "appeared to him out of the pages of a book and ... warned him that she had eyes everywhere," and making good on this promise, her first reminder, when he tries to seal himself in an iron-walled room, is "a tiny, poisonous creature [that] had crept through a crack and bitten him" (17–18). An all-seeing goddess of snakes and spiders, Manasa Devi is uncontainable and infectiously metatextual. And her legend points both toward the future and to further dimensions. When Nilima tells her informer it makes little sense to her, he tells her first, "The legend is filled with secrets and if you don't know their meaning it's impossible to understand," and second, "But some day, when the time is right, someone will understand it and who knows? For them it may open up a world that we cannot see" (18).

Deen will fall into the Gun Merchant's steps, eventually coming to see the world through his eyes, and the legend itself will get several significant retellings. Already when Deen meets Horen and discusses the tale with him, he finds Horen emphasizes and even adds different aspects to it. In Horen's retelling, the Gun Merchant suffers not because the goddess extraordinarily plagues him but because he is too proud to recognize the powers she represents. Believing he can continue to profit from his trading as he evades her grasp, he continues to expose others, including his wife and children, to fatal calamities. In a sense, the Gun Merchant's continual attempts to immunize himself, to relocate to more fortunate and fortified sites, brings bare life ever nearer. What stands out in Horen's memory is the bare-life-inducing drought that first afflicts the merchant's homeland: "a drought so terrible that the streams, rivers and ponds had dried up and the stench of rotting fish and dead livestock had hung heavy in the air. Half the people had died of starvation; parents had sold their children and people had been reduced to eating carcasses and cadavers." The merchant moves downriver, even as his boats are shattered by a huge wave, and he manages to find a safe haven for his family and the wealth he salvages. But even then, when he leaves for commerce in the city, a flood strikes his supposedly "large and solid house" and his wife and family are killed by invading "swarms of snakes and scorpions," as though venom represents concretely that which evades immunizing hubris (60). But not all of Horen's additions are tragic. He also remembers a good ship captain, the Muslim Nakhuda Ilyas, who rescues the merchant early on when, fleeing his domestic disasters, he is captured by bandits who enslave him. Ilyas purchases and frees the merchant and together they travel to various strangely named islands before the return journey that Nilima has recounted. When Deen also learns from Horen that the Muslim family that currently watches over the shrine now has one descendent left, the teenager Rafi who ekes out a living from fishing, he's eager to meet and interview him. Fortuitously running into Rafi when he finally makes it to the shrine, Deen learns more of the Gun Merchant's legend.

Rafi helps Deen decode some of the hieroglyphic symbols etched into the temple's façade and reinforced over time with pottery shards. While Deen correctly interprets symbols for the Gun Merchant and the pirates, he has more difficulty understanding the symbols for Captain Ilyas, two of the oddly named islands on the captain and merchant's itinerary, and two strange circular markings. In particular, a circle within a circle and a circle within a circle that is then marked with four lines crossing it stump him. Although Rafi helps him understand the first circular symbol stands for Gun Island or Bonduk-dwip, he claims not to remember the meaning of the second symbol (but much later he will indicate it represents an eight-legged spider). He acts as though he too finds the names of the islands that the merchant and captain visit nonsensical (supposedly the "Land of Palm Sugar Candy" and the "Land of Kerchieves" or *Taal-misrir-desh* and *Rumaali-desh*). But he usefully adds that the circle within a circle stands for Gun Island because "not only was Bonduk-dwip an island, it was an island within an island—hence the circle enclosed by another circle" (81). Affecting disbelief, Rafi calls the legend "just a fairytale" and adds, "No one can rule over snakes" (82). But when, humoring him, Deen agrees and says that of course the temple has no connection to Manasa Devi, the tables turn and Rafi asks why he says so. Deen shocks Rafi by arguing that if it were truly a powerful shrine to the goddess, it would have a resident snake, a cobra perhaps. Unbeknownst to Deen, a cobra does live in the shrine and Rafi had spotted it behind Deen when first encountering him. This same venomous snake will rise up as Horen and Tipu return to collect Deen, and protecting Deen, Tipu will be bitten by it, setting off a chain of important events for the novel. Many of these events will involve further animal epiphanies and connections made via technological devices. Interestingly, it is Deen's visit to the physical temple and his encounter with the legend's visual symbols that initiate the tale's enactive dimension. From this encounter on, the legend will map out the events to follow, as though Deen not only retraces its steps, but also calls forth its world.

But the tale will get its most significant retelling when Deen recounts it to Cinta and she interprets its symbols and strange place names. Invited by her to a Los Angeles conference celebrating a museum's acquisition of a rare edition of *The Merchant of Venice*, Deen looks forward to the break. Ever since returning to

Brooklyn, he's felt haunted by his Sundarbans trip and the strange texts and video calls he keeps receiving from Tipu. Although at the time of the cobra attack Deen was able to coordinate via cellphone with Piya to have the necessary and rare antivenin treatment delivered for Tipu, Tipu seems not to have fully recovered from the effects of his initial delirium. He begins sending unusual messages that lead characters in fateful directions, strongly encouraging, for example, Deen to attend the California conference to meet up with Cinta (about whom Tipu should have no knowledge). And indeed, several strange things happen to Deen on his trip, from his spying through his plane window a snake in the grasp of an eagle to the conference proceedings' getting disrupted and relocated due to raging west coast wildfires. Remarkably, this environmental upset occurs even as historians discuss the catastrophes, "famines, droughts, and epidemics" among them, of the Little Ice Age in the seventeenth century (135). While the speaker of this relevant lecture entitled "Climate and Apocalypse in the Seventeenth Century" is derided for suggesting a link between that era's environmental catastrophes and its "extraordinary intellectual and creative ferment" and for stressing the era's significance for our time, Cinta tells Deen she is in full agreement with his arguments (138). She suggestively puts her sense of the past in the terms of after-death communication when she claims it's as if "the Little Ice Age is rising from its grave and reaching out to us" (139). The otherworldly significance of the past is further underscored when Cinta gives the conference's closing lecture, reflecting on the Venice of that time and startling Deen by calling the Jewish enclave (the original ghetto), "an island within an island" (149). Not only this, but she adds that the Arabic speaking merchants trading with Venice then called it "Banadiq," which came not only to be a word for the notable items of trade— "hazelnuts, bullets, and guns"—but also found its way into a word some Persians and Indians used (and still do) for guns: "*bundook*" (150–1). Startled into the realization that the Gun Merchant (Bonduki Sadagar), who traveled to Gun Island (Bonduk-dwip), may actually be a merchant who journeyed to Venice, Deen later tells Cinta the rest of the tale, showing her a key symbol. She translates *misr* in *Taal-misrir-desh* to mean Egypt (not Sugar Palm Candy Land), a place known for its sugar crystallization process and deduces that *rumaal* in *Rumaali-desh* refers to Turkey, site of the fort of Rumeli-Hisari (153). She also notes that the symbol for Captain Ilyas is the Hebrew letter aleph and deduces that he was Jewish. Putting the tidbits together, Cinta reconstructs a tale of a merchant from eastern India who flees the climate catastrophes of the Little Ice Age as they strike his home, then is captured by enslaving pirates who take him to Goa where he is bought and freed by a Portuguese Jewish merchant fleeing the Inquisition. The two team up, traveling and trading their way from the Maldives to Egypt to Istanbul, fending off environmental and political upheaval at every turn until they make it to Venice, the crucial turning point before the merchant's return home. Cinta further exhorts Deen that to truly understand the legend and to understand why it has found its way to him at this time, he must journey to Venice, and specifically its ghetto.

Cinta's belief that Deen must follow his inquiry through to a meaningful end is based on her capacious understanding of stories. When Deen first tells her of the Gun Merchant's temple and legend, he finds it contradictory that this enshrined and clearly meant to be preserved story is not written down and can be transmitted only orally. But Cinta sees nothing strange in the injunction against writing and suggests that the shrine builders, far from wanting to give the story the closure a written text might imply, might instead have wanted it to "reach out into the future" (140). Asked how mere stories can do this, she stakes a dimensionist claim in historical terms:

> In the seventeenth century no one would ever have said of something that it was "just a story" as we moderns do. At that time people recognized that stories could tap into dimensions that were beyond the ordinary, beyond the human even. They knew that only through stories was it possible to enter the most inward mysteries of our existence where nothing that is really important can be proven to exist—like love, loyalty, or even the faculty that makes us turn around when we feel the gaze of a stranger or an animal. Only through stories can invisible or inarticulate or silent beings speak to us; it is they who allow the past to reach us.
> 140–1

When Deen is incredulous, Cinta remarks on the truism that humans are different from animals because of the human ability to tell stories, but then she turns this belief on its head:

> But what if the truth were even stranger? What if it were the other way around? What if the faculty of storytelling were not specifically human but rather the last remnant of our animal selves? A vestige left over from a time before language, when we communicated as other living beings do? Why else is it that only in stories do animals speak? Not to speak of demons, and gods, and Indeed God himself? It is only through stories that the universe can speak to us, and if we don't learn to listen you may be sure that we will be punished for it.
> 141

Ominously suggesting the planet's animal self has not only been stalking and eavesdropping but has been trying to get our attention for a long time and has been using a form of proto-communication to do it, Cinta unsettles Deen. He then experiences a sense of spectral contamination, recalling that in Brooklyn he "had been haunted by the feeling that something that had long lain dormant in the mud of the Sundarbans had entered me" (141). And indeed, the story of the Gun Merchant acts as a preternatural venom, precipitating events and creating connections that resist explanation.

The Unaccountably Strange

Without the notion that Manasa Devi haunted the Gun Merchant and is now haunting Deen there may seem to be little reason for him to see an eagle with a snake in its talons from his airplane window. The reasons for the eagle's dropping the snake so close to the plane may be elaborated on but they aren't fully explained. We're left to make what we will of the idea of a form of planetary communication that can move humans and nonhuman animals as though they exist in a legend. Those who become vehicles for the legend's recurrence become vehicles through which many of the novel's inexplicably strange events occur. But it isn't only the legend that enables an inexplicably strange strand in the text. Although centered on a goddess, the Gun Merchant's story features mainly male characters. Another key strand in the novel, however, involves Cinta and her daughter Lucia. Both strands of extraordinary occurrences require a hub-character, someone through whom other characters connect, creating the convergences necessary for the novel to reach its end. Tipu acts as a crucial vehicle that enables the Gun Merchant's legend to be channeled into the present, but it's Deen himself who becomes the agent through which Cinta's story, via the Gun Merchant legend, reaches its culmination. In this way, the novel's conception of character is as both channeling focal point and mediating presence for the never entirely explicable. This is to say characters are always potentially avatars, a quality highlighted in *Gun Island* by the fact that nearly all of them travel under aliases, quick nickname versions of their given names. As avatars, they all carry the potential to act as portals for what Cinta calls "invisible or inarticulate or silent beings," or what Nilima's informant called "a world we cannot see"—that is, other dimensions.

This avataric function of characters appears most obviously in Tipu, a character of queer and highly mediated animacy whose uncanny animal encounter and its aftereffects spark forms of multi-perspectival and multi-temporal awareness. When he's bitten by the shrine's resident cobra, Tipu enters into an altered state that endows him ever after with a form of inexplicably enhanced consciousness. His expanded consciousness reaches ever outward through his ties to other characters, through many media, and throughout his journeys. When Rafi comes to Tipu's aid and immediately sucks some of the venom from his bite wound, inadvertently swallowing some himself, Horen says as long as it goes to his stomach and not into his bloodstream, he'll be safe. But Rafi reiterates a truth the text upholds: "If a cobra puts something in you ... you can never be rid of it. That's what my grandfather used to say" (84). After, when Rafi joins the others on the boat and tries to soothe Tipu, the two express a feeling of déjà vu recognition, even though they've never crossed paths previously. As Tipu appears to hallucinate shadowy figures coming for him but also snakes swarming and protecting him, Deen insists there's no one there. But Rafi rebuffs Deen, affirming the truth of Tipu's experience. The two form a bond, eventually becoming a couple, and in the moment, Deen marvels:

> They could not have been more unlike each other, Tipu with his ear stud and highlights, and Rafi with his shaggy hair and feral wariness, yet an odd bond seemed to have arisen between them; it was as if the venom that had passed from Tipu's body into Rafi's mouth had created an almost carnal connection.
>
> 89

Here Mel Y. Chen's biopolitical focus in *Animacies* on immunity's troubling "coextant figure" of toxicity, a figure that for Chen is not entirely accounted for in Esposito's immunity paradigm, becomes relevant (194). If the political manipulation of the border between "lifeliness or deathliness" (193), or the animate and inanimate, becomes refined in the twentieth-century belief in personal immunity and "an integral and bounded self" (194), then the threat posed by toxins becomes especially affronting. Fittingly, for Chen, toxicity and intoxication—both phenomena highlighted in Tipu's case—suggest ambivalence and queer affect, as "toxicity incontrovertibly meddles with the relations of subject and object required for even the kind of contractual immunitary ordering that Esposito suggests" (195). Although Chen doesn't reflect on animism specifically, their understanding of toxins both opens up space to see forms of animism troubling strict immunity paradigms and allows us to ally queerness to this process. Failing to uphold "rationality's favorite partner, the *human* subject," but "rather defaulting" to various objects and "other sexual orientations," toxicity for Chen cuts across multiple categories of things and beings, reminding us of "the interanimation that surrounds us" (221) and a time before humanity's "insistence on a radical segregation of self and world fueled by a bellicose antagonism" (195). Initiated by a sacred site's venomous snake, the queer and uncanny bond between Tipu and Rafi also blurs temporal boundaries, as it harkens back to an earlier time, specifically to the Gun Merchant legend. When a delirious Tipu insists Rafi tell him his real name, Rafi discloses that his parents had actually named him Ilyas after the revered Muslim saint of the shrine, the captain who freed and sailed with the merchant. Struggling against the shadows he sees, Tipu then exclaims that they must call Piya to warn her about Rani, the nickname of the dolphin RN1 that she tracks and towards whom Piya feels an affinity. And this warning initiates a series of unexplained premonitions Tipu will have throughout the text, distinguished only by its being delivered at least partly in person.

Many of Tipu's other prescient alerts either will occur remotely via mysterious calls and texts or will be reported secondhand, making him not only a ghost in others' machines, but also a watchful presence a few steps ahead of others' machinations. Even in this first instance, when Deen works up the courage forty-five minutes later to repeat Tipu's warning about Rani over the phone to Piya, she reports having gotten a phone alert from the tracking device with which she's equipped the dolphin, one that warns of a beaching, at exactly the time of Tipu's utterance. Similarly, Piya will later receive an initially untraceable email reporting the details of a mass beaching of the dolphins she studies. When an internet search reveals no such beaching, she's puzzled. She becomes even more puzzled when she sees the date of the report is a week in the future, but she reshuffles her travel schedule to be on site, observers in tow, at the projected time. And a tragic mass beaching does occur. Later a tech-savvy friend helps her trace the email to Tipu, who has by that time left India en route to Europe along with Rafi. Moving through dubious networks of traffickers (the pirates of our time), the two get separated close to Turkey (*Rumaali-desh*) with Rafi carrying onto Italy (to Venice or Bonduk-dwip, Gun Island) and Tipu changing course to head to Egypt (*Taal-misrir-desh*). While Piya tries to believe in a reasonable chain of events that will explain the beaching report—specifically, a supposed whistleblower who, wanting to help in the fight against a toxic refinery upriver, informs Tipu who then informs her of a chemical dumping that would likely cause a beaching—no such whistleblower is ever found. Instead, we learn of further mysterious communications from Tipu as he fights not only for Piya's cherished ecosystem but also for the rights of his fellow migrants as they are exploited and abused by traffickers as well as rejected by governments. His both prescient and constantly mediated presence makes him a medium in more than one sense. And indeed, when Deen returns to Brooklyn, his impromptu computer chats with Tipu address the very phenomena—beings of an ambiguous nature and the expanded forms of communication possible amongst them—that typify Tipu's life after the cobra's bite. Popping up in an on-screen chat window, Tipu first renews contact with Deen by asking whether the Bangla word "bhuta" means ghost. Dictionary in hand, Deen responds, "All I can tell you is that the Bangla word 'bhoot' or 'bhuta' comes from a basic but very complicated Sanskrit root, 'bhu', meaning 'to be', or 'to manifest'. So in that sense 'bhuta' means 'a being' or 'an existing presence'" (114). Stretching this term for ghost by asking whether it can then be applied to humans and nonhuman animals as beings and gaining Deen's agreement, Tipu then wonders why it gets restricted to ghosts. Deen answers that the word can imply past states, hence former beings, but Tipu presses him further, asking whether a word for both being and past being implies "the past wasn't past? That the past was present in the present?" He then, failingly, tries to get Deen to assent to ghosts' existence, spurring him to abruptly end the chat and slam his laptop shut. Tipu's later pop-up topics will include shamanism, animal communication, demonic possession, and the Apocalypse. However hyperbolic these exchanges may initially seem, Deen does have occasion on his subsequent travels to further reflect on their topics. Later in Italy when a shouted warning—surprisingly in Bangla—from a nearby construction worker helps Deen avoid a falling masonry slab and Deen realizes the worker is Rafi, who has joined a Bangladeshi crew, he returns to the concepts of his first online chat with Tipu:

> Suddenly I remembered my exchange with Tipu about that mysterious Sanskrit root *bhu*, which means simultaneously 'being' and 'becoming' and much else as well. It seemed to me then that only a word derived from this root could account for our presence in the Ghetto: Rafi and I were both *bhutas* in the sense of being at once conjunctions and disjunctions in the continuum of time, space, and being.
>
> 170

Through these meditations on bhutas inspired by a cobra-bitten Tipu, Deen arrives at an understanding of all beings, nonhuman and human, as interdimensional, simultaneously ghostlike and future-oriented. His sense of being becomes truly transmigrating.

Fittingly, it is in migrating, crossing from Asia to Iran and then through a Kurdish village into Turkey, that Rafi loses Tipu, whose presence then becomes even more transcendental and pivotal for the text. Tipu initially prepares for a second attempt at entry into Turkey, but what causes him to then change course and take on this transcendentally enhanced role in the text is a visionary dream.

Rafi says that Tipu reports dreaming of an angelic Ethiopian woman and decides he has to find her. When he claims to have located and contacted her in Egypt, Tipu travels there and Rafi loses touch with him completely. It is only when Rafi, now arrived in Venice, sees a newspaper story of a refugee boat headed for Sicily that he rediscovers Tipu, his face visible in the story's accompanying photo of the refugees. Tipu comes to inhabit an eye of a storm when Ghosh orchestrates his characters' arcs so that they will all converge in a confrontation at sea as protesters from both sides of the refugee controversy set out to either thwart or enable their boat's safe entry to Italy.

The journey to rendezvous with the refugees takes on transformational significance not only for the world, but also for Cinta personally, and her storyline includes many of the novel's other unusual occurrences. The refugees' "Blue Boat" becomes the messianic counterpart to the biopolitical "armed lifeboat" that Ghosh decries in *The Great Derangement*. As one character puts it:

> If a fleet of civilian vessels shows up to support the refugees ... then maybe it'll speak to the world's conscience. Across the planet everyone's eyes are on the Blue Boat now: it has become a symbol of everything that's going wrong with the world—inequality, climate change, capitalism, corruption, the arms trade, the oil industry. There's a lot of hope that this will be a historic moment. Maybe now, while there's still time to make changes, people will wake up and see what's going on.
>
> 218

While not explicitly making such wide-ranging claims, Cinta admits to coming along on the vessel her documentarian niece has rented and that Deen, Rafi, and even Piya will board, because she hopes to see a special event happen, perhaps a miracle. Having translated the legend's final strange island name, "The Island of Chains," or in Bangla, "Shikol-dwip," as "Siqilla" in Arabic and thus Sicily, Cinta sees special significance in the Blue Boat's course (269). It's en route to "The Island of Chains" that the legend's captives rise up against the imprisoning pirates as all kinds of sky and sea creatures come to their aid. Yet inexplicable occurrences have also been trailing Cinta for some time. When Deen first meets her long ago, she is a notorious widow, her Mafia-exposing journalist husband and their young daughter having died on a road trip when his Maserati's brakes mysteriously gave out. Early in the morning of their planned drive to meet her, Cinta had called from the conference she was attending saying she had a bad feeling. But her husband had brushed her worries aside and assured her she could call them anytime on the road. She successfully does so a first time, but later when she distinctly hears her daughter's voice call out to her in her hotel room and tries the number again, she gets only static. Patrolmen later find them dead in the car after it has fallen down a mountainside. Ever since, she has felt haunted by her daughter's presence. And indeed, when Tipu pops up on Deen's computer to video chat and encourage him to attend the Los Angeles conference, his explanation for even knowing of Cinta seems related to Lucia: "Maybe someone whispered something in my ear. Maybe I got a secret pal who knows your friend very, very well and wants to be sure you don't chicken out of your meeting in LA" (123). Cinta also reports having heard her daughter's voice years ago when, full of grief and despair after the tragedy, she had neglected herself, contracted pneumonia, and been hospitalized. From her hospital room, she had heard Lucia's voice telling her, "This is not your time, you must fight to stay alive," and predicting, "something will happen to renew your faith in the world ... if you die now, neither you nor I will ever find peace" (147). Deen becomes a further vehicle for Lucia's presence while also enabling the circumstances that allow Cinta, before she reunites with her daughter, to be present at a hopeful event. After his conference trip to California, when he travels to Italy and stays in Cinta's creaky Venice apartment, the dwelling itself seems to give him an uncanny feeling. In one instance, he encounters a bird pecking at the window, then experiences "an odd feeling at the back of my neck," later hearing a thump that we're led to infer is caused by Lucia's favorite storybook, a tale of a Sundarbans tiger, falling to the floor (231–2; 181–2). These feelings will intensify on the novel's final boat voyage, with Deen falling asleep and then waking to find that toys left behind from previous rescue missions have seemingly rearranged themselves so that several dolls are staring at him. And Cinta's niece Gisa, having tried unsuccessfully on the boat to check on her own family over the phone, will report mysteriously hearing a girl's voice cut through to tell her that her children are fine. Strangely, the voice calls Gisa Ella, Lucia's nickname for her. Finally, in Deen's last conversation at sea with a weakened, fading Cinta, she claims to be "celebrating with Lucia, my daughter" and adds, "She is here with me" (311).

In a novel that could easily subordinate its spiritualist strain to character psychology, geopolitical advocacy for Indigenous belief, or even its own explicit concern with planetary ecology, it's significant that it not only lets spirit belief stand, but makes it part of its cosmopolitan core. Significantly, as a historian of the Inquisition, Cinta refuses to see spirit belief in orientalist terms. Early on in the novel when Deen hosts Cinta in Calcutta and he is surprised by her enthusiasm for popular jatra performances of folk epics, he calls their audiences "simple and uneducated" and proclaims himself unwilling "to go along with a whole lot of superstitious mumbo-jumbo" (36). And Cinta rebukes him, citing such words as "supernatural" and "superstitious" as religious themselves, popularized by the Inquisition that sought to eradicate the beliefs it so labeled. She adds a remark that, as we saw in Chapter 3, André Alexis's *Days by Moonlight* upholds: "I can tell you that to this day there are many people in France and Italy for whom witches and spirit-possession are just simple facts of life" (37). Cinta's remarks recall cosmopolitan theorist Isabelle Stengers's in "Reclaiming Animism" when she underscores the irony of contemporary condescension towards past witches and witch hunts: "our pride in our critical power to 'know better' than both the witches and the witch hunters makes us the heirs of witch hunting." Through Tipu and Cinta, the novel advances a belief in the spiritual that is persistently, pervasively cosmopolitan, with Tipu aligned with technology's present and near future and Cinta a spokesperson for the extended life of past eras. If the Gun Merchant's tale has been waiting to open up an invisible world, Tipu is a crucial portal for that world's entry. But the legend was also said to be waiting for the right person and the right time. If Tipu represents and embodies the future-oriented, intangible, and inexplicable elements of the world the legend wants to convey, Deen becomes the focal point for its current timeliness. Many of his encounters with elements from the tale's world may seem strangely repetitive to him, as though mythic motifs keep popping up in front of him, but not all of these moments are entirely unexplainable. As we'll see, several of these occurrences are also all too ecologically explicable. If Deen's exchanges with Cinta often serve to reinforce his recent experiences' spiritual dimension and place them in historical context, their contemporary earthly significance usually comes through in his conversations with Piya. Ghosh sets *Gun Island* the distinctive task of bringing these two strands into convergence, so that the extra-human can be conceived of in both otherworldly and creaturely terms.

The Strange Explained

If, as theorists like to point out, the uncanny (*umheimlich*) is literally the unhomely, then the loss of homes and habitats we currently see on a planetary scale for so many species has made the eerily familiar expansively so. Piya makes this point when she meets up with Deen in the Sundarbans shortly after Tipu's cobra bite and they follow up on Rani's tracker alert. She explains that increased toxic dumps all over the world have increased fish kills, with "thousands of dead fish floating on the surface or washed up ashore." When leaders of pods have to avoid their usual places for hunting, a kind of existential dislocation occurs.

Ghosh has Piya imagine entering the mind of such animals, and when she does so, she speaks simultaneously to the feelings of refugees:

> 'And it must be hardest on Rani, knowing that the young ones depend on her. There she is, perfectly adapted to her environment, perfectly at home in it—and then things begin to change, so that all those years of learning become useless, the places you know best can't sustain you any more and you've got to find new hunting grounds. Rani must have felt that everything she knew, everything she was familiar with—the water, the currents, the earth itself—was rising up against her.'
>
> 106

Deen remarks, as is fitting for a sense of the uncanny, on these words' familiar ring, mentioning this is what he's been told also about the people who have to leave the Sundarbans. Piya agrees, summing up a state of global homelessness with the words, "We're in a new world now. No one knows where they belong any more, neither humans nor animals" (106). But for longtime readers of Ghosh, this moment is uncanny for an additional reason. Piya's statement that Rani "must have felt everything she knew, everything she was familiar with ... rise up against her" might recall the words of the unnamed narrator of *The Shadow Lines* when he remarks that the particular fear of civil violence and riots "is a fear ... that the spaces that surround one, the streets that one inhabits, can become, suddenly and without warning, as hostile as a desert in a flash flood" (200). For those who hear such an echo, Deen's words after hearing Piya, "The words had an oddly familiar ring" (106), will themselves have a knowing sound. This sense of an expansive uncanny, larger than any ecological or textual frame, sends ripples throughout the text and takes numerous out-of-place animals as its bearers.

For Piya nonhuman animals are already centers of convergent and expansive meanings, ones that bridge the human and the nonhuman. When Deen returns to Brooklyn and Tipu begins contacting him, Deen gets in touch with Piya, now in Oregon, who in the course of conversation reports a recent large die-off of Sundarbans crabs. Her remark that they are a keystone species will remind readers of *The Hungry Tide* of her meditation on crabs there, and fittingly, that meditation merges the dimensions of the human and nonhuman. Her guide Fokir fishes for crabs, and his work leads her to find the river dolphins she seeks. She muses that as someone born in July, crabs might rule over her fate, but also wonders why the ancients would allot crabs a zodiac sign. Recalling a lecture describing the ways crabs sift through mud, freeing trees from debris, she sees their value for intertidal forests, and in perceiving the confluence of her education and research, Fokir's livelihood, crabs' environmental role, and her zodiac sign's importance for her, she decides phrases such as "keystone species" might mean many things (118–19). Likewise, her discussion of crabs with Deen in *Gun Island* leads her to the topic of bark beetles, insects that feed on trees, increasing such trees' likelihood of spreading fires in dry weather. She says when her friend Lisa, an entomologist, noticed their incursion into the west coast mountain forests and tried to warn local officials, she was rebuffed. Piya reports that when wildfires later broke out, Lisa was threatened and blamed for supposedly starting them in a desperate effort to prove herself right and garner more research money. As though channeling Cinta, Piya compares the threats Lisa receives to "the Dark Ages," with "women being attacked as witches!" (120). Piya then goes on to become Deen's source of information for many of the out-of-place animals he finds on his travels. Although many of these take the form of snakes and insects and so recall Manasa Devi, they also emerge in strained environments. The eagle that drops the snake directly in Deen's view, for example, is inexplicably odd, but Deen sees it while flying over the wildfires, watching circling raptors, and contemplating the fact that wildfires are a boon to birds of prey, since the loss of tree cover they cause exposes animals on the ground to the birds' gaze. Similarly, when Deen takes a break from the LA conference to meet Cinta's niece Gisa at her nearby home in Venice, they go to the beach and a yellow-bellied sea snake lethally bites Gisa's dog. This snake is then revealed, via Deen's later email exchange with Piya, to be an unusual species there, newly washing up on California beaches due to warming ocean temperatures. Spiders and shipworms join this series when Deen then takes Gisa up on her offer to journey to Venice, Italy and help with her documentary on migrants there by serving as a translator able to interview Bangladeshis. Staying in Cinta's apartment before she returns, he finds a large spider one evening sitting on his laptop. He snaps a photo before the spider leaves through the window and sends it to Piya, who forwards it to a colleague. She later informs Deen it's a brown recluse, known for its venomous bite and, predictably, known to be moving further north than usual because of Europe's new hotter climate.

Similarly, the shipworms that seem to plague Deen and Cinta when she returns home and meets up with him in Italy fall into this category of the ecologically explicable uncanny. Yet they also present complexities, since Deen is no longer able to see them in purely scientific terms. Rather than a remotely contacted Piya, Cinta explains the link to global warming this time, noting that Venice's higher lagoon temperatures account for the destructively invasive shipworms they find on a nighttime walk to an embankment. Forced to run when the worms gnaw away the rails of the very pier where they are standing, Deen and Cinta slip and stumble on more of them as they fall to the planks. Underscoring a hybrid interpretation of this strange experience, at once ecological and otherworldly, Deen reflects, "It was as though the earth itself had sent out tentacles to touch us, to feel the texture of our skin and see whether we were real" (252). And here he seems to have arrived at Cinta's understanding of his recent experiences, one in which the terms of spirit possession and climate change are not mutually exclusive, and human-centered experience is dislodged as the measure of the real. Earlier when Deen had told Cinta that he knew he shouldn't find himself so unsettled lately, since he accepted that global warming scientifically explained all these species' extended ranges, she claimed that those who in the time of the Inquisition felt possessed were not so different from him. She describes both those caught in the feeling of being possessed and those caught in the forces of climate change as "beset by a feeling that inexplicable forces are acting upon them in such a way that they are no longer in control of what happens to them" (235). But she also makes a crucial distinction whereby our ancestors experienced the threat of loss of will and loss of presence in an inverse manner to our contemporary version of this state. She claims that whereas the people of the past might have habitually felt "their sense of their presence in the world" fail them if they couldn't prevail against potentially hostile elements, and thus spirit possession might have been a readily imaginable state, today "that sense of presence slowly fades" because it doesn't need to be asserted "in a world of impersonal systems" where it's easily "lost or forgotten" and "it's easier to let the systems take over" (236). In contrast to both losses of presence, Cinta sees in Deen's retracing of the Gun Merchant's legend, neither possession nor impersonal fading, but "awakening," a heightened sensitivity to planetary forces that the world's impersonal and presence-robbing systems have blocked out (237). In this way, Cinta provides a model for the scientifically explainable to nonetheless become a vehicle for the otherworldly, a vehicle or a portal.

In-between Entities

Just as the novel's conception of character is avataric, it depicts locations and objects as remarkably porous. *Gun Island* may give the impression that there is a special passageway, almost a wormhole, from Venice, California to Venice, Italy, or from contemporary Venice to the seventeenth century's Bonduk-dwip, but it also intriguingly links the Italian Venice to another city. "That there is a strange kinship between Venice and Varanasi has often been noted," Deen himself notes, elaborating, "both cities are like portals in time; they seem to draw you into lost ways of life. And in both cities, as nowhere else in the world, you become aware of mortality." A maintenance of the past merges with "evidence of the enchantment of decay, of a kind of beauty that can only be revealed by long, slow fading" (165). As a place where persistence and impermanence converge to create a sense of slow-motion entropy, Venice lends an apt setting to Deen's mental time travels in which inhabiting the Gun Merchant's perspective becomes a portal to further speculative realms, ones in which the centrality of material human experience is continually displaced.

Arriving at Venice's Ghetto, Deen immediately tries to imagine it through the Gun Merchant's eyes, and although he does conjure up a vision to himself of the Merchant, imagining a tall turbaned man, his perspective suddenly shifts: "a strange thing happened; I seemed to slip through an opening, or a membrane, so that I wasn't looking at the Merchant's predicament from his own point of view but rather from the perspective of his pursuer, the goddess herself" (166). Following this train of thought, Deen finds the word "goddess" less and less fitting for Manasa Devi, who comes to seem more a mediator and even a medium unto herself than a divinely sovereign figure:

> 'Goddess' conjures up an image of an all-powerful deity whose every command is obeyed by her subjects. But the Manasa Devi of the legend was by no means a 'goddess' in this sense; snakes were not so much her subjects as her constituents; to get them to do her bidding she had to plead, cajole, persuade. She was in effect a negotiator, a translator—or better still a *portavoce*—as the Italians say, 'a voice carrier' between two species that had no language in common and no shared means of communication. Without her mediation there could be no relationship between animal and human except hatred and aggression.
>
> 166–7

A sort of prosopopoeia of proto-communication or an earthly goddess of communication's grounds of possibility, Manasa Devi seems to stand both for and at a threshold. Her figure preserves a story that is at once about a broader world trying to get our attention and also is a remnant itself of a broader form of communication. And the Merchant's tale suggests, Deen muses, that trouble comes when mediation is rendered impossible, when humans deny such a voice, obsessively pursue profit, sequester themselves, yet "recognize no restraint in relation to other living things" (167). In a sense, humanity's exaltation of human language as supremely exemplary of communication does even the worlds in which humans find themselves a disservice and injustice. Deen's contemplation of the *portavoce* urges us to see language as not so much possessed as carried, and *Gun Island*'s love of portals can be seen as consonant with its appeal to communication at a level of the proto.

Accordingly, the novel's treatment of books and its weaving of a multidimensional literary matrix reminiscent of Zebra's in Van der Vliet Oloomi's *Call Me Zebra* can also be read as part of its appeal to proto-communication and its project to decenter human language-based exceptionalism. Books, too, become portals, objects in transit and transition, and one book in particular takes on an archetypal, and even arche-typographic significance. On the heels of an unpleasant encounter with a loan shark with whom Rafi has had dealings as he's tried to raise money for Tipu's crossings (a loan shark who threateningly references Thomas Mann's *Death in Venice*), Deen wanders by a small bookstore in the Ghetto. In its window he finds a poster for a book exhibit of Aldo Manutius's 1499 printing of the allegory *Hypnerotomachia Poliphili* or *The Strife of Love in a Dream* by Francesco Colonna. Thinking of Manutius as Venice's Gutenberg and the "Michelangelo of print," Deen recalls his work:

> He designed the prototypes of some of the most widely used fonts of our day, including Bembo, and Garamond (my personal favourite); it was Manutius who invented italics, introduced the semicolon and gave the comma its distinctive hooked shape. As if this were not enough, he also created the ancestor of the modern paperback, because of which he is credited with forever changing our relationship with the written word: it was only after Aldo Manutius that people began to read not for instruction, or edification, or for purposes of piety, but purely for pleasure.
>
> 225

Not only does Ghosh nicely allot a semicolon to the sentence that details Manutius's introduction of it, but also in this almost McLuhanesque meditation on a medium, he credits the paperback with inaugurating the pleasure of reading text. This musing will become linked to further ones on the creatureliness of the *Hypnerotomachia*, the importance of the Bembo family, and the current relationship of books to phones. All of these meanderings will work to move Deen from reinhabiting the perceptual world of the Gun Merchant to contemplating a rich matrix of shifting media. Indeed on his walk to the exhibit, Deen imagines not only all the old bookshops that Cinta (as though employing the method Benajmin famously ascribes to the flaneur in his *Arcades Project* [5]) has told him once existed at particular sites, but also the Merchant passing by them, seeing "a universe of books" (226). When he beholds the exhibit's vitrines and screens displaying the *Hypnerotomachia*, the rare text seems to serve a similar function for Deen to the Gun Merchant's shrine, now washed away, as though it picks up a relay of meaning or represents a further step back in retracing the revelations the Gun Merchant experienced. What Deen recalls of the allegory immediately recalls the shrine and its legend:

> Scrolling through the pages I began to remember bits of the story: it was told in the voice of a man who sets off to search for an always absent beloved and finds himself lost in a forest where he is surrounded by savage animals—wolves, bears and hissing serpents. He wanders on and on until he falls into an exhausted sleep and dreams a dream in which he is dreaming a dream at once terrifying and erotic, filled with fantastical creatures, sculptures and monuments, some of which are engraved with cryptic messages in Latin, Greek, Hebrew and Arabic. In this dreamt-of dream voices and messages emanate from beings of all sorts—animals, trees, flowers, spirits ...
>
> 227

Deen infers from the similarity between the text's dream images and the Sundarbans shrine that the Gun Merchant beheld these same pages, and not only this, but that when Manasa Devi was said to have emerged from the pages of a book, this was the one. He begins to feel not only that he is seeing through the Merchant's eyes, but that his presence is close by. Most importantly, Deen's sense that he "had entered the dreamtime of the book" (228) allows him to uncannily invert the customary hierarchies of waking consciousness and dreams, the human and the nonhuman, and the real and fantastical:

> As this started to come back to me I had an uncanny feeling that I too had lost myself in this dream; it wasn't so much that I was dreaming, but that I was being dreamed by creatures whose very existence was fantastical to me—spiders, cobras, sea snakes—and yet they and I had somehow become a part of each other's dreams.
>
> 227

The imagined ties between the Merchant and the early book culture of Venice will tighten when Deen on a later city walk with Cinta will pass by the Palazzo Bembo. She will point out its having belonged "to the family of the great poet Pietro Bembo," and Deen will add, "After whom Manutius named the Bembo font?" (238). And cosmopolitanizing the Bembo family history as well as linking it to the text's core legend, Cinta will remark on the descendent Ambrosio Bembo, a contemporary of the Merchant's who traveled to and from India, and whom, she speculates, the Merchant might have met. Through the Merchant, his imagined steps and eyes, a universe of bookshops, printing presses, pages, typefaces, mediator-deities, dreamers, forests, fantastical creatures, poets, and travelers opens up, spans West and East, and dissolves temporal barriers. Far from resisting modes of modernity, Manasa Devi as mediator is shown to be fluent in them.

Two final instances act as capstones to this use of Aldo Manutius as a way to move musings on books towards metatextual and extra-dimensional meditations on media. In the voyage to rendezvous with the Blue Boat of refugees, tempestuous weather will strike with serpentine twisters appearing in the sky. In the midst of this extreme weather, Deen will remark to himself, "The sight was nothing like I had ever seen before; it seemed to belong not on the earth of human experience but in the pages of some unworldly fantasy, like the *Hypnerotomachia Polyphili* [sic]" (276). Both a knowing nod to the reader that the novel's final events will depart from customary realism and a returning of ur-book history to the unworldly, the earth that is not of human experience, this last reference sets up the ending even as it completes the *Hypnerotomachia*-centered textual strand. But the book is not done with meditating on dreams, books, or Manutius. Talking to one of Venice's Bangladeshi residents about what inspires migration, Deen hears a very different reference to "the dream." Rather than voicing the notion that we inherit dreams, their stories and images, as a vestige of our animal self, Palash sees the dream that fuels travel and migration, the fantasy that surrounds such a place as Venice, for example, as specifically human. Even if foreigners come to Venice for a typically Italian experience, ignoring all the Bangladeshis who are working in the hospitality industry's menial jobs to make that dream happen, Palash lets it go, excusing the dreamers with the language of rights: "And why not? Every human being has a right to a fantasy, don't they? It is one of the most important human rights—it is what makes us different from animals" (291). Attributing the perpetuation of such dreams to the screens of phones and TVs, their ability to act as portals to other worlds, he sparks a reminiscence in Deen:

> I remembered the restlessness of my own youth and how it had been fed by another, very powerful medium of dreams—novels, which I had read voraciously, especially savoring those that were about faraway places. I thought of teenage years and all the time I had spent hunting for cheap paperbacks in the alleys and back lanes of Calcutta (Aldo Manutius might well have had me in mind when he pioneered the publication of inexpensive books; I was addicted to them in much the same way that people of Palash's generation were to their phones).

292

Thinking of reading as a way "of escaping the narrowness of the world I lived in," Deen then, almost as though he's learned to do this from Cinta, flips the observation and asks himself, "But was it possible that my world had seemed narrow precisely because I was a voracious reader?" (292). He concludes that novels had achieved what the eighteenth century suspected they would and what myriad visual media do today. All are "instruments of ... uprooting," but the latter create "dreams," "desires," and "restlessness" with "the power of the billions of images that now permeate every corner of the globe" (292–3). Ghosh's novel refers to its existence as a novel, reminds us of the novel's traditional role as a transporting vehicle, and signals awareness of this role's current supplanting by newer media. Acknowledging the raised stakes in a world of globally pervasive smart technology and constantly transferred images, Deen's musings raise the question of what else, what other mediations these media can carry. If Manasa Devi had to appear to the Merchant from the pages of an allegory to get him to build a physical shrine, a material marker, what could emerge from global media to make a difference that matters?

Arrival Times

The novel will provide a somewhat utopian answer amidst some of our present world's most recognizably dystopian features. Taking place in the politically anomalous topos of the ocean, or, in Deen's rendering of a phrase from Bengali legends, "*sasagara basumati*—'the ocean'd earth'" (295), the conclusion brings together not only many character strands but also many political spokespeople and nonhuman species.[6] In a gathering that merges the explicably and unaccountably strange, we witness the hoped for miracle-at-sea. Several migrating species—long-finned pilot whales, Risso's dolphins, striped dolphins, fin whales, and sperm whales among them—join the boats heading towards Sicily. When Deen asks an observing Piya whether such a multispecies migration event is normal in those waters, she hedges, responding, "It depends on what you mean by normal ... It changes from season to season" (288) and later refers to it as "just a little bit unusual." Nonetheless, the passengers traveling with them cheer on and even toast with wine and grappa the frolicking dolphins, and Cinta refers to the sightings teasingly as "maybe miraculous?" (293). But as they near the Blue Boat, the *Lucania* and its crew encounter xenophobic protesters, TV journalists, and Italian warships. The clash of causes and looming threat of violence fill Deen with a sense that for the anti-migrant forces, "there was something truly apocalyptic, not least because the anger on display was so clearly fuelled by fear" (299). Sighting even more whales and dolphins in the distance, Deen and Piya notice them circling and leaping in the air at the same spot, and Piya now admits she can't account for such strange behavior. When the skies then fill with millions of migrating birds, Rafi says the obvious: "It's just as it says in the story—the creatures of the sky and the sea rising up" (306). And, as if signaling the way that this final chapter entitled "The Storm" will come to both reprise and rewrite the ending of *The Hungry Tide*, Cinta uses "the Italian word for a flock of birds in flight" as she points to them and says, "*Uno stormo.*" Deen himself refers to the whirling circles of the birds above as "a halo" and the circle of sea creatures below—now glowing with a bioluminescence that causes Piya to declare, "I don't believe it!"—as a "chakra" (307). When the Italian Navy on site acts independently to rescue the migrants, the commander, Admiral Vigonovo, whose family is known to Cinta through their shared religious congregation, defends his actions by saying he has not contravened the government but rather taken literally its statement that only a miracle could save the refugees. But Piya backpedals, whispering to Deen, "He's wrong you know—there's a scientific explanation for everything that happened there. It was just a series of migratory patterns intersecting in an unusual way." And when Deen inquires further about the bioluminescence, she insists that the dynos that might cause it are capable of migrating a long way, and that "animal migrations are being hugely impacted by climate change so nothing is surprising now," but adds ominously, "I'm sure we'll see more of these intersecting events in the future" (309). But shifting from the future back to the present, Deen presses the question of why now, and there Piya stops short, claiming not to know, but simply to be grateful. When Admiral Vigonovo is told he has broken the law, he proclaims, "I have acted in accordance with the law of the sea, the law of humanity and the law of God" and is left to defend himself from accusations of following "religious beliefs over [his] orders" (310).

In several ways, the final chapter of *Gun Island* refuses to stand down from its spiritual position. But in others, it attempts a careful negotiation, one that can be seen via an extended comparison with Benjamin. Not only do the miraculous multitudes of swarming species garner sympathy for the refugees, but an interview with Piya and Rafi recounting the latter's love for and separation from Tipu gets uploaded to social media at just the right moment. Support from global activists and private donors rushes in. Looking for Cinta after all the drama, Deen finds her not simply weakened and resting in her cabin but claiming to be celebrating with her lost daughter Lucia, who has now, at last, come for her. She tries to thank Deen for fulfilling a long-held intuition of hers, one dating back to "the very first time we talked, outside that library in the midst of that

Midwestern snow," when, she says, "I knew that one day you would give me a great gift, a boon" (311). Refusing to hear this, Deen runs for Gisa and a doctor and, taking too long to find one, returns to find Cinta already dead. Turning over her words, Deen stands at her cabin door, unable to bear entering the room with the doctor. "Now at last I had an inkling of why she had chosen to bestow her friendship on me," he reflects, adding, "it was as if she had had an intuition that someday we would bring each other *here*, to this juncture in time and space— and not till then would she find release from the grief of her separation from her daughter." Between Piya's ecological prophecies and Cinta's uncanny intuition, Deen finds himself in Admiral Vigonovo's position of having to adjudicate in the face of many explanations, many laws. For Benjamin, messianism already had to navigate its way past certain forms of spiritualism.[7] But for Ghosh, this tension unfolds in a distinctive way in the context of an era he agrees to call the Anthropocene.

Insisting on stopping at the here and now before contemplating past seeds of the future, Deen partly repeats a Benjaminian posture. In standing at the threshold, Deen embodies many refusals: his immediate refusal to enter and see his dread fulfilled, his earlier refusal to believe Cinta's claim that death is approaching, his refusal even earlier to accept Piya's deflection from the present, her shift from beholding the unbelievable in the moment to foreseeing a future filled with incredible multispecies behavior, and finally, his refusal for so long to acknowledge Cinta's world of intuitive possibilities, her having foreseen this moment and moved toward it all along. When we think of the famous words with which Benjamin's "On the Concept of History" ends, it's easy to place greater emphasis on the last line than on its predecessors:

> We know that the Jews were prohibited from inquiring into the future: the Torah and the prayers instructed them in remembrance. This disenchanted the future, which holds sway over all those who turn to soothsayers for enlightenment. This does not imply, however, that for the Jews the future became homogeneous, empty time. For every second was the small gateway in time through which the Messiah might enter.
>
> 397

Benjamin's lines emphasize prohibition and disenchantment as much as portals and messianism, and in doing so, repeat points he makes in his much earlier, and notably surrealism-inspired, text "One-Way Street." In the subsection named for the mysterious "Madame Ariane," he has strong words for those who use psychics to grasp the future:

> He who asks fortune-tellers the future unwittingly forfeits an inner intimation of coming events that is a thousand times more exact than anything they may say. He is impelled by inertia, rather than by curiosity, and nothing is more unlike the submissive apathy with which he hears his fate revealed than the alert dexterity with which the man of courage lays hands on the future. For presence of mind is an extract of the future, and precise awareness of the present moment is more decisive than foreknowledge of the most distant events. Omens, presentiments, signals pass day and night through our organism like wave impulses. To interpret them or to use them: that is the question. The two are irreconcilable. Cowardice and apathy counsel the former, lucidity and freedom the latter. For before such prophecy or warning has been mediated by word or image, it has lost its vitality, the power to strike at our center and force us, we scarcely know how, to act accordingly. If we neglect to do so, and only then, the message is deciphered. We read it. But now it is too late.
>
> 482–3

It's Gisa who says, "We came too late," and then the novel's final two words, "Cinta's gone." But this is just after Deen in the doorway reports feeling "something like the touch of a hand, brushing gently against my cheek," but stops himself from calling Cinta's name, claiming to have "realized that it was just a draught, created by the opening of the cabin door" (312). Ghosh maintains Deen's sensitivity at the cost of its full acknowledgment, and in this way, keeps him from becoming completely a predictor of futures or after-the-fact interpreter of signs. His intuitions can remain inklings, his fleeting feelings brushed off. In Benjamin's peculiar temporal logic in "One-Way Street," it's after we drop a cup that we feel its gaze beheld us strangely, knowingly just before. We taunt ourselves with the knowledge we should have had, the aura of what we could have seen. These are the co-opted, retrofitted futures he warns against, leaving us the question of how to reverse this temporal formula. For the Benjamin of "One-Way Street," it's a matter of the body, ourselves as organism, what Cinta might call our animal selves that can feel the unmediated wave and act, with "presence of mind," just in time.

But Cinta's conception of humanity's formerly acknowledged animal self and its modes of communication might not fully align with Benjamin's "One-Way Street" cautions against prophecy and mediation by word or image. Although we might see a Benjaminian element in Deen's self-imposed restrictions, Benjamin's principles can also seem opposed to the ones Deen, with Cinta's help, must rely on as he decodes the legend of the Gun Merchant and comes to feel through the power of Manasa Devi the forces on behalf of which she mediates. In *The Great*

Derangement Ghosh uses various phrases to describe such forces' agency and mediation, referring to "those uncanny instances in which *the planet* seems to have been toying with humanity" (22); "the uncanny impression that *global warming* has long been toying with humanity" (80) or asking whether "*the Anthropocene* has become our interlocutor, [and whether] it is indeed thinking 'through' us" (83; italics mine). For Deen getting to the bottom this conversation is a hermeneutical and at times prophetic activity. For the Benjamin of the "Madame Ariane" fragment, interpretation creates a scene at which it arrives too late. Yet both Ghosh and Benjamin are interested in types of conveyance that aren't fully captured in a human utterance. "Madame Ariane: Second Courtyard on the Left," might lead us to see a kind of communicability, on the one hand, in the usable "inner intimation," "precise awareness of the present moment," and the "Omens, presentiments, signals" that move through us like waves or else, on the other hand, in the "would have, could have, should have" thoughts we ascribe to entities after the fact. There's the conveyable we might see either in what was or what should have been conveyed, the intuition that can be seen to have spoken for itself, or else, unattended to, can be seen to have left a trail of smoke over everything.

Ghosh, by contrast, turns at the close of his first chapter, "Stories," in *The Great Derangement*, to Eduardo Kohn's *How Forests Think* for a model of more-than-human communication, one that poses the questions of whether "to think about the Anthropocene will be to think in images" and will "require a departure from our accustomed logocentrism" (83).[8] He draws this idea of imagistic Anthropocenic communication from Kohn's notion that the nonhuman world communicates through patterns and forms:

> In *How Forests Think*, the anthropologist Eduardo Kohn suggests that "forms"—by which he means much more than shapes or visual metaphors—are one of the means that enable our surroundings to think through us … we are constantly engaged in patterns of communication that are not linguistic: as, for example, when we try to interpret the nuances of a dog's bark; or when we listen to the patterns of birdcalls; or when we try to figure out what exactly is portended by a sudden change in the sound of the wind as it blows through the trees. None of this is any less demanding, or any less informative, than, say, listening to the news on the radio.
>
> 82

Ghosh's phrasing, however much his thought is derived from Kohn's, lets us bring into analogy Benjamin's impulse waves and the airwaves, organic communication and telecommunication, and he turns specifically to the nonhuman, citing dogs, birds, and trees as key exemplars and purveyors of such patterned information. Yet for the particularly restrictive Benjamin of "One-Way Street," prophecies and warnings that become "mediated by word or image" have already lost vital force, the power that can move us simply by moving through us. One wonders whether this nuance of difference between Ghosh and Benjamin occurs because Benjamin is speaking of organism but not specifically of ecology, perhaps even organism without need of ecology, in the same way that at the end of "One-Way Street" he speaks of a "cosmic experience" exemplified in astrology but belied by astronomy.

There in the final subsection "To the Planetarium," Benjamin engages in a revolutionary form of planet-thinking that harkens back to ancient experience. "Nothing distinguishes the ancient from the modern man," he tells us, "so much as the former's absorption in a cosmic experience scarcely known to later periods," and he adds, "Its waning is marked by the flowering of astronomy at the beginning of the modern age" (486). He speaks of a human ability to perceive correspondences that elsewhere he calls "the mimetic faculty." In "Doctrine of the Similar," he writes of both nature and human beings as generating similarities and humans, who are particularly gifted in the capacity for imitation, as formerly able to widely perceive similarities. But, he claims, employing a word for perceptual world that Jakob von Uexküll uses in relation to animals, "clearly the perceptual world [*Merkwelt*] of modern human beings seems to contain far fewer of those magical correspondences than did that of the ancients," and he cites the example of astrology. "We must assume," he guides us as a step to understanding ancient astrology, "in principle that processes in the sky were imitable, both collectively and individually, by people who lived in earlier times; indeed, that this imitability contained instructions for mastering an already present similarity." Even if we no longer have a feel for such cosmic correspondence, its link to "the moment of birth" in astrology suggests a principle for tracking this faculty: "The perception of similarity is in every case bound to a flashing up" (695). It is to such a "flashing up" that Benjamin also appeals in "On the Concept of History" when he writes of historical materialism's method in theses V and VI and claims, "The true image of the past flits by. The past can be seized only as an image that flashes up at the moment of its recognizability, and is never seen again" (390); that "it is an irretrievable image of the past which threatens to disappear in any present that does not recognize itself as intended in that image"; and that "Analyzing the past historically does not mean recognizing it 'the way it really was.' It means appropriating a memory as it flashes up in a moment of danger. Historical materialism wishes to hold fast to that image of the past which unexpectedly appears to the historical subject in a moment of danger." If the danger forestalled by allying image to flashes, interpretation to recognizabilty, is "becoming a tool of the ruling classes" and "conformism" (391), then it's worth asking of Ghosh's of communication in images, who is speaking and what a *Merkwelt* of ecology might mean for form.

The vital source for Ghosh, what he means by "the planet," "global warming," and "the Anthropocene," is Gaia. This is seen when he describes the mindset underlying questionable urban planning as one that's "trained to break problems into smaller and smaller puzzles" and concludes, "it is a perspective that renders the interconnectedness of Gaia unthinkable" (56). If the term marking our epochal awareness of our species' geological impact, the Anthropocene, notably has man at its root, the name for the hypothesis that planetary life can be seen as part of a self-regulating system is equally telling. This hypothesis from an era of awareness of global warming is named not for women, a population unhabituated to standing for their species, but for an archetypally feminine goddess, the Greek goddess of the earth. The Anthropocene and Gaia come to form an unequal gendered pair, a couple in which species man confronts planetary feminine in an epoch that didn't have to happen. Manasa Devi might be said to serve as an avatar of Gaia in *Gun Island*, with Cinta becoming her vanishing prophet, a spokesperson for a portavoce. It might appear that Ghosh lets Cinta, for a time, carry on the business for which Benjamin's Madame Ariane and her clientele are admonished. Or one could say that in Deen's many uncanny encounters, whether through nature or technology, Ghosh is giving Gaia, rather than the man of revolutionary action, the upper hand. To let Gaia speak through the Anthropocene, Ghosh makes allowances for a mode of communication that takes many forms and leaves many signs. If Ghosh leaves more room for protracted interpretation, with omens, presentiments, and signals that, beyond merely coursing as waves, take readable form in myth and hieroglyph, it may be because he associates more possible mediations with more species and he wants to be sure to include the nonhuman in his imagined uprisings. Indeed, he intends a strong critique of logocentrism, a textual exceptionalism he sees moving from the Abrahamic religions through the Protestant Reformation and print technology into pictureless Western novels, "as if every doorway and window that might allow us to escape the confines of language had to be slammed shut, to make sure humans had no company in their dwindling world but their own abstractions and concepts" (83–4). However much Ghosh accords with Benjamin's desire to seize a revolutionary present and wrest both the future and the past from appropriating teleologies, his Anthropocenic need for prophetic imagistic thought means he still needs to pass through a metaphorical second courtyard on the left before every second can become a small gateway.

If Ghosh's novel shows Gaia thinking through many forms, it's fitting that its ending offers a vision of salvation mediated by many female figures. We know that Cinta has long been awaiting a reunion with her daughter Lucia, and in the final chapter she feels this longing fulfilled. In addition, the angelic Ethiopian woman of Tipu's prophetic dreams comes to be at the center not only of the uprising of refugees, but also the miraculous multispecies swarming at sea. And she is another epiphanic figure, an avatar not only of Manasa Devi, but also of Benjamin's angel of history and Venice's famous Black Madonna. When Tipu journeys to Egypt to find this woman who's appeared in his dreams, he ends up, we later learn, in a connection house run by human traffickers notorious for trading in human organs. When this woman is brought there as part of a "motley lot, consisting of Ethiopians, Eritreans, Somalis, Arabs and Bengalis," the house is struck by a mysterious tornado that overwhelms the traffickers, freeing the refugees who then manage to seize one of their boats. When Deen, Piya, Cinta, Gisa, and Rafi sail out to meet the Blue Boat, amidst the swirling cetaceans and swarming birds, they spot the Ethiopian woman standing at the boat's prow:

> The woman lifted her arms now, raising them until they were level with her shoulders, palms facing upwards. And almost instantly a funnel-like extrusion appeared in the storm that was spinning above us. It began to extend downwards, forming a whirling halo above her head.
>
> She stood absolutely still for what was perhaps only a moment, with a halo of birds spinning above her, while down in the water a chakra of dolphins and whales whirled around the boat. And then an even stranger thing happened: the colour of the water around the refugee boat began to change. In a few moments it was filled with a glow, of an unearthly green colour, bright enough that we could see the outlines of the dolphins and whales that were undulating through the water.
>
> 307

Cinta's remark just before, as what she calls "*Uno stormo*" begins to coalesce, sets the Ethiopian woman up as having theologically historical significance. "Time itself is in ecstasy," Cinta marvels, adding, "I had never thought I would witness this joy with my own eyes, pouring over the horizon" (306). In addition to channeling, along with Manasa Devi (and hence Gaia), Benjamin's messianic time and storm-from-paradise-propelled angel, the Ethiopian woman reprises the role of Venice's Black Madonna—but with a key reversal. In their earlier

Venetian urban wanderings and retracing of the Merchant's likely footsteps, Deen and Cinta come to the church honoring the Blessed Virgin who is credited with saving Venice from the Plague in the 1600s. Entering the Santa Maria della Salute, Cinta describes the famous Black Madonna there in Manasa Devi-like terms as "The Panaghia Mesopanditissa, Madonna the Mediator" or "she who stands between us and the incarnate Earth, with all its blessings and furies" (243). And she adds the figure was brought from Crete, a city known for worshipping "A-sa-sa-ra-me ... the Minoan goddess of snakes." Deen hears the church's bells reverberate throughout the dome and muses, "It was as if a voice were crying out from the past to remind the world that the limits of human reason and ability become apparent not in the long, slow duration of everyday time, but in the swift and terrible onslaught of fleeting instants of catastrophe." His thoughts link this divine female protector from plagues to the temporality that Benjamin famously opposes to "homogeneous, empty time" and that Ghosh himself wants to rescue from Apocalypse, preferring to underscore "instants of catastrophe." In a final temporal flourish, Ghosh ends this chapter entitled "Warnings" with Cinta gesturing to the church floor's mosaic with its Latin motto, exhorting Deen, "Remember these words, *caro*, think of them whenever you despair of the future: *Unde origo inde salus*—'From the origin salvation comes'" (244).

The Black Madonna of the Santa Maria della Salute returns us to Esposito's immunity paradigm. In *Immunitas: The Protection and Negation of Life*, Esposito claims that the "images of besieged cities, fortified castles, and territories surrounded by potential invaders that filled pages of English, French, and Italian political treatises between the sixteenth and seventeenth centuries offer tangible evidence" of an "obsession with self-protection" in which open borders and open-to-infection bodies are linked. He cites as inaugural moments of this obsession the epidemics of the sixteenth century, syphilis and the plague, and Girolamo Fracastoro's treatises in which "Galenic humoral theory was flanked and then opposed by the theory that disease is communicated through contamination caused by the body's intake of tiny infectious agents (*semina*) of exogenous nature, and therefore by means of a mechanism structurally different from the endogenous processes involved with the putrefaction of bodies." The idea of bodily infection brought on by alien contaminating seeds becomes part of a "common horizon of meaning" in which "contact with unfamiliar cultures and ethnicities" can likewise stir anxiety (123). It's striking that en route to the Santa Maria della Salute, Cinta describes the decades just before the Merchant's arrival as ones not only of catastrophic weather and hence hunger, but also of an epidemic brought in by foreigners, first "German soldiers" and then "a diplomat."

No stranger to the immunity paradigm, seventeenth-century Venice responded, Cinta tells Deen, accordingly:

> The disease was not new to Venice; there had been other outbreaks of the plague before and much had been learnt from them: many tracts had been published on governing *la peste* and permanent boards of health had been set up as far back as the fifteenth century. You could even say that modern sanitary protocols, for dealing with epidemics, were invented in Venice. So when the great plague of 1630 broke out the city fathers were not slow to act.
>
> 241

Cinta's remarks make Venice a point of origin for the immunity paradigm, but also for its inversion, since Venice is miraculously saved by its faith in an imported Madonna, one that while it is enshrined in their famous church, also harkens back to the Crete where it was made, a Crete famous for its snake goddesses. And as Joanne M. Ferraro notes, Venice itself owes its origins to "fishing peoples ... Venetia's refugees, who preferring the boggy terrain of the lagoon and the littoral to the aggressive Lombard tribes that were colonizing northern Italy, scattered along the mud flats and salt marshes" of the area, a region in which "There was no firm shoreline separating land and sea, only the slippery mud and fluid margins that made settlement so precarious" (2; 3). Fluid borders, founding refugees, inaugural epidemic awareness, and a far-reaching goddess all characterize the text's Venice as a concentrated point from which an idea of salvation might come.

Before Deen feels the draft from the cabin door's opening brush his cheek and Gisa closes the novel by declaring Cinta "gone," he returns to that moment in the Santa Maria della Salute. As he thinks of Cinta's foreknowledge that they would arrive "*here*, to this juncture in time and space—and not until then would she find release from the grief of separation from her daughter," he claims:

> In that instant of clarity I heard again that familiar voice in my ear, repeating those words from La Salute—*Unde Origo Inde Salus*—"From the beginning salvation comes," and I understood what she had been trying to tell me that day: that the possibility of our deliverance lies not in the future but in the past, in a mystery beyond memory.
>
> 312

Deen's reflections recall the endings of two of Ghosh's prior, perhaps foreknowing, novels: *The Shadow Lines* in which an unnamed narrator, having received the account of the way his mentor and cousin Tridib sacrificed himself amidst a riot, feels "grateful" for this "glimpse ... of a final redemptive mystery" (246), and *The*

Hungry Tide in which Fokir sacrifices himself for Piya but also meets his death knowing he has intuited his dead mother calling for him days before. But Deen's words also intriguingly rescript Cinta's translation of La Salute's Latin motto. Whereas she had exhorted Deen to remember, "From the origin salvation comes," he now thinks, "From the beginning salvation comes," inspiring us to consider the difference. Writing of ideas and art in *Origin of the German Trauerspiel*, Benjamin distinguishes origin from genesis in terms resonant with his "Theological-Political Fragment":

> By "origin" is meant not the coming-to-be of what has originated but rather what originates in the becoming and passing away. The origin stands as eddy in the stream of becoming and vigorously draws the emerging material into its rhythm. In the naked, manifest existence of the factual, the original never allows itself to be recognized; its rhythm stands open only to a dual insight. On the one hand, it demands to be recognized as restoration, and on the other hand—and precisely on account of this—as something incomplete and unclosed. Determining itself in every origin-phenomenon is the formation in which, again and again, an idea confronts the historical world, until it lies there complete in the totality of its history. The origin, then, does not arise from the facts attested but concerns their fore- and after- history.
>
> 24–5

Like Deen's aquatic chakra, this stream eddy is multiply mysterious—something amenable more to double vision than direct recognition, restorative yet unfinished, a formation, a confrontation with history complete only in the "totality of its history," an immanent +/– 1 that with respect to time is best described in after/before terms. The "origin" of Benjamin's text and Cinta's utterance, recalled as requested later by Deen, is easy to elide. It's easy looking back, to make this fleeting, ambiguous 1 a beginning. If Samuel Weber, deriving his own +1 from Benjamin's oeuvre in his imaginative study *Benjamin's -abilities*, attributes Benjamin's "seemingly inexhaustible ability to come up with striking, unexpected, and above all compelling formulations and insights, however enigmatic these may be," —in other words, flashes or formations—at least partly to his unusual way of nominalizing verbs by adding the suffix "ability" or "ibility," then Deen's other rephrasing seems equally notable. Not only does he depart from "origin," but he also shifts from salvation to "the possibility of our deliverance," in other words, deliverability, akin, no doubt, to an image we can see, perhaps with double vision, only in its moment of recognizability. It's as if Deen wants to say through his various shiftings that whether we save ourselves or not, we've been worthy of deliverance right from our start.

Postscript: Seeing Past Curses

If *Gun Island* is not only (or even just barely) a novel unto itself with its own specific textual existence but also a gesture to an expansive over-novel, a Ghoshian literary convergence it's especially good at affording us glimpses of, then his 2021 *The Nutmeg's Curse* makes for a comprehensive afterword. "A powerful work of history, essay, testimony, and polemic," as its inner flap has it, Ghosh's study of what he now calls our "planetary crisis" in the context of settler colonialism's long history of extraction and extermination extends many of the arguments seen in the interplay between *Gun Island* and *The Great Derangement*. The seventeenth-century Dutch takeover of the Indonesian Banda Islands, their policy of seeking to entirely eliminate its existing population, and their attempts to violently bend the environment to their will for the supposed sake of the spice trade all form a horrific primal scene, and not merely for colonialism. The Dutch acted, Ghosh tells us, "not just as colonists but also philosophers; it was their violence, directed at 'natives' and the landscapes they inhabited, that laid the foundations of the mechanistic philosophies that would later be attributed to their contemporaries, like Descartes and Mandeville, Bacon and Boyle" (37). What Ghosh calls a "resource curse" ensues when the colonizers find that their economic and environmental control can never be complete. Demand for a ready supply can fade, spicy food can be cast as morally unsavory, and it can seem necessary to control resources, restricting clove cultivation to one island, nutmeg to another, while bitterly, and often failingly, battling the landscapes' vegetational habits along the way (74). Moreover, paranoia can take hold, and a widescale massacre of Indigenous people be sparked by as little as the drop of a lamp. A portrait in miniature of the logic that leads to the Anthropocene, the colonial history of the Banda Islands has spectral aftereffects that also evoke spiritual dimensions, much like the ones *Gun Island* appeals to.

The book provides many intertextual echoes of scenes from *Gun Island* as though giving us a view of its seed material. Visiting the Banda Islands in 2016, Ghosh notes, for example, the leftover, restored but empty, colonial mansions. As he tours one with a room that allowed a suicidal Dutch administrator to look out at a well where the bones of slaughtered Bandanese leaders were deposited, Ghosh understands why it's said to be haunted. In a Deenlike moment when he's left alone by the window, he feels a draft even though no door or window is open. He describes "an uncanny sense that someone, or something, was in the room with me—a presence that was a shadow of something human and yet nonhuman" (248). And just as he gives fuller rein to intuitions Deen shies away from, Ghosh also lets himself voice directly Cinta's views on the nonhuman and narrative while proposing a mission for art. He reiterates, "that far from being an exclusively human attribute, the narrative faculty is the most *animal* of human abilities" and concludes, "if those nonhuman voices are to be restored to their proper place, then it must be, in the first instance, through the medium of stories" (204).

Also giving fuller voice to Gaian politics, Ghosh devotes a chapter to her eponymous hypothesis, but underscores her multifarious nature, both motherly and monstrous, as described by Hesiod. Acknowledging planetarity's multiform nature beyond even the mythic qualities of Gaia, Ghosh proposes an alternative avatar for the time of the Anthropocene. Appearing three times (83; 171; 198) and highlighting its radical yet agentive otherness (what Spivak would call planetarity's being in the species of alterity) is the fictitious planet Solaris. If postcolonial literature was said to be the empire writing back, Ghosh tells us that "the Earth's responses [to climate change] are increasingly reminiscent of the imaginary planet after which the Polish science fiction writer Stanislaw Lem named his brilliant novel, *Solaris*: when provoked by humans Solaris begins to strike back in utterly unexpected and uncanny ways" (83). Additionally intriguing in Ghosh's choice of alternatives is his decision, despite drawing on anthropological work that moves in the direction of animism (Davi Kopenawa and Bruce Albert's *The Falling Sky*, for instance), to advocate instead under the banner of vitalism. Both terms arguably come with unfortunate European baggage, whether colonial or biopolitical, and Ghosh notes such risks when, discussing extreme right-wing appropriations of ecology, he concedes, "This is not to say that a vitalist politics will always and necessarily be benevolent in intent: that is very far from being the case (ecofascism does not lack for shamans)" (233). Yet despite these counterpoints and concessions, the book, perhaps more than *The Great Derangement*, conveys hope, especially shamanic hope.

The Nutmeg's Curse both provides material for an explanation of global anglophone fiction's intensified engagement with indigeneity as well as spirituality, and it provides examples of life beyond extractivist limits. If global anglophone literature is crafting its own dimensionisms and turning to Indigenous beliefs and lifeworlds for inspiration, this may bespeak a macro mimetic faculty. For Benjamin, the mimetic faculty was already cosmic in nature, and just as the formations of what Ghosh repeatedly calls "official modernity" may have depleted it (for Benjamin astronomy and the First World War are notable), the violence to Indigenous lifeworlds with their broad perceptions of vitality and animacy, a violence Ghosh describes as a form of "omnicide," could also justifiably be called a form of "cosmocide." But this cosmocide, unfortunately, is itself amenable to expansive imitation, and Ghosh repeatedly underscores the idea that humans are "essentially mimetic creatures" for good and ill (196). *The Nutmeg's Curse* tells of a disturbing, and likely unforeseen by elitist early colonizers, global mimesis of settler colonialism, even for countries with strikingly divergent colonial histories. Citing India, he summarizes, "The upshot is that India, where the historic model of colonialism was very different from that of settler colonialism, is now striving to remake itself in the image of settler colonialism" (233). This is to say that the model of uprooting and oppressing Indigenous people, often forest-dwellers with a history of protecting biodiversity, while desecrating and toxifying their sacred sites and homelands in the name of resource extraction, tourism, and even misguided or corrupt conservation policies has become a norm imposed across multiple planetary environments. The hybrid spirits of much global anglophone fiction might seek, then, to bear witness to this settler-colonialist model's expansion, to look for what's being lost, and to explore what can be reconstituted—an admittedly ambivalent undertaking.

Ghosh holds out hope for cosmopolitan vitalism, a hybrid political mode that allows those from any historical or religious background to connect to the spirits of the land. He cites approvingly the Bandanese writer Des Alwi who claimed to be of Arab, Chinese, Javanese, Manadonese, and Sumatran descent, and whose memoir describes a highly hybrid Banda Naira culture of the 1930s in which "all were considered Bandanese if they followed Bandanese customs and spoke the Bandanese-Malay dialect" (qtd. in *Nutmeg's* 245). Interestingly, these customs included belief in spirit protectors and these Bandanese included even the descendants of colonial Europeans, by that time a minority group. Ghosh expresses a hope that language, custom, and community when attuned to the landscape and to animate forces beyond the human can collectively act to connect and ground a people whatever their past trajectories, as though "the vitality of the place itself ... creates commonalities between the people who dwell in it, no matter what their origin" (221). It's perhaps this vision that, as we saw in Chapter 3, André Alexis, born in Trinidad with its similar history of exterminationist colonialisms and diverse communities formed from the descendants of transported laborers, both parodies and embraces.

But the echo that resonates across his recent writing most strongly, that offers Ghosh the greatest solace, and that allows him to extend such solace to his readers comes from a story of his mother who died in August 2020. She appears to be an inspirational source for Tipu's venom-induced otherworldly visions as well as the idea of a Madonna extending from the past an offer of future salvation, yet there isn't really an anthropological, ecological, or psychological explanation for the experience he describes. Although sadly COVID-19 prevented Ghosh from traveling to Kolkata during his mother's last days, he recalls a prescient moment from 2018. Hospitalized for chronic respiratory illness, she reaches from her bed for Ghosh's and his wife Debbie's hands. Entering what he calls a trance, she describes welcoming figures and a creaturely presence: "There was something wrapped around her, she said, a creature that was holding her in a protective embrace, so that no harm could come to her—a snake. This was astonishing to hear, for she had had a great terror of snakes all her life." Yet she repeats that she's not afraid, there's nothing to fear, and seems disappointed when alarmed medical staff give her a potassium infusion that returns her to wakefulness. Ghosh concludes that "whatever she saw on the other side had inspired not dread, but longing." And he reports, despite partly envying her her vision, feeling "a sense of reassurance, thinking that she, who had always been a little bit shamanic, would make sure that when my own time came I too would be granted such a vision" (216).

Part Three

Spirals

5

Expected on Earth: Distributive Redemption in Zeyn Joukhadar's *The Thirty Names of Night* and Tanya Tagaq's *Split Tooth*

1. Cusps

In many of the texts I consider, other dimensions emerge as Indigenous beliefs filtered through disingenuous observers, as though a certain version of the global anglophone novel can only cusp on the realms it finds so inspiring. Choo focuses on either the Chinese or the British Malayan community and often presents us with mixtures: Malay and Indigenous tribal beliefs either mingled with Chinese traditions or else reported on from a colonial perspective. Her protagonists constantly strive for peace and wholeness amidst a sense of commercially and colonially expansionist space, warped character fates, and older conceptions of distinctively human virtue now led astray. Likewise, Alexis's Alfred Homer longs for a primal and rooted connection to the Ontario landscape, but it's one he has to establish virtually in projected dimensions. His highly ambivalent tale simultaneously exemplifies two approaches to indigeneity. First, Homer's story can be considered a version, perhaps a parodic one, of Joshua Whitehead's "Indigiqueer Idyll," a "pseudo-settler vision quest" that moves through Indigenous land, appropriating tropes of indigeneity but erasing Indigenous people's presence (229). But second, it might recreate a process of naturalization that Robin Wall Kimmerer in her chapter "In the Footsteps of Nanabozho" describes with its subtitle, "Becoming Indigenous to Place" (205). Ghosh too seems to put stock in this process, noting its power in *The Nutmeg's Curse*. Although in the Indonesian Banda Islands, Indigenous people were largely eradicated by the Dutch and various types of transported unfree laborers took their place, by the 1990s, Ghosh reports, citing anthropologist Philip Winn, that the Bandanese people of Lonthor had created their own form of communal identification with the landscape. While for the most part these Bandanese ceased to claim ancestral ties to the land, nonetheless they saw it as animated by unseen spirits that they, across religious differences, revered with rituals. Ghosh culminates this line of thought on a hopeful note:

> For those who experience the Earth as Gaia, as a living, vital energy, a landscape doesn't spring to life because its inhabitants happen to share a common origin. It is, rather, the vitality of the place itself that creates commonalities between the people who dwell in it, no matter what their origin.
>
> This may well have been the primordial process through which humans were indigenized and assimilated into landscapes everywhere around the planet—for after all, except for one small part of Africa, nowhere on Earth can people be said to be truly native, in the sense of having come into being on that soil.
>
> 221

Holding out hope for what he might call vitalist cosmopolitics, Ghosh may be less ambivalent and more comfortable calling forth the goddess Manasa Devi in *Gun Island*. Yet she comes through not only tentacularly but also tentatively—via multiple layers of legends and text, and he further filters her presence through his highly discomfited and skeptical protagonist Deen. Van der Vliet Oloomi's Zebra alone, exceptional in so many ways, inverts this persistent pattern according to which protagonists, even as they reach out for something other-dimensional and primal, act as reader proxies and protective filters. Highly deracinated and given to hyperbole, she embraces her extra-human multidimensional matrix as though she has no alternative. With no mundane ground to stand on, she has no room for rejecting or othering multiple dimensions. It's her readers who might follow her lover Ludo in responding to her over-the-top proclamations with rolling eyes. Given these examples, one might wonder what it would mean for literary fiction to do what many feel our times call for and what genre fiction has no trouble doing: make itself at home in radically alternative worlds.

Indigenous scholar Kyle Whyte argues, however, that our current times aren't alone in feeling the pressing need to imagine alternatives and that the counterfactual has long been crucial to Indigenous understandings of storytelling and time. In his essay "Indigenous science (fiction) for the Anthropocene: Ancestral dystopias and fantasies of climate change crises," Whyte takes issue with the ghastly worlds many climate crisis fictions imagine, as though contemplation of the Anthropocene uniquely presents us with a glimpse of apocalypse. These "horrific science-fiction scenarios," writes Whyte, "can erase Indigenous peoples' perspectives on the connections between climate change and colonial violence" (225). From such perspectives, apocalypse is not new and the narrative features often associated with science fiction are not marginalized modes of imagining. Indeed, the conditions Whyte finds in many post-apocalyptic climate fictions are telling: "rationing, government assistance, major extinctions, social unrest, drastic measures, and defaced landscapes." He parallels this list with conditions Indigenous peoples detail having already endured: "ecosystem collapse, species loss, economic crash, drastic relocation, and cultural disintegration" (226). Thus, from an Indigenous point of view, the imagined crises accompanying the Anthropocene can be seen as colonially created catastrophes that have just taken longer to catch up to the colonizer (227). In keeping with this more complicated view of historical time, Whyte describes the ways that many Indigenous conceptions of temporality are not simply ones of unilinear progression. Instead, based on Anishinaabe concepts according to which a single word can mean both ancestor and descendant, he outlines a view of time as spiraling. "Spiraling time," he writes, "refers to the varied experiences of time that we have as participants, within living narratives involving our ancestors and descendants." He adds, "spiraling time, then, may be lived through narratives of cyclicality, reversal, dream-like scenarios, simultaneity, counterfactuality, irregular rhythms, ironic un-cyclicality, slipstream, parodies of linear pragmatism, eternality, among many others" (229). Not surprisingly, he quotes Indigenous scholar Grace Dillon remarking, "In fact, incorporating time travel, alternate realities, parallel universes and multiverses, and alternative histories is a hallmark of Native storytelling tradition, while viewing time as pasts, presents, and futures that flow together like currents in a navigable stream is central to Native epistemologies" (qtd. in Whyte 229). It's likely this sort of storytelling tradition that many current global anglophone novels long for and are in their own strangely ambivalent ways both cathecting and reckoning with. Asking in times felt to be fateful how one might have changed one's fate easily becomes asking how one might change one's sense of time. In asking these questions, such novels reach out for interlocutors.

Spiraling time allows for movement and communication across the borders between the living and spirits. The dead are not simply dead and gone, nor are they necessarily the undead with unfinished business. Whyte's concomitant notion of intergenerational "counterfactual dialogue" means it was never assumed the dead's work was done in one lifetime nor that after that time their part of the conversation was over. As continued presences, spirits in spiraling time are animated interlocutors, and in this way, spiraling time opens up space for reckoning but also accords well with universes for animists. A counter to expiring time, spiraling time lets us imagine many "otherwises" and even try to carry some of them forth. Thus, Whyte concludes, on the one hand, that those who consider themselves allies need to recognize their true relationship to the fantasies of their ancestors and entertain the possibility that the agency they exercise in even the choice to advocate on behalf of Indigenous people might be part of a dominance wished upon them: "Perhaps it is all part of allies' ancestral fantasies that their descendants would have the privilege of unlimited individual and collective agency to exploit Indigenous peoples *and* the privilege of claiming moral high ground as saviors." But, on the other hand, he also acknowledges the at times violent past of his own people and in doing so, he invokes the potential for change: "Yet when we engage in dialogic narratives through counterfactual space, we can connect ourselves to the errors of our ancestors and work to change how we do things today so as to learn needed lessons to pass on to future generations" (238). The legacies of colonialism can create a sharply ambivalent engagement with spiraling time and its narrative analogues in many of the global anglophone novels I analyze. The degree to which counterfactual dialogue can be made explicit might be the degree to which there will be room for change, placing the literary novel, with all the traditionally change-resistant qualities that Ghosh cites in *The Great Derangement*, at a potential disadvantage.

Yet the words with which Whyte describes spiraling time and counterfactual dialogue's power to inspire change aren't without European analogues. For readers of European cultural theory, some of Walter Benjamin's most famous sentences can seem echoed in Whyte's final lines:

> We are always in dialogue with our ancestors as dystopianists and fantasizers. Would the hidden interests of our descendants really involve their finding out that our current generation tried to cover up the errors of our ancestors? I will leave this question as a topic to engage for another time.
>
> 238

It's interesting to compare these lines to Benjamin's remarks on weak messianism in the second thesis of "On the Concept of History." There he considers the envy we might feel in the present towards our own and others' past chances at happiness in contrast to the envy we tend not to feel towards those in the future. He suggests that in the cases of both our regard for moments we could have seized in our own time and in our thoughts of the past, we're concerned with ideas of redemption, and this thought suggests further speculations:

> If so, there is a secret agreement between past generations and the present one. Then our coming was expected on earth. Then, like every generation that preceded us, we have been endowed with a *weak* messianic power, a power on

which the past has a claim. Such a claim cannot be settled cheaply. The historical materialist is aware of this.

390

In the same way that we behold the future with expectation, so the past has beheld us, and in a way that still exerts a claim and calls for awareness. Admittedly, Whyte's "hidden interests" and Benjamin's waiting to be settled claim both sound like unfinished business, intergenerational haunting, whether from our descendants or from our ancestors. But just as descendants and ancestors might be invoked by the same word for some, so ghosts in the kinds of novels I'm investigating might not be ghosts alone.

2. Not Alone

In Zeyn Joukhadar's novel of 2020, *The Thirty Names of Night*, the protagonist who comes to be known as Nadir is rarely without the ghost of his mother, a presence he mournfully addresses throughout as "you." But this ghost isn't there to settle a score. Rather, we see by the end that Nadir's mother has likely been helping to orchestrate an outcome, a longed for reunion whose significance she wouldn't have perceived while living. In helping bring together Nadir's grandmother and her secret beloved, the ghost of Nadir's mother fulfills a generational wish and allows Nadir to benefit from witnessing it. It's as though the threads of our lives are better woven into patterns by those looking and working from the fabric's other side. And the novel works to make us view its threads from this perspective. At the same time, out-of-place animals—birds—appear or swarm at odd moments. These appearances have all the fatefulness of those in Ghosh's *Gun Island*, and although we might infer urban sprawl and climate change explain some of these events, no one dwells on such explanations. It's as though Joukhadar's characters move in a world a few steps beyond Ghosh's where such occurrences may still be worth casually remarking but not more than cursorily explaining. Nadir's opening captures the both personally and collectively mournful mood with which such animals are beheld: "Tonight, five years to the day since I lost you, forty-eight white throated sparrows fall from the sky. Tomorrow, the papers will count and photograph them, arrange them on black garbage bags and speculate on the causes of the blight" (1). While we never do get a satisfactory official explanation, Nadir, listening to the birds' crashes, recalls his ornithologist mother's words: "Migrating birds, you used to say, the city's light can kill" (2).

Even more than *Gun Island* does, this novel contravenes any ethical injunction against making animals bearers of meaning for humans. This is true not just in the way birds are simultaneously ornithological objects, psychoanalytic objects, i.e., charged markers of a lost maternal presence and hence stand-ins for a "lost object," and indices of environmental disruption.[1] Nadir is also a visual artist fascinated by birds' distinctive appearance, and he is retracing the history of a crucial precursor: Laila, early immigrant from Syria, painter of birds, and, we come to discern, the secret beloved of his grandmother. The novel, again akin to *Gun Island*, has no qualms in aligning animal and human migrations and even extending this migration metaphor to modes of becoming. As Laila reflects in one of the sections she narrates, "Migrating birds will navigate around the smoke of New York's factories. How different the world would look if it had any mercy toward migrations undertaken as a last resort against annihilation" (221). While birds generally carry this charged sense of transformational precarity, a rare type of a bird close also to Ghosh's heart, the ibis, fascinates three generations of Nadir's Syrian-American community: Laila, suspected of having sighted and illustrated it; Nadir's mother, ornithologist and collector of many of Laila's prints; and Nadir himself, who retraces their steps to locate Laila's lost illustration, a quest that ultimately reunites his grandmother with Laila. And this bird's name, *Geronticus simurghus*, contains a reference to the simurgh, the magical phoenix-like bird of Persian poet Farid ud-Din Attar's 1177 text *The Conference of the Birds*. The emblematic ibis at the heart of *The Thirty Names of Night* in becoming multiply allegorical becomes also multidimensional, a living entity continually surpassing signs.

A condensation of so many types of meaning, this bird might seem to be Joukhadar's dreamtiger. When Laila first sees three of them, they suffer in imagined comparison, a brief counterfactual cross-referencing, with her mother's past accounts, as they themselves take spiral flight:

> The waxing moon emerged from behind a cloud, illuminating the frozen field. Three shapes slid across the moon in silhouette, narrow as knives, their black wings sleek, their long, curved beaks. The birds were iridescent, huge, like my mother's stories of the birds that followed the night. As they spiraled away into the forest, I imagined that nothing, not even those moon-slicked wings, could be as lovely and true as the stories I'd been fed as a child. Nothing was ever as beautiful as it was promised.
>
> 222

Yet when Laila finally catches up to them in the forest, her dreamlike experience is the complementary opposite of Borges's. Instead of being an approximation of the tiger that can never be captured, her vision of *Geronticus simurghus* itself exceeds all former reference points:

> Out of breath, I surmounted one final ridge. I arrived in a clearing of furled ferns and young red oaks, and the smell of wet earth was everywhere. I squinted in the falling light, and there they were: thirty arrow-shaped birds with shimmering feathers, long curved beaks, their faces shimmering iridescence. I had never seen anything like them. It seemed then that all the knowledge I considered encyclopedic had been only part of the story, and that the world was big enough to contain more than I have ever dreamed. I have learned nothing from emulating Audubon ... Studying paintings of posed specimens has brought me no closer to the essence of things, nor has copying the patterns of spotted eggshells or the fine bones of a bird's foot. How foolish I've been to search for a sign in these things when all along, right here before me in the hush of evening, something so holy was alive without a name.
>
> I pulled out my notebook and set my box of paints on a stone nearby. I began to sketch.
>
> 227

In this dimensionist moment, Laila's world expands and not only does the text need to gesture to another medium, painting, but Laila's past training and former methods must also be surpassed. Yet what's also intriguing is that the ibises here don't return the artist's gaze.

This is so because the rare ibis *is* the artist, is the chance that one could be in the world, make oneself and make one's way there, while being significantly other to the ways one has felt beheld. Aisla Chang in an NPR interview with Joukhadar remarks on birds in the book being both a "binding thread" across characters' stories and animals that "just sort of appear out of nowhere sometimes." Asked what birds represent to him, Joukhadar replies:

> Well, I think that I wanted there to be a relationship between birds and memory and the sacred. I chose, for example, when I was thinking of this mysterious bird that I wanted to sort of feel real without necessarily being real, I was thinking a lot about the relationship between the ibis and the sacred in many Southwest Asian and North African cultures. And so ultimately, when I think about birds, I think about the fact that Nadir is also sort of the rare bird that, for some of the world, isn't really supposed to exist. And yet, he does.
>
> qtd. in Chang

Chang notes that Joukhadar wrote Nadir's story of transitioning to become a trans man while Joukhadar himself was likewise coming out as trans. Asked about the experience of writing the novel during that pivotal period and about the importance of resurfacing queer history, Joukhadar interestingly appeals to ancestral time:

> For me, it was really powerful to know that I was not alone and that I was sort of held in—this is how I think of it—that I was sort of held in the net of history; that I had all of this history behind me, that there were all of these other Arab American people who had had all of these other lives that had led up to mine in some way, that their stories were a part of my story and that as I was trying to envision a future for myself, I had to know this history in order to move forward. I had to know where we had come from in order to know how to move ahead.
>
> qtd. in Chang

Far from severing the threads of weak messianism, denying any ancestral claim on one's agency for self-making, this experience of queer becoming reaches out to spirits and lives of forebears.

The rare ibis isn't so much an ancestral self that looks on its artist descendants in acknowledgment or affirmation. It's an iridescence, a focal image for a distributed energy that radiates out, holding many beings as if in a net, or, we might say, a matrix. Eduardo Kohn conceives of a distributed self in relation not to the artistic pursuit of animals, but rather in the context of the Amazonian Runa people's hunting practices. Because an expectant father is believed to add vigor to his unborn child by having frequent sex with the child's mother, he is deemed energy depleted, and thus expectant fathers in a hunting party are seen as easy targets and tempting lures for wild pigs. Using them as bait for these pigs and then allowing flanking males to close in for the kill sets up a new prey/predator dynamic, one in which it might seem that some Runa men have taken on a prey identity. But far from absolutely transforming the Runa via these lures into objects of predation or "meat," this tactic, Kohn argues, maintains Runa male selfhood at a higher level: "the Runa—here a sort of distributed self in the figure of the group of hunters acting in unison—are reinstated as the true predator, and the pigs become meat, thanks to the temporarily desubjectified state of the expectant father" (124). Joukhadar's rare ibis isn't so much meat as material to be mediated along many outwardly radiating lines, but it likewise allows for identity amidst distribution.

And yet it's important to recognize that the heady anthropological concept of the relational or distributed self might itself be the product of a distribution, a more widely cast net than is often delineated. As Jadran Mimica notes, the idea of a de-individualized, highly relational, and often especially corporeal self (as opposed to a supposedly Western mode of hyper-individualization) can be traced back to Western ideas that aren't based in ethnography: Nietzsche's philosophy as well as L. Von Bertalanffy's theories of primitive animals and unicellular organisms. Tracking this inheritance as well as its unwitting ethnographic reiterations, Mimica quotes ethnologist Maurice Leenhardt's shocking conclusions about Melanesian selfhood to particularly sobering effect: "'the native is filled with the world's pulse, he does not distinguish the world from his body'. And further: 'the Melanesian is unaware that the body is an element which he himself possesses'" (qtd. in Mimica 219). Rather than uncritically projecting the relational self onto non-Western others, obscuring the concept's history in the Western imagination, we need to recognize what *The Thirty Names of Night* is especially skilled at portraying: the multiple forms of the self and ideas of distribution that can emerge across contexts. Following both Whyte and Benjamin, we might trace spirals, radiating lines and distributive networks, without drawing a line that places a romanticized unself outside an imagined West's borders. Laila's tracking and memorializing of the ibis, Nadir's mother's following of Laila's career and instilling of ornithological knowledge in Nadir, and Nadir's choice of an Arabic word for "rare" in his eventual naming of himself as Nadir—all these point to a spiraling animacy that both circles out from and gives back to the past, suggesting an ever-unfolding pattern and distributive redemption. Just as Laila must use both words and paint as she depicts the rare ibis, Nadir's journey crucially involves not only his living grandmother's generation but also his departed mother's presence. In moving from one expressive form to another and from the dead to the living, both strands of the novel, Laila's and Nadir's, are essentially mediumistic, and the bridge that is built between them is what allows for Nadir's sense of being not so much gazed upon, but "expected on earth," a sense of intuitively beheld becoming that allows for his self-naming.

Accordingly, the novel allows Nadir to fulfill his quest without his precisely taking hold of its object—a single complete print by Laila of *Geronticus simurghus*. In the midst of the culminating gathering—the conference—Nadir brings about and that includes his mother's spirit, his elders, his peers, and multiple scattered incomplete works of Laila's art, he thinks of something like Whyte's "question as a topic to engage for another time": "One day, someone will try to explain us as they once tried to explain this, and they will not have the words" (284). These words glance sideways, foresee their speaker and companions being looked upon, but cast this glance forward to a point that annuls "the words." A recursive dimensionist paradox, the lines call out to their readers, implicitly asking them to inhabit the perspective that casts a gaze back but asking them also not to add further words. NPR's Chang admits upon finishing the book to "wondering, does transition ever end?" And Joukhadar, responding personally, thinks no, that his transition "doesn't have an endpoint because I think that it's true to the experience of being human because we are all constantly becoming all the time." Neither Joukhadar nor Nadir advocates for having multiple simultaneous selves in precisely Zebra's manner, but all three, unlike Ji Lin, Ren, Deen, or even Alfred Homer, in some way tap into a force that both speaks through them and allows them to insist on their own words. It isn't that they move through an Indigenous and historically overdetermined space whose digitlike tentacles reach out to them—as an uncanny omen, power, or reminder. It's that in reaching out to the ways forebears might have incompletely anticipated them, they engage a multidimensional animacy, one that future interpreters will fail to grasp in one medium.

It's no surprise, then, that one of the literary novels of the last five years that gives fullest representation to nonhuman spirits and extra-human dimensions is also the least restricted to one medium. Indigenous Canadian writer and singer Tanya Tagaq meditates across media on multiple dimensions, circling time, cusps, and the power of sound beyond words in her 2018 work *Split Tooth*. While Tagaq's novel explicitly moves through Indigenous and historically overdetermined space, and this space does have forces that reach out and through characters, the novel is hardly tentative or eerily tentacular in engaging these forces. Rather, Tagaq's narrator moves in a world in which the presence of extra-human energetic forces is pronounced, precise, pervasive, and a clear premise for what ensues. Her book, far from the pictureless Western novel Ghosh decries as blocking out the multifarious communicability of patterns and forms beyond words, exists in more than one version and makes use of many media. A mixture of fiction, diary writing, poetry, Jaime Hernandez's line drawings, and, in its audio version, the Inuk throat singing Tagaq is famous for, *Split Tooth* communicates in every way possible. And Tagaq, like Ghosh and Kohn, associates this broad conception of communication with interspecies understanding. In an interview with Mike Doherty of *Maclean's*, she reflects on the power of sound without words:

> When it comes to art, I've found if you boil things down to greatest common denominators, then everyone will be able to understand. That's why with music, it was easy for me to remove language, because people are responding to sound, which can carry intent. That's why interspecies relationships work. Your dog doesn't understand English; we don't understand the crows ... People can

understand body language and sound, so by the removal of language, I found it a lot easier to find common ground with people, and then afterwards, when you have people's interest, you can bring up things like MMIW [Missing and Murdered Indigenous Women] or Indigenous rights or whatever it is you're standing by when it comes to art.

qtd. in Doherty

Dedicated to "*the Missing and Murdered Indigenous Women and Girls, and survivors of residential schools*," the book is clear in its advocacy and in marking out the intergenerational trauma it takes on.[2] Tagaq's prose is multiply layered and the net her characters are held in, far from being uniformly affirming, is often highly charged.

Set in the 1970s and 1980s, the era of Tagaq's youth, in the part of arctic Canada's Northwest Territories now recognized as Nunavut, the novel opens with children fleeing adults' drunken violence. With the residential school system that was designed to sever family connections and forcibly assimilate children long in place, the adults are scarred and the children are their potential victims as well as victims of the molesting and abusive teachers they themselves face regularly. They cower in closets, endure being touched by teachers, but also roam the land freely as spring creates thaws and summer brings on twenty-four hour sunlight. Many times come together in this setting. The seasonal thaw is associated not just with cycles, but also with environmental history:

> The freeze traps life and stops time. The thaw releases it. We can smell the footprints of last fall and the new decomposition of all who perished in the grips of winter. Global warming will release the deeper smells and coax stories out of the permafrost. Who knows what memories lie deep in the ice? Who knows what curses? Earth's whispers released back into the atmosphere can only wreak havoc.
>
> 6

"Earth's whispers" conjure deep history as wordless sound, and elsewhere sound is associated with the interdimensional: "Sound is its own currency. Sound is a conduit to a realm we cannot totally comprehend. The power of sound conducts our thoughts into emotions that then manifest in action" (55–6). This use of sound as a spiritually energetic force can seem shamanic, and indeed shamans are referred to, but also described as tied to an interrupted history:

> My mother never speaks to me in Inuktitut anymore. Residential schools have beaten the Inuktitut out of this town in the name of progress, in the name of

> decency. Everyone wanted to move forward. Move forward with God, with money, with white skin and without the shaman's way.
>
> 50

Later we are told of a shaman whose body "had rotted at the town dump, rejected from the public graveyard by the Anglican ministers" (118). And yet in the midst of this landscape that seems to have progressivist historical time imposed on it, where in the 1970s and 1980s global warming can already be palpably discerned, and where the dead can be dumped unceremoniously, the children at the novel's outset feel enlivened, as "children on the cusp of puberty seem to understand that this magic time will end soon" (11). There is a sense of such in-between time as particularly memorialized in *Split Tooth*.

Nonhuman animals and extra-human energies are everywhere in this world and sensed especially by these children "on the cusp." Evading their parents, they get together to binge on junk food and found cigarette butts, float across ponds on Styrofoam pieces from an abandoned construction site, and even swallow baby trout whole. Amidst these rogue activities, latent memories awaken. Tagaq's narrator remarks about the trout:

> I let it swim down my esophagus; its tail tickled all the way down to my tummy. It was delightful. The flesh was so fresh. Something awoke in me, an old memory; an ancient memory of eating live flesh. It is a true joining of flesh to flesh. My spine straightened. When flesh is eaten live, you glean the spirit with the energy.
>
> 16

This same energy is present, though not consumed, in the lemmings she feeds, the newts she plays with placing under her tongue, and the foxes, real and spiritual, that pop up throughout the text. And this same sense of awakened memory appears in a scene of near spirit possession when the narrator is eleven and the kids have gathered in an empty house. Feeling "something enter the room," the narrator explains, "My real self recognizes the feeling, recognizes the place this being came from, where it lives. There are other realities that exist besides our own; it is foolish to think otherwise. The universe is conscious" (30). Deciding to explore this sensation, to let the being in and let her own spirit temporarily out, she claims that even though the incoming spirit seems not to be good, she is "not afraid, only curious. I don't feel like prey. I too am a predator." Time seems to stop and although everyone else senses nothing, her cousin catches her eye, and acts accordingly:

> We both instinctively know what to do. Where did the knowledge come from? No one has taught us how to do this, but the ritual is old and living in our bones.

> Just as giving birth is involuntary, we fall into rank to facilitate a process we don't comprehend yet. She bends over and rests her head on my lap, and I feel a click in the unphysical place, like two puzzle pieces snapping together. She pushes her energy into mine, and we become one being Ourselves.
>
> 31

Anchored by her cousin, the narrator explores "the unphysical place," as if astral projecting, and gauges the vengeful energy of the entity that has entered the room. But before this murderous, now quasi-canine, spirit can superimpose his face onto her eyes and inhabit her body, she returns to it, pushing him away, painfully snapping back into form. When she feels "an electrical current" pass through her and makes an unusual twitch, she scares all the children other than her cousin. The narrator and her cousin enjoy this risky shared moment in which they, like the Runa hunting parties Kohn describes, have inverted typical prey/predator dynamics by becoming a conjoint force—part lure, part anchor—and this chapter captures in miniature the logic of much of the novel.

Split Tooth doesn't engage with spirit realms to exalt an idea of the supernatural as either Indigenously utopic or imaginatively deconstructive. The novel is explicit about not only its spiritual episodes, but also the instances of self-harm as well as sexual and substance abuse that exist in this community and are traumas repeatedly marking its history. The narrator seems to take on this mixed energy in her strange but enlivening encounters with the "other realities that exist besides our own." And the novel's core otherwordly event in which the narrator, now teenaged, gives birth to magical twins after being impregnated by the energy of the Northern Lights underscores this. The twins' mysterious birth speaks simultaneously to the position of Tagaq's generation, the intergenerational trauma that preexists her, and the forces of the "conscious universe" that appear fantastical but are "foolish" to ignore.

Discussing with Anupa Mistry of the *Globe and Mail* her generation's stories of the Northern Lights, Tagaq reports a belief, one repeated in the novel also, "That if you whistle at the Northern Lights, they'll look down and see your mouth and cut off your head and use it as a football ... So kids would whistle and sing at the Northern Lights and run away, scared" (qtd. in Mistry). The exact provenance of this belief and its percentage of kid innovation are unclear in the interview; it seems left to inhabit an intriguing in-between zone of cultural memory and childhood creativity, a spirit that animates much of the novel. Indeed, and perhaps not unlike Alexis's sense of parody and the perverse, Tagaq describes the novel as an exercise in making fun of herself and perhaps also the readers who might most mystify her art. Speaking to Doherty about reviewers who liken her throat singing to spirit possession, she reflects:

> All these years performing and knowing what it feels like and what I'm thinking, and having that outside gaze—most often, the colonial gaze—observing and processing my work, I sometimes would scoff at the way people will very readily believe what general society has spoon-fed them. In almost the same breath, they'd reduce something from the "other culture" to something exotic. It's seen as folklore, and ridiculous. I'm often laughing when people talk to me about shamanism, and sometimes I'll flip it over: "Well, was Jesus a shaman? So you're telling me that there's a dude in the sky who has magic, invisible sperm that knocked up this woman without touching her, and she had a baby, and he died for three days and came back to life?" Everything surrounding Christianity seems completely mythological to me. So when people want to call my art possession or exorcism, or they want to call Inuit belief systems folklore or tokenize them, well, I'm not going to attempt to control that narrative. When it comes to the book, I was giggling. I'm always kind of making fun of myself.
>
> qtd. in Doherty

As with Joukhadar's words referring to "the words" others won't have and thus insisting on their own presence, Tagaq's world in *Split Tooth* asks to be taken on its own terms, and these terms are inseparable from the narrator's age and generational position, the position of a cusp.

Likewise, the magical twins the narrator gives birth to embody two starkly different energies that suggest two different orientations to generational time. Savik, the boy, focuses others' latent negativity, concentrating and feeding off its energy, as he makes those who hold him or live with him sick. It's as though he condenses the illness—the shame, self-loathing, and mourning as well as malice—that haunts this community. He "seems to grow stronger when he bears witness to suffering." By contrast, Naja, his sister, has a voice that "heals anxiety and [makes] plants want to grow towards her" (156). Essentially a predator, Savik fatally drains others, while Naja, the healer "weaves peace from thin air" (157). When Savik's power leads to the death of the narrator's uncle and then threatens her father and boyfriend, the narrator knows she must return the inseparable twins the Northern Lights has given her. The energy they represent can't remain in such concentrated form in the narrator's habitual world, but having become the agent of their emergence and now their return, the narrator herself loses her ties to that world.

In a culminating yet ambiguous ending, she returns to the sea ice, site of her spirit journey and the merging with the Northern Lights that impregnated her, to release her children to the water. Savik metamorphoses there into a seal and "absorbs" Naja as they become one animal, a seal that, she says, before it swims away, "looks up at me with love and hatred, death and life" (181). Two dreamlike sequences then end the novel, the first one in which the narrator, having given up her children, longs for her own death. She describes a painful suicide that rips her soul from her body but also "blocks [her] journey into the spirit world" (182). Full of regret, she declares, "I leave my body to search for Savik and Naja. I leave my body and hitch a ride with the wind. I am not human now; I am only Lament. The wind is the only song. This is why the Arctic wind screams" (183). The second sequence flashes back to a time when the narrator's mother prayed to her own recently departed mother to know the narrator's fate, whether she was destined for heaven or hell. The narrator's grandmother revealed the truth to the narrator instead, coming to her in a dream and describing her crucial role to play in hell. There the spectral narrator would pretend to preside over the souls destined for the worst of all fates—to fall through holes and become absorbed by hell, made "part of the malevolent force of destruction and evil, causing malice and murder in the living world." With a sense of distributive agency, the narrator, rather than aiding the forces of hell's predation, says she would instead "spread myself over the hole to act as a net and catch the soul. I would then absorb the thousand years of agony, feeling it all at once, and the soul would be revived." Her grandmother claims this is an agonizing but honored role, and the narrator says she wakes from the dream "already hurting, and have been ever since" (187).

These two dreamlike sequences might represent two extra-human destinies for the human, one in which the narrator becomes the wordless sound and force of lament itself and the other in which she takes up the painful task of distributed redemption. Like Zebra, Tagaq's protagonist channels a traumatic history and self-annihilating urges into a realm of the disincarnate that speaks beyond words with mere sound, noises. And likewise, both imagine these realms, even their hellish versions, as still potentially navigable. In Tagaq's case, the navigational reference points bespeak familiarity with a shamanic world, however much Tagaq is also aware of shamanism's appeal for a colonial gaze. Disincarnate dimensions can be traversed with intention and spiritual energy, leaving bodies provisionally aside. And others, not exclusively human, can conjoin in such spirit journeys forming a collective that can link contemporary individuals but also beings across times. Zebra draws on her family line to imagine a textual net of Indra, Joukhadar a net of rare forebears, and Tagaq a net in hell to catch lost souls. Tagaq's vision might seem the least idealized. In a poetic chapter entitled "Topography of Pity," she claims, "We look upon the scarred earth with pity/

What have we done to her?" And her lines here, bemoaning mineral extraction, accord easily with ecological pleas made in the name of Gaia. Yet she ends the poem with speculations that eschew easy appeals to Mother Earth: "Perhaps she looks upon us not with the love of a mother/But with the same indifference we lend to our lungs/With the same indifference/That we give the homeless human" (28). One could infer that the idea of a biopolitical Gaia that places us in a zone of indistinction, unremarkable mere life, is ironically far more conceivable from the roaming perspectives of animism, however reclaimed, than from oikos-oriented ecology. It's perhaps this more comprehensive urge, a concept of redemption that can take on and absorb the force of wordless lament, that Tagaq expresses in her lines, "One must trust/in a world that has been perfect/in its distribution of chaos" (45).

Recalling Gaia: A Note in Ending

In Memory of William Irwin Thompson, 1938–2020

I have always been fascinated by blackouts and eclipses. My mother remembers a candlelit dinner in the hospital amidst the Northeast blackout of 1965. It darkened our Boston the day after I was born. Years later in 2003, I was back in Boston, again at a hospital—this time picking my father up after heart surgery—when the Niagara Mohawk power grid failed. It darkened large parts of the Midwest and Northeast—the Niagara Mohawk power grid ironically covering parts of the same territory Robin Wall Kimmerer writes about as the Indigenous "Maple Nation." While my family in Toronto and Ann Arbor, then my city of residence, bore the brunt of the blackout, this time Boston was spared. Returning to my father and my birth city, I missed a repetition.

In 1965, they say, some of the blackout's effects were mitigated by the full moon. It's strange to think of everyone newly noticing it. But the lockdown periods of COVID-19 provide similar examples of newly perceived nature. Reports of a temporary decrease in pollution, of clearer skies, and of animals that drew closer all became familiar.

This book has been written in a mix of darkness and unexpected light. COVID-19 casts the most obvious shadow. Begun in a 2019–20 sabbatical, the manuscript was already focused on uncanny animals and their ties to spirit dimensions. I was trying to articulate my sense that writers interested in worlds beyond the human were invoking worlds ever more radically beyond. And such an intensely shared collective experience—however unevenly felt also—as a pandemic only sharpened these concerns, made them seem more poignant. But this wasn't the only sharp experience occurring in the midst of this book's journey. The care my father began to need in 2003 intensified over the following years, and he had gone into a marked decline by 2018 before dying in November 2020. Whenever we discussed precautions he should take in a brand-new and pre-vaccine COVID-19 world, he, ever the cultural historian interested in cultural phenomenology, would say, "It's the plague mentality." Yet as drained and even confused as he could be in those days, he would nonetheless find moments to gather his strength and ask me about my book. There was so much I wanted to tell him about it that I held back. I didn't want to burden conversations or overwhelm with information. We communicated somewhat telegraphically towards the end. But, ever fond of names and wordplay, he would ask me its title, chapter titles, and so on.

I wanted to say it's about the hypercubes you love, the Escher exhibit at the Vorpal Gallery you took me to see, the book of his art you bought me there, the book you also bought me on hyperspace when I was in grad school, or the autographed copy of Madeleine L'Engle's *A Swiftly Tilting Planet* that was a birthday present, I think, when I turned twelve. How he loved tesseracts, the number 4, and what he called hieroglyphic thinking. Now I wonder, why did I return to those topics just as he was leaving but never have a full conversation about them, about what I was doing? It's like returning to the scene of a blackout but continuing to use the cover of darkness rather than the light of the moon or the remaining electricity an eccentrically failing grid has granted you.

One of the bright lights of my father's career was his work on Gaia. I think of him as a theorist of the planetary, an early advocate of planetary culture. These interests converged meaningfully with those of the authors of the Gaia hypothesis—James Lovelock and Lynn Margulis—and Bruce Clarke has thoughtfully detailed the role Lindisfarne, my father's Celtically named intellectual organization, played in bringing together theorists of Gaia as well as of autopoiesis. As one of the most powerful yet mythically charged vehicles for beholding the symbiotic and the planetary, Gaia exerts an admittedly mixed influence on my thought. Its earth mother name makes it hard to disentangle from the fraught gender politics of the 1970s and 1980s counterculture, yet its capacious conceptual reach makes it hard also to evade. Perhaps coming to terms with Gaia while trying to sift through varying concepts of the planetary is like longing for a day of fine weather when you can finally row to the lighthouse.

While Godrevy Lighthouse sends beams through the text of Woolf's famous novel, I've wondered about Gaia, does it cast a shadow? A concept so holistic in some versions, so meta in others, and, in its maternal guise, so prone to Kleinian oscillations—providentially good, then catastrophically monstrous—seems to obscure even its shadows, as though it has none that don't come from us. In writing about planet-thinking in novelists who, other than Amitav Ghosh, don't explicitly attend to Gaia and in not exploring in greater detail my sense of planet-thinking in relation to various models of Gaia—my urge, for example, not to oppose planet-thinking to either the global or to animism—I've let my thought grow a little like a shade-loving plant beneath a cluster, albeit complex, of family and friendly thinkers from whom I still draw inspiration.

I remember Lovelock, holding his wife Sandy's hand, saying at a Lindisfarne conference at Esalen that there could be both a god and a goddess. And this for me opens up the possibility of planetary animacies with many names, many faces. My father saw as key to the development of planetary culture what he called "the planetization of the esoteric," the world's wisdom traditions becoming a kind of commons, and I both grapple with this concept and see that what this book describes might be read in this vein. He called himself a druid, and a stone from the island Iona was his most prized possession. I think of myself as an informal animist. When I accidentally drop objects, I find myself addressing them, spontaneously apologizing. When I told my father the name of this book, he said, "anima mundi," which I misunderstood as his accusing me of piety. Later I rediscovered it was the name of one of his poems. He was citing a link. Likewise, I would love for there to be multiverse of animate worlds and worldly animisms, turtles all the way up and out, so that we could go on hailing them with infinite names, provisional addresses.

Notes

Introduction

1 Particularly salient is Laura A. White's *Ecospectrality: Haunting and Environmental Justice in Contemporary Anglophone Novels* but also Sharae Deckard's "Ecogothic" chapter in *Twenty-First-Century Gothic: An Edinburgh Companion* as well as Andrea Riemenschnitter's "Beyond Gothic: Ye Si's Spectral Hong Kong and the Global Culture Crisis." White, along with the Derrida she cites, conceives of the spectral as including both spirits and ghosts and perceives its use in global anglophone fiction as more than simply past or present-oriented, but rather as a call also for an environmentally just future. While she explores fictions from cultural settings with non-Western conceptions of animacy and reflects on what in her texts may be beyond Derrida's scope or inaccessible to various outside readers, she prefers not to refer to animism directly and to take readerly lacunae as occasions for a further if more self-reflective sense of haunting (39; 85). Riemenschnitter compellingly quotes Salman Rushdie to declare, "Ghosts are messengers of unfinished business," and expounds the need to rethink a series of formations: global capitalism in the wake of late nineties' conflicts and crises, the modernist belief in progress in the wake of expanding wealth gaps and proliferating dispossessions, and industrial acceleration in the face of its toxic environmental effects. She concludes, "the shift toward ghostlore featuring not only the clamor of wronged humans but also the grievances of an abused planet increasingly informs art production on the threshold of the 21st century" (155–6).

2 For two famous examples, see Anna Lowenhaupt Tsing's *The Mushroom at the End of the World* (158–9) and Donna Haraway's *Staying With the Trouble* (39–40).

3 Readers of Haraway's *Staying With the Trouble*, which Marder doesn't discuss in this essay, might perceive an overlapping of their ideas, in particular, with regard to her recurring invocations of "terra" and "Terrapolis," the chthonic and Chthulucene (as alternative to the Anthropocene), and her cautionary approach to the mythic content in simplistic notions of Anthropos or Gaia. I see these overlapping thinkers nonetheless differentiating themselves in their negativities, in Haraway's case with her sustained suspicion toward the sky and astral thinking and in Marder's case, with his four conceptual "never-beens." She, as Ghosh will do in *Gun Island*, turns to tentacular goddesses of snakes and spiders, and in a characteristic moment remarks of a series of such goddesses, "Potnia Theron/Melissa/Medusa give faciality a

profound makeover, and that is a blow to modern humanist (including technohumanist) figurations of the forward-looking, sky-gazing Anthropos." For her, "chthonic ones are precisely not sky gods, not a foundation for the Olympiad, not friends to the Anthropocene or Capitalocene, and definitely not finished" (53). Marder's dialectically paradoxical earth that has never been, by contrast, can be registered in the elusive "geo" of such sky-focused locutions as "planetary geology" and thus his conceptually multiply stratified earth might have trouble fitting into Haraway's notion of a concretely chthonic "becoming-with."

4   It's worth noting that an additional important influence for Pheng Cheah is Hannah Arendt, particularly her discussion of world alienation in the final chapter of *The Human Condition*. Moreover, in his epilogue to *What Is a World?*, Cheah also turns to Benjamin's "The Storyteller," but less for its geological sensibility and more for its understanding of the story's "power of temporalization" (322), which is to say there Benjamin "elucidates how stories open up a world by suggesting that finitude is structural to their form" (321). This moment is additionally interesting, however, because here Cheah links Arendt to Benjamin, remarking of "The Storyteller," "it was first published in English translation in a volume edited by Hannah Arendt and resonates with her views on stories" (322). While I likewise trace a line of thought back to Benjamin here in my introduction, I discuss both Cheah and Arendt in Chapters 1 and 2.

5   While I intend the term "interanimism" to refer to interrelated animisms and the multidimensionality their many perspectives entail, I want to note that Mathieu Thiem has also used this word on his blog *The Woven Song*. More a conception of interrelated becomings than a theory of animisms per se, his use differs from mine in being both more capacious, that is, a theory of existence, and more restricted in that it denies specific existence to gods and spirits and thus excludes what might be called the supernatural. Citing Karen Barad's influential concept of "intra-action," he defines interanimism as "the notion that existence is mutually inspiring and co-creating itself, animating its interbeing through intra-active relationships" and asks, "Rather than seeing the world filled with particulated essences or souls, what would reality be like if we saw all matter as an emergent function of relationships and agency as the phenomenology of entanglement?" This focus on "interbeing," a term that recalls Buddhist writer Thich Nhat Hanh's book of that name, leads to a deconstruction of the individualist self in favor of entangled becomings: "We trade out the essentialism for diffractive uniqueness that can never be considered separated from the process of interbeing nor entirely collectivized by any essential totality." And this deconstruction seems related to Thiem's claim that he doesn't "abide super-naturalism like other folk do in the magical communities." Thus gods and spirits for him become respectively "the long lived intellects of ecosystems and bioregions" and "the liminal agencies of the rocks, the trees, the rivers and all the other functionaries of the more than human world."

6 I argue this in *Novel Creatures*, but see also Marc Lucht and Donna Yarri's edited volume *Kafka's Creatures*.
7 While she doesn't explicitly discuss animism and focuses more on their haunting role in political imaginaries, Carla Freccero makes a similar case for wolves in the fifth chapter, "Wolf, or *Homo Homini Lupus*" of the "Monsters" half of *Arts of Living on a Damaged Planet*:

> Wolf is everywhere in the western imagination. From werewolf trials and fairy tales to postmodern wolf-human hybrids, the wolves that prowl through moral fables are clothed in political allegories, dragged unwittingly into juridical encounters, and, most recently, stand in for the queerness of transpecies becomings. Wolves and werewolves are ancient and familiar enemies and monsters, and they are emergent figures in the Anthropocene, both through their disappearance and "reintroduction" in discussions of vanishing species and habitats, and through recent imaginative refigurations of wolf-human becoming in the age of the holobiont, spawning new imaginaries for communities of the living (M91).

8 See Hannah Gould; Casper Bruun Jensen and Anders Blok; Fabio R. Gygi; and Timo Kaerlein for such spirited engagements with Allison's book.

Chapter 1

1 The titles of two foundational texts, Pheng Cheah's and Bruce Robbins's edited volume *Cosmopolitics: Thinking and Feeling Beyond the Nation* and Rebecca Walkowitz's *Cosmopolitan Style: Modernism Beyond the Nation*, indicate this investment that might be compared to recent multispecies cosmopolitanisms such as Amitav Ghosh's in *The Great Derangement* or Donna Haraway's in *Staying with the Trouble* that emphasize perspectives that are "beyond the human" or "more than human."
2 While I mean here to refer casually to the expanded elliptical space, defined by the dual foci of source and host cultures, in which for Damrosch a world literature text can move (283), it's important to note that Gayatri Spivak in "The Stakes of a World Literature" defines his world literature model by other coordinates: "I want to keep emphasizing that even this pattern, many steps down from Kant's stark world, is upstream from the story of colonialism's (Goethe) and capitalism's (Marx) insistence on world literature" (*Aesthetic* 459). Accordingly, she warns that if one of the qualifications for world literature eligibility is "a sort of archetypal unity in humankind," a sense of a common human story made visible by readers' expanded education in languages and history, then Damrosch's theory becomes

"A good creed that points at a level playing field in a selective past when the present builds itself on false promises." She adds, citing Gramsci, the caution, "what is selected out is the space of subalternization that must be disavowed for a polity to function" (464). This tension between a level plane along which entities might move and a lingering sense of a space selected out seems crucial to the ambiguous appeals to extra-human spirit dimensions in global anglophone novels such as *The Night Tiger*.

3 See Agamben's *The Open: Man and Animal* (13–16).
4 See Casanova's *The World Republic of Letters* (171).

Chapter 2

1 See Ghosh's "Imperial Temptations" in *Incendiary Circumstances* (28).
2 Indeed, Zebra's matrix in which texts "mirror each other in a series of replicas" might seem to recall the fabled net of Indra, important for Hinduism and Buddhism.
3 It wouldn't be hard to apply aspects of Nicolas Abraham and Maria Torok's classic essay "Mourning *or* Melancholia: Introjection *versus* Incorporation" generally, but the novel might also interestingly invert some of their specific descriptions of "The Intrapsychic Tomb" whereby "Inexpressible mourning erects a secret tomb inside the subject. Reconstituted from the memories of words, scenes, and affects, the objectal correlative of the loss is buried alive in the crypt as a full-fledged person, complete with its own topography." While Zebra does claim to receive signals from her departed parents and imagined matrix, they are far from "cryptic" and the matrix is hardly a "whole world of unconscious fantasy ... that leads its own separate and concealed existence" (130). If anything, the Matrix is melancholic mourning rendered multidimensionally expansive, and Taüt is her crypt externalized, animalized, and surreally companionate.

Chapter 3

1 While a *Toronto Star* article of November 8, 2017 ran with the headline "Toronto is now majority visible minority. What about your neighbourhood?" (Cole et al.), the city's report on public health cites the 2016 Census as reporting that people of a so-called "visible minority" made up 52 percent of the population, but adds a footnote explaining, "The term 'visible minority', no longer appropriately reflects the composition of Toronto's population. The term is used here however, to be consistent with the term used in 2016" (Fleiszer et al. 9).

2   In this regard, Anna Lowenhaupt Tsing's *The Mushroom at the End of the World: On the Possibility of Life in Capitalist Ruins* is a book that resembles *Days by Moonlight*; it not only advocates for countering historical erasures by telling landscape-focused stories rooted in details, but also contains botanical sketches, visual details, throughout (111; 158–9). In addition, it highlights the importance of the dead, remarking of the key nonhuman life form it investigates, the matsutake mushroom, "Although matsutake is known for its relations with living trees, it can get some nutrients from dead ones too," and thus it illustrates the importance of remembering, "The dead, too, are part of social worlds" (279).

3   Interestingly, Whitehead outlines this category in relation to YA literature, but its structure and features—including a spirit-questlike journey through a "green world" cast as both Indigenous and queer that consolidates protagonists' identities and "embeds settlers further into the nation state" (224)—can be applied, as I further discuss in Chapter 5, to *Days by Moonlight*.

Chapter 4

1   Both Ursula Kluwick and Sarah Nuttall have analyzed important connections and divergences between *The Hungry Tide* and *Gun Island* in their thematic treatment of and structural innovations in response to climate change, specifically aquatic conditions, with the former arguing for a flood-aware "diluvial" form and the latter a rainfall-conscious "pluvial" narrative mode. Both also recognize that increased awareness of such accelerating conditions as increased flooding and rainfall alters the traditional dimensions of realism such that what once might have seemed a departure from narrative norms—extreme weather depictions or unusual animal appearances, for example—now can be read as realistic and relevant, as though literary codes themselves experience a rising water table. While Nuttall embraces Ghosh's uncanny, links it to a James Lovelock-inspired Gaian view of the planet as "a dynamic, self-regulating system that defies logical explanation," and even sees Ghosh engaging not merely planetary but cosmic stakes in his storytelling (461), Kluwick appears puzzled at what she sees as Ghosh's swerve to the "supernatural" in his later novel's climax (74), as though it's unclear why an aquatically enhanced realism shouldn't have sufficed, especially since it would be more in line with Ghosh's apparent eschewing in *The Great Derangement* of genres outside of traditional literary fiction. Seeing *Gun Island* as tied to not only *The Hungry Tide* but also *The Calcutta Chromosome*, however, allows us to retrace a history of dimensionist genre experiment in his work that precedes his explicit turn to ecology. Moreover, given his interview with Gill, it might make more sense to see him not as quitting realism

for the sake of magical realism, but rather as reaching for something like a "preterrealism."

2 For a critical reading of Ghosh's treatment of a character cast as subaltern see Victor Li's "Necroidealism, or the Subaltern's Sacrificial Death."

3 For a relevant study of critical attitudes toward apocalypse in Indian English texts, including *The Hungry Tide*, see Sagnik Yadaw and Rupsa Roy Chowdhury's "Resisting the Apocalypse: Representing the Anthropocene in Indian English Literature."

4 See Pramod K. Nayar's "The Postcolonial Uncanny: The Politics of Dispossession in Amitav Ghosh's *The Hungry Tide*" as well as Sharae Deckard's "Ecogothic."

5 See in particular the opening to Convolute M in *The Arcades Project* (416).

6 Readers looking for intertexts might consider J. G. Ballard's *Rushing to Paradise* here, with its at-sea activists, island setting, theological resonances, and emphasis on world media.

7 And indeed Jacques Derrida in a text that, as we've seen, has become influential for world literature discussions as well as literary interpretations of specters and haunting, his *Specters of Marx: The State of Debt, the Work of Mourning, and the New International*, writes also of delicate negotiations where messianism and politics are concerned: "Well, what remains irreducible to any deconstruction, what remains as undeconstructible as the possibility itself of deconstruction is, perhaps, a certain experience of the emancipatory promise; it is perhaps even the formality of a structural messianism, a messianism without religion, even a messianic without messianism, an idea of justice—which we distinguish from law or right and even from human rights—and an idea of democracy—which we distinguish from its current concept and from its determined predicates today" (59). More akin to my approach, Sam Durrant looks to Benjamin's historical materialism as offering a salutary influence for new animist thought. In his essay "Critical Spirits: New Animism as Historical Materialism," he claims, "Both new animism and historical materialism are utopian in their investment in a spirited, more than human world, but the latter also seeks to promote what I call a *critical* spiritedness," and he further clarifies, "The critical spirit that I seek to invoke consists in a double gesture: firstly, in an affirmative belief in the animated or spirited nature of our more than human world, and secondly an auto-critical awareness of the pitfalls of romanticising this belief, a vigilance concerning the ways in which any desire to re-enchant the world is liable to co-optation by the nature industry" (50;53). Moreover, Durrant finds, as I will proceed to, a rich resource in Benjamin's writings on similarity.

8 For a critical reading of "thinking in pictures," one that inspires to me weigh Ghosh's and Kohn's thoughts against Benjamin's, see Anat Pick's second chapter of *Creaturely Poetics: Animality and Vulnerability in Literature and Film*, particularly her discussion of Temple Grandin's work and the risks of easy appropriations of it into animal studies that leave crucial questions of creaturely ethics unanswered (64–70).

Chapter 5

1. It's worth comparing Joukhadar's multiple uses of birds to Haraway's capacious interest in pigeons in *Staying With the Trouble*: "As spies, racers, messengers, urban neighbors, iridescent sexual exhibitionists, avian parents, gender assistants for people, scientific subjects and objects, art-engineering environmental reporters, search-and-rescue workers at sea, imperialist invaders, discriminators of painting styles, native species, pets, and more, around the earth pigeons and their partners of many kinds, including people, make history" (29).
2. While not addressing *Split Tooth* specifically in *Staying with the Trouble*, Haraway also admires the advocacy and world-making of Tagaq's art, in particular in her album *Animism*, of which she says, "Materialist, experimental animism is not a New Age wish nor a neocolonial fantasy, but a powerful proposition for rethinking relationality, perspective, process, and reality without the dubious comforts of the oppositional categories of modern/traditional or religious/secular. Human-animal knots do something different in this world" (164).

Bibliography

Abraham, Nicolas, and Maria Torok. "Mourning *or* Melancholia: Introjection *versus* Incorporation." *The Shell and the Kernel: Renewals of Psychoanalysis*, vol. 1, edited and translated by Nicholas T. Rand, University of Chicago Press, 1994, pp. 125–38.

Abram, David. *The Spell of the Sensuous: Perception and Language in a More-Than-Human World*. Vintage, 1997.

Agamben, Giorgio. *The Open: Man and Animal*. Translated by Kevin Attell, Stanford University Press, 2004.

Agamben, Giorgio. *State of Exception*. Translated by Kevin Attell, University of Chicago Press, 2005.

Agamben, Giorgio. *Profanations*. Translated by Jeff Fort, Zone, 2007.

Agamben, Giorgio. "We Refugees." Translated by Michael Rocke, *Migropolis: Venice/Atlas of a Global Situation*, vol. 1, edited by Wolfgang Sheppe et al., Hatje Cantz, 2010, pp. 120–5.

Agamben, Giorgio. "The Invention of an Epidemic." *European Journal of Psychoanalysis*, 26 Feb. 2020, www.journal-psychoanalysis.eu/coronavirus-and-philosophers/. Accessed 22 Jan. 2022.

Alexis, André. *Pastoral*. Coach House, 2014.

Alexis, André. *Fifteen Dogs*. Coach House, 2015.

Alexis, André. "Last Word: André Alexis on a Matter of Style." *Quill & Quire*, 26 Mar. 2015, quillandquire.com/authors/2015/03/26/last-word-andre-alexis-on-a-matter-of-style/. Accessed 21 Feb. 2020.

Alexis, André. "Of a Smallness in the Soul." *Canadian Notes & Queries*, 2 Feb. 2016, notesandqueries.ca/essays/andre-alexis-of-a-smallness-in-the-soul/. Accessed 1 Oct. 2022.

Alexis, André. *The Hidden Keys*. Coach House, 2016.

Alexis, André. *Days by Moonlight*. Coach House, 2019.

Allison, Anne. *Millennial Monsters: Japanese Toys and the Global Imagination*. University of California Press, 2006.

Anasuya, Shreya Ila. "Interview: Amitav Ghosh on the Novels, Commerce and Sociology of Climate Change." *The Wire*, 22 July 2016, thewire.in/books/amitav-ghosh-interview-climate-change. Accessed 21 Feb. 2020.

"Announcing the 2019 PEN/Faulkner Award Winner." *PEN/Faulkner*, 29 Apr. 2019, www.penfaulkner.org/2019/04/29/announcing-the-2019-pen-faulkner-award-winner/. Accessed 22 Jan. 2022.

Arendt, Hannah. "We Refugees." *The Jewish Writings*, edited by Jerome Kohn and Ron H. Feldman, Schocken, 2007, pp. 264–74.

Bailly, Jean-Christophe. *The Animal Side*. Translated by Catherine Porter, Fordham University Press, 2011.

Bakhtin, Mikhail. *The Dialogic Imagination: Four Essays*. Edited by Michael Holquist, translated by Caryl Emerson and Michael Holquist, University of Texas Press, 1986.

Bakhtin, Mikhail. *Problems of Dostoevsky's Poetics*. Edited and translated by Caryl Emerson, University of Minnesota Press, 1999.

Benini, Stefania. *Pasolini: The Sacred Flesh*. University of Toronto Press, 2015.

Benjamin, Walter. "One-Way Street." *Walter Benjamin: Selected Writings, Volume 1, 1913–1926*, translated by Edmund Jephcott, edited by Marcus Bullock and Michael W. Jennings, Belknap Press of Harvard University Press, 1996, pp. 444–88.

Benjamin, Walter. "Doctrine of the Similar." *Walter Benjamin: Selected Writings, Volume 2, 1927–1934*, translated by Rodney Livingstone and Others, edited by Michael W. Jennings et al., Belknap Press of Harvard University Press, 1999, pp. 694–8.

Benjamin, Walter. "Theological-Political Fragment." *Walter Benjamin: Selected Writings, Volume 3, 1935–1938*, translated by Edmund Jephcott and Others, edited by Howard Eiland and Michael W. Jennings, Belknap Press of Harvard University Press, 2002, pp. 305–6.

Benjamin, Walter. *The Arcades Project*. Translated by Howard Eiland and Kevin McLaughlin, Belknap Press of Harvard University Press, 2002.

Benjamin, Walter. "On the Concept of History." *Walter Benjamin: Selected Writings, Volume 4, 1938-1940*, translated by Edmund Jephcott and Others, edited by Howard Eiland and Michael W. Jennings, Belknap Press of Harvard University Press, 2003, pp. 389–400.

Benjamin, Walter. "The Lisbon Earthquake." *The Storyteller Essays*, edited by Samuel Titan, translated by Tess Lewis, New York Review of Books, 2019, pp. 17–23.

Benjamin, Walter. *Origin of the German Trauerspiel*, translated by Howard Eiland, Harvard University Press, 2019.

Benjamin, Walter. "The Storyteller: Reflections on the Work of Nikolai Leskov." *The Storyteller Essays*, edited by Samuel Titan, translated by Tess Lewis, New York Review of Books, 2019, pp. 48–73.

Benjamin, Walter. *The Storyteller Essays*, edited by Samuel Titan, translated by Tess Lewis, New York Review of Books, 2019.

Boomgaard, Peter. *Frontiers of Fear: Tigers and People in the Malay World, 1600–1950*. Yale University Press, 2001.

Borges, Jorge Luis. "Dreamtigers." *Dreamtigers*, translated by Mildred Boyer and Harold Morland, University of Texas Press, 1993, p. 24.

Borges, Jorge Luis. "The Other Tiger." *Dreamtigers*, translated by Mildred Boyer and Harold Morland, University of Texas Press, 1993, pp. 70–1.

Borges, Jorge Luis. "The God's Script." *Labyrinths: Selected Stories and Other Writings*, edited by Donald A. Yates and James E. Irby, translated by L. A. Murillo, New Directions, 2007, pp. 169–73.

Botar, Oliver A. I. "Charles Sirató and the Dimensionist Manifesto." *Dimensionism: Modern Art in the Age of Einstein*, edited by Vanja V. Malloy, MIT Press, 2018, pp. 19–47.

Broglio, Ron. "Thinking with Surfaces: Animals and Contemporary Art." *Animals and the Human Imagination: A Companion to Animal Studies*, edited by Aaron Gross and Anne Vallely, Columbia University Press, 2012, pp. 238–58.

Carter, Sue. "The Latest from Andre Alexis: Ontario Landscapes Filtered through a Psychotropic Drug." *Toronto Star*, 21 Feb. 2019, www.thestar.com/entertainment/books/2019/02/21/the-latest-from-andre-alexis-ontario-landscapes-filtered-through-a-psychotropic-drug.html. Accessed 21 Feb. 2020.

Casanova, Pascale. *The World Republic of Letters*. Translated by Malcolm DeBevoise, Harvard University Press, 2007.

Chakrabarty, Dipesh. "The Climate of History: Four Theses." *Critical Inquiry*, vol. 35, no. 2, 2009, pp. 197–222.

Chan, Margaret. "The Sinophone Roots of Javanese Nini Towong." *Asian Ethnology*, vol. 76, no. 1, 2017, pp. 95–115.

Chang, Ailsa. "'The Thirty Names of Night': A Story of Self-Discovery and Self-Acceptance." *NPR*, 30 Nov. 2020, www.npr.org/2020/11/30/940196969/the-thirty-names-of-night-a-story-of-self-discovery-and-self-acceptance. Accessed 22 Jan. 2022.

Cheah, Pheng, and Bruce Robbins, eds. *Cosmopolitics: Thinking and Feeling Beyond the Nation*. University of Minnesota Press, 1998.

Cheah, Pheng. *What Is a World? On Postcolonial Literature as World Literature*. Duke University Press, 2016.

Cheah, Pheng. "Worlding Literature: Living with Tiger Spirits." *Diacritics*, vol. 45, no. 2, 2017, pp. 86–114.

Chen, Mel Y. *Animacies: Biopolitics, Racial Mattering, and Queer Affect*. Duke University Press, 2012.

Choo, Yangsze. *The Ghost Bride*. William Morrow, 2014.

Choo, Yangsze. *The Night Tiger*. Flatiron, 2019.

Choo, Yangsze. "Kindle Notes and Highlights." *Goodreads*, 2019, www.goodreads.com/notes/41124373-the-night-tiger/13384834-yangsze-choo?ref=abp. Accessed 1 Oct. 2022.

Choo, Yangsze. *Yangsze Choo*. WordPress, yschoo.com/. Accessed 22 Jan. 2022.

Clarke, Bruce. *Gaian Systems: Lynn Margulis, Neocybernetics, and the End of the Anthropocene*. University of Minneosta Press, 2020.

Coetzee, J. M. *The Lives of Animals*. Edited by Amy Gutmann. Princeton University Press, 1999.

Cole, Matthew, et al. "Toronto Is Now Majority Visible Minority. What about Your Neighborhood?" *Toronto Star*, 8 Nov. 2017, www.thestar.com/news/gta/2017/11/08/toronto-is-now-majority-visible-minority-what-about-your-neighbourhood.html. Accessed 22 Jan. 2022.

Cunningham, Joel. "In Which Author Zen Cho Is Interviewed by Her Husband about the True Queen." *B&N Reads*, 20 Mar. 2019, www.barnesandnoble.com/blog/sci-fi-fantasy/in-which-author-zen-cho-is-interviewed-by-her-husband-about-the-true-queen/. Accessed 1 Oct. 2022.

Damrosch, David. *What Is World Literature?* Princeton University Press, 2003.

DasGupta, Amrita. "Hydrocultural Histories and Narratives: Insights from the Sundarbans." *Ecology, Economy and Society—the INSEE Journal*, vol. 3, no. 2, 2020, pp. 169–78.

Deckard, Sharae. "Ecogothic." *Twenty-First-Century Gothic: An Edinburgh Companion*, edited by Maisha Wester and Xavier Aldana Reyes, Edinburgh University Press, 2019, pp. 174–88.

Deleuze, Gilles, and Felix Guattari. *A Thousand Plateaus: Capitalism and Schizophrenia*. Translated by Brian Massumi, University of Minnesota Press, 1987.

Derrida, Jacques. *Specters of Marx: The State of the Debt, The Work of Mourning, and the New International*. Translated by Peggy Kamuf, Routledge, 1994.

Doherty, Mike. "The Surprising Sounds and Sides of Tanya Tagaq." *Maclean's*, 12 Nov. 2018, www.macleans.ca/culture/books/tanya-tagaq-on-her-desperate-attempt-to-alleviate-indigenous-suffering/. Accessed 11 Aug. 2021.

Doniger, Wendy. "Epilogue: Making Animals Vanish." *Animals and the Human Imagination: A Companion to Animal Studies*, edited by Aaron Gross and Anne Vallely, Columbia University Press, 2012, pp. 349–53.

Durrant, Sam. "Critical Spirits: New Animism as Historical Materialism." *new formations: a journal of culture/theory/politics*, vol. 104, 2022, p. 50–76. Project MUSE muse.jhu.edu/article/845873. Accessed 24 Jan. 2023.

Durrant, Sam, and Philip Dickinson. "Editorial." *new formations: a journal of culture/theory/politics*, vol. 104, 2022, p. 4–14. Project MUSE muse.jhu.edu/article/845873. Accessed 24 Jan. 2023.

Esposito, Roberto. *Immunitas: The Protection and Negation of Life*. Translated by Zakiya Hanafi, Polity, 2014.

Esposito, Roberto. "Cured to the Bitter End." *European Journal of Psychoanalysis*, 28 Feb. 2020, www.journal-psychoanalysis.eu/coronavirus-and-philosophers/. Accessed 13 Mar. 2020.

Esposito, Roberto. "Biopolitics and the Coronavirus: A View from Italy." *The Philosophical Salon*, 31 Mar. 2020, thephilosophicalsalon.com/biopolitics-and-coronavirus-a-view-from-italy/. Accessed 22 Jan. 2022.

Ferraro, Joanne M. *Venice: History of the Floating City*. Cambridge University Press, 2012.

Fleiszer, Paul, et al. *T.O. Health Check: An Overview of Toronto's Population Health Status*. Toronto Public Health, 2019.

Foucault, Michel, et al. "Coronavirus and Philosophers." *European Journal of Psychoanalysis*, Mar. 2020, www.journal-psychoanalysis.eu/coronavirus-and-philosophers/. Accessed 13 Mar. 2020.

Fraser, Scott. "The Complicated Place of André Alexis in Black CanLit." *Hamilton Review of Books*, 15 May 2020, hamiltonreviewofbooks.com/blog/2020/5/15/the-complicated-place-of-andr-alexis-in-black-canlit. Accessed 1 Oct. 2022.

Freccero, Carla. "Wolf, or *Homo Homini Lupus*." *Arts of Living on a Damaged Planet: Monsters of the Anthropocene*, edited by Anna Tsing et al., University of Minnesota Press, 2017, pp. M91–M105.

Gardner, Martin. *Mathematical Carnival*. Alfred A. Knopf, 1975.

Ghosh, Amitav. *The Glass Palace*. Penguin Canada, 2000.

Ghosh, Amitav. *Calcutta Chromosome: A Novel of Fevers, Delirium, & Discovery*. Perennial, 2001.

Ghosh, Amitav. "Imperial Temptations." *Incendiary Circumstances: A Chronicle of the Turmoil of Our Times*. Houghton Mifflin, 2005, pp. 26–31.

Ghosh, Amitav. *The Hungry Tide*. Houghton Mifflin, 2005.

Ghosh, Amitav. *The Shadow Lines*. Houghton Mifflin, 2005.

Ghosh, Amitav. *Sea of Poppies*. Picador, 2008.

Ghosh, Amitav. *The Great Derangement: Climate Change and the Unthinkable*. University of Chicago Press, 2017.

Ghosh, Amitav. *Gun Island*. John Murray, 2019.

Ghosh, Amitav. "Beyond the End of the World: Human and Non-Human after the Collapse of 'Civilization.'" Keynote Address for Penn Program in Environmental Humanities, 7 May 2020, ppeh.sas.upenn.edu/index.php/events/pre-recorded-keynote-address-live-q-amitav-ghosh.

Ghosh, Amitav. *The Nutmeg's Curse: Parables for a Planet in Crisis*. University of Chicago Press, 2021.

Gill, Harsimran. "'My Book Is Not an Apocalyptic Book at All. I Guess I'm Leaving Hope as a Possibility': Amitav Ghosh." *Scroll.in*, 17 Jun. 2019, scroll.in/article/927202/my-book-is-not-an-apocalyptic-book-at-all-i-guess-im-leaving-hope-as-a-possibility-amitav-ghosh. Accessed 21 Feb. 2020.

Gould, Hannah. "From Spirits to Superfans." *Asian Geographic*, 1 June 2016, www.asiangeo.com/culture/from-spirits-to-superfans/. Accessed 22 Jan. 2022.

Gygi, Fabio R. "Robot Companions: The Animation of Technology and the Technology of Animation in Japan." *Rethinking Relations and Animism: Personhood and Materiality*, edited by Miguel Astor-Aguilera and Graham Harvey, Routledge, 2018, pp. 94–111.

Hall, Matthew. "In Defence of Plant Personhood." *Religions*, vol. 10, no. 5, 2019, p. 317.

Haraway, Donna J. *Staying with the Trouble: Making Kin in the Chthulucene*. Duke University Press, 2016.

Harrington, Anne. *Reenchanted Science: Holism in German Culture from Wilhelm II to Hitler*. Princeton University Press, 1996.

Henderson, Linda Dalrymple. *The Fourth Dimension and Non-Euclidean Geometry in Modern Art*. MIT Press, 2013.

Jensen, Casper Bruun, and Anders Blok. "Techno-animism in Japan: Shinto Cosmograms, Actor-network Theory, and the Enabling Powers of Non-human Agencies." *Theory, Culture & Society*, vol. 30, no. 2, 2013, pp. 84–115.

Johnson, Ryan. "A Critique of 'Literary Worlds' in World Literature Theory." *Journal of World Literature*, vol. 3, no. 3, 2018, pp. 354–72.

Joukhadar, Zeyn. *The Thirty Names of Night*. Atria, 2020.

Kaerlein, Timo. "The Social Robot as Fetish? Conceptual Affordances and Risks of Neo-Animistic Theory." *International Journal of Social Robotics*, vol. 7, no. 3, 2014, pp. 361–70.

Kimmerer, Robin Wall. *Braiding Sweetgrass: Indigenous Wisdom, Scientific Knowledge and the Teachings of Plants*. Milkweed, 2013.

Kluwick, Ursula. "The Global Deluge: Floods, Diluvian Imagery, and Aquatic Language in Amitav Ghosh's *The Hungry Tide* and *Gun Island*." *Green Letters: Studies in Ecocriticism*, vol. 24, no. 1, 2020, pp. 64–78.

Kohn, Eduardo. *How Forests Think: Toward an Anthropology beyond the Human*. University of California Press, 2013.

Kuklis, Megan. "Journeymen: Travels with an Order of Timbits." *Literary Review of Canada*, June 2019, reviewcanada.ca/magazine/2019/06/journeymen/. Accessed 21 Feb. 2020.

Kurniawan, Eka. *Man Tiger*. Translated by Labodalih Sembiring, Verso, 2015.

Kurniawan, Eka. "Eka Kurniawan on Indonesia and Magical Realism." Interview by J. R. Ramakrishnan. *Electric Lit*, 28 Jan. 2016, electricliterature.com/eka-kurniawan-on-indonesia-and-magical-realism/. Accessed 24 Aug. 2021.

Li, Victor. "Necroidealism, or the Subaltern's Sacrificial Death." *Interventions: International Journal of Postcolonial Studies*, vol. 11, no. 3, 2009, pp. 275–92.

Lucht, Marc, and Donna Yarri, eds. *Kafka's Creatures: Animals, Hybrids, and Other Fantastic Beings*. Lexington, 2010.

Malloy, Vanja V. "From Macrocosm to Microcosm: Examining the Role of Modern Science in American Art." *Dimensionism: Modern Art in the Age of Einstein*, edited by Vanja V. Malloy, MIT Press, 2018, pp. 71–97.

Malloy, Vanja V. "Introduction." *Dimensionism: Modern Art in the Age of Einstein*, edited by Vanja V. Malloy, MIT Press, 2018, pp. 1–16.

Marder, Michael. *Plant-Thinking: A Philosophy of Vegetal Life*. Columbia University Press, 2013.

Marder, Michael. "What Is Plant-Thinking?" *Klesis*, vol. 25, 2013, pp. 124–43.

Marder, Michael. "For a Phytocentrism to Come." *Environmental Philosophy*, 2 May 2014, doi: 10.5840/envirophil20145110.

Marder, Michael. "For the Earth That Has Never Been." *Stasis*, vol. 9, no. 1, 2020, pp. 60–75.

Massumi, Brian. "Translator's Foreword: Pleasures of Philosophy." *A Thousand Plateaus: Capitalism and Schizophrenia*, by Gilles Deleuze and Felix Guattari, University of Minnesota Press, 1987, pp. ix–xv.

Medley, Mark. "After the Giller, André Alexis Seeks to Complete His Masterpiece." *Globe and Mail*, 23 Sep. 2016, www.theglobeandmail.com/arts/books-and-media/after-the-giller-andre-alexis-seeks-to-complete-his-masterpiece/article32024640/. Accessed 21 Feb. 2020.

Mencius. *Mencius*, translated by D. C. Lau, Penguin, 1970.

Mimica, Jadran. "Un/knowing and the Practice of Ethnography: A Reflection on Some Western Cosmo-ontological Notions and Their Anthropological Application." *Anthropological Theory*, vol. 10, no. 3, 2010, pp. 203–28.

Mistry, Anupa. "'This Book Was Written for My Own Heart': Tanya Tagaq on *Split Tooth*." *Globe and Mail*, 24 Sep. 2018, www.theglobeandmail.com/arts/books/article-this-book-was-written-for-my-own-heart-tanya-tagaq-on-split-tooth/. Accessed 11 Aug. 2021.

Murakami, Haruki. "The Elephant Vanishes." *The Elephant Vanishes: Stories*, translated by Alfred Birnbaum and Jay Rubin, Vintage, 1993, pp. 307–27.

Nancy, Jean-Luc. "Riposte by Jean-Luc Nancy to Roberto Esposito." *European Journal of Psychoanalysis*, Feb. 2020, www.journal-psychoanalysis.eu/coronavirus-and-philosophers/. Accessed 13 Mar. 2020.

Nancy, Jean-Luc. "Viral Exception." *European Journal of Psychoanalysis*, 27 Feb. 2020, www.journal-psychoanalysis.eu/coronavirus-and-philosophers/. Accessed 13 Mar. 2020.

Nayar, Pramod K. "The Postcolonial Uncanny: The Politics of Dispossession in Amitav Ghosh's *The Hungry Tide*." *College Literature*, vol. 37, no. 4, 2010, pp. 88–119.

Nuttall, Sarah. "Pluvial Time/Wet Form." *New Literary History*, vol. 51, no. 2, 2020, pp. 455–72.

O'Yeah, Zac. "'What We Have to Think About, Above All, Is How to Slow Down': Amitav Ghosh." *The Hindu*, 25 Apr. 2020, www.thehindu.com/books/what-we-have-to-think-about-above-all-is-how-to-slow-down-amitav-ghosh/article31414696.ece. Accessed 26 Apr. 2020.

Pasolini, Pier Paolo. *Theorem*. Translated by Stuart Hood, Quartet, 1992.

Pick, Anat. *Creaturely Poetics: Animality and Vulnerability in Literature and Film*. Columbia University Press, 2011.

Ray, Sangeeta. "Towards a Planetary Reading of Postcolonial and American Imaginative Eco Graphies." *A Companion to Comparative Literature*, edited by Ali Behdad, and Dominic Thomas, John Wiley & Sons, Incorporated, 2011, pp. 421–36.

Redhill, Michael. "An Interview with André Alexis." *Brick: A Journal of Reviews*, vol. 62, 1999, pp. 50–6.

Riemenschnitter, Andrea. "Beyond Gothic: Ye Si's Spectral Hong Kong and the Global Culture Crisis." *Journal of Modern Literature in Chinese*, vol. 12, no. 1, 2014, pp. 108–56.

Riemenschnitter, Andrea. "Flower Spirits, Drifting Leaves, and Trees of Transcendence: Reflections on Plants in Leung Ping-kwan's Poetry." *Interventions*, vol. 20, no. 8, 2018, pp. 1188–208.

Saussy, Haun. "The Dimensionality of World Literature." *Neohelicon*, vol. 38, no. 2, 2011, pp. 289–94.

Sirató, Charles Tamko. "The Dimensionist Manifesto." *Dimensionism: Modern Art in the Age of Einstein*, edited by Vanja V. Malloy, MIT Press, 2018, pp. 170–9.

Spivak, Gayatri Chakravorty. *An Aesthetic Education in the Era of Globalization*. Harvard University Press, 2012.

Stengers, Isabelle. "Reclaiming Animism" *e-flux Journal*, no. 36, 2012, www.e-flux.com/journal/36/61245/reclaiming-animism/. Accessed 14 Oct. 2021.

Rajiva, Jay. *Toward an Animist Reading of Postcolonial Trauma*. Routledge, 2021.

Tagaq, Tanya. *Split Tooth*. Penguin Canada, 2018.

"Tesseract." *Wikipedia: The Free Encyclopedia*, 21 Jan. 2022, en.wikipedia.org/wiki/Tesseract. Accessed 22 Jan. 2022.

Thiem, Mathieu. "Interanimism: On the Mutual Inspiration of a Dreaming Earth." *The Woven Song*, 23 May 2017, wovensong.wordpress.com/2017/05/23/interanimism-on-the-mutual-inspiration-of-a-dreaming-earth/. Accessed 22 June 2021.

Thompson, Hilary. *Novel Creatures: Animal Life and the New Millennium*. Routledge, 2018.

Titan, Samuel. "Introduction." *The Storyteller Essays*, by Walter Benjamin, edited by Samuel Titan, New York Review of Books, 2019, pp. vii–xviii.

"Trudeau: 'There's No Place for the State in the Bedrooms of the Nation.'" *CBC Digital Archives*, 2021, www.cbc.ca/archives/entry/omnibus-bill-theres-no-place-for-the-state-in-the-bedrooms-of-the-nation. Accessed 22 Jan. 2022.

Tsing, Anna Lowenhaupt. *The Mushroom at the End of the World: On the Possibility of Life in Capitalist Ruin*. Princeton University Press, 2015.

Tu Weiming. "Confucian Spirituality in Contemporary China." *Confucianism and Spiritual Traditions in Modern China and Beyond*, edited by Fenggang Yang and Joseph Tamney, Brill, 2011, pp. 75–96.

Uexkull, Jakob von. *A Foray into the Worlds of Animals and Humans: with A Theory of Meaning*. Translated by Joseph D. O'Neil, University of Minnesota Press, 2010.

Van der Vliet Oloomi, Azareen. *Call Me Zebra*. Houghton Mifflin Harcourt, 2018.

Viveiros de Castro, Eduardo. *The Relative Native: Essays on Indigenous Conceptual Worlds*. Hau Books, 2015.

Walkowitz, Rebecca. *Cosmopolitan Style: Modernism Beyond the Nation*. Columbia University Press, 2006.

Weber, Samuel. *Benjamin's -abilities*. Harvard University Press, 2010.

White, Laura A. *Ecospectrality: Haunting and Environmental Justice in Contemporary Anglophone Novels*. Bloomsbury, 2020.

Whitehead, Joshua. "'Finding We'Wha': Indigenous Idylls in Queer Young Adult Literature." *Queer as Camp: Essays on Summer, Style, and Sexuality*, edited by Kenneth B. Kidd and Derritt Mason, Fordham University Press, 2019, pp. 223–40.

Whyte, Kyle P. "Indigenous Science (Fiction) for the Anthropocene: Ancestral Dystopias and Fantasies of Climate Change Crises." *Environment and Planning E: Nature and Space*, vol. 1, no. 1–2, 2018, pp. 224–42.

Wilkinson, Darryl. "Is There Such a Thing as Animism?" *Journal of the American Academy of Religion*, vol. 85, no. 2, 2017, pp. 289–311.

Yadaw, Sagnik, and Rupsa Roy Chowdhury. "Resisting the Apocalypse: Representing the Anthropocene in Indian English Literature." *Postcolonial Interventions*, vol. 4, no. 2, 2019, pp. 358–77.

Index

Index note: the prefix n refers to the notes.

Abraham, Nicolas 209 n.3
Abram, David 18–19
Acker, Kathy 82
Agamben, Giorgio 28–9, 44, 84–6, 108–9, 135–6
Alexis, André 15, 28–9, 99–134, 141, 183, 187
Ali, Agha Shahid 80
Allsion, Anne 17
Alwi, Des 183
Animacies 157
animals 1–3, 65–9, 83–93, 105–6, 146–7, 151; *see also* were-animals
birds 86–7, 88–90, 191–3, 212 n.1
Animals and the Human Imagination 1
animism 2–3, 11–12, 15–18, 157, 205, 206 n.1, 212 n.2; *see also* interanimism
anomie 108–9
Anthropocene 27, 30, 58–9, 95, 172, 176–7
apocalypse 147–51, 188–9, 211 n.3
The Arcades Project 167, 211 n.5
Arendt, Hannah 33–4, 71, 83–5, 207 n.4
avatars 3, 13, 29, 146–7, 156–7, 176, 182

Bailly, Jean-Christophe 2
Bakhtin, Mikhail 27–8, 56, 90–1, 93, 107–12, 127–8, 133
Ballard, J.G. 211 n.6
Banda Islands 181–3, 187–8
Beecroft, Alexander 62
Benini, Stefania 104
Benjamin, Walter 4–5, 7–8, 24, 79, 167, 172–5, 180, 190–1, 207 n.4, 211 n.5
biocentrism 14
biopolitics 27, 85–6, 135–9
birds 86–7, 88–90, 191–3, 212 n.1
Black Madonna, Venice 177–8, 179
blackouts 203
Boomgaard, Peter 42–3
Borges, Jorge Luis 13, 53, 82, 86, 91–3

Botar, Oliver A.I. 54
Braiding Sweetgrass: Indigenous Wisdom, Scientific Knowledge, and the Teachings of Plants 1
Buddhism 62, 70, 209 n.2

The Calcutta Chromosome 29, 139, 140, 143, 149
Calder, Alex 75
Call Me Zebra 27–8, 54–6, 64–5, 105, 141, 201
synopsis 70–96
carnivals 107–9, 111–12, 127–8
Casanova, Pascale 50
Chakrabarty, Dipesh 27, 58–9
Chang, Aisla 193–4, 196
Chan, Margaret 43
Chariandy, David 103
Cheah, Pheng 26–7, 33, 34–7, 59–61, 64–9, 70, 144–6, 207 n.4, 208 n.1
Chen, Mel Y. 49, 157
Childhood 103
China 43–6
Choo, Yangsze 26–7, 33–53, 106, 141, 187
Chowdhury, Rupsa Roy 211 n.3
Cho, Zen 41–2
chronotope 28, 110–12, 134
circles 75, 81
Clarke, Bruce 147, 204
Cliff, Michelle 64
climate change 58–9, 137–9, 176–7, 188, 210–11 n.1
Coetzee, J.M. 13
colonialism 3, 15–16, 41–3, 181–3, 190
communication 142–3
"The Complicated Place of André Alexis in Black CanLit" 102
Confucianism 47–9
Costello, Elizabeth 13
COVID-19 pandemic 25, 135–7, 203–4
cultural involution 43

Dalí, Salvador 90
Damrosch, David 35, 208–9 n.2
Dasgupta, Amrita 147
Days by Moonlight 15, 28–9, 101–2, 103–4, 106, 110–12
   synopsis 113–34
the dead 3, 189–91
Dead Souls 105, 107, 111
Deckard, Sharae 206 n.1, 211 n.4
Deleuze, Gilles 19, 20–2, 150
Derrida, Jacques 24, 144, 206 n.1, 211 n.7
Dickinson, Philip 15, 17–18
Dillon, Grace 189
dimensionism 2–3, 20–2, 27, 52–3, 54–96, 101, 144, 146; *see also* multidimensionality
Dimensionism: Modern Art in the Age of Einstein 54
Doherty, Mike 196, 200
Doiniger, Wendy 1
Don Quixote 105
Dreamtigers 13
Duchamp, Marcel 19, 75
Durrant, Sam 15, 17–18, 211 n.7

earth 3–10, 22, 23–4, 204–5; *see also* Gaia
earthquakes 7–8, 10
eclipses, solar 74–5, 99–100, 112, 203
ecological devastation 3, 206 n.1; *see also* climate change
Ecospectrality: Haunting and Environmental Justice in Contemporary Anglophone Novels 206 n.1
Eddy, Mary Baker 100
Einstein, Albert 2, 3, 19, 24, 53, 75, 99–100, 110–11
"The Elephant Vanishes" 2
Eliade, Mircea 104
environment 3, 206 n.1; *see also* climate change
Esposito, Roberto 29, 135, 136–8, 157, 178
ethnography 22–3, 42
ethology 2, 11, 22, 67
exiles 33–4, 83–6, 137–8
extra-human 26, 196–202; *see also* spirits

Farah, Nuruddin 64
fetishism 15, 16–17

Fifteen Dogs 103, 106
flat, two dimensional 72–4
A Foray into the Worlds of Animals and Humans 67–9
foreknowing 51–3
"For the Earth That Has Never Been" 5
fourth dimension 99–102, 107–8, 133
The Fourth Dimension and Non-Euclidean Geometry in Modern Art 54
Fraser, Scott 102–3
Freccero, Carla 208 n.7
Frontiers of Fear: Tigers and People in the Malay World, 1600–1950 42
Fu Manchu 49

Gaia 5, 147, 176–7, 182, 204–5, 210–11 n.1
Galimberti, Umberto 104
Gardner, Martin 107
geological impact of humans 58–9; *see also* Anthropocene
geophilosophy 6
Geronticus simurghus 191–3
Ghosh, Amitav 5, 6–7, 8–10, 16, 19, 29, 64–5, 135–84, 187–8, 208 n.1
The Ghost Bride 35, 50, 141
ghosts 3, 191, 206 n.1
Gill, Harsimran 139–40, 210–11 n.1
Gilmour, David 102
The Glass Palace 148
global 4–5, 64–5
globalization 3, 9–10, 59–60, 137–8
global warming 58–9, 137–9, 176–7, 188, 210–11 n.1
"The God's Script" 13
Goethe, Johann Wolfgang von 60, 114
Gogol, Nikolai 105, 107, 111
The Golden Flower Pot 105
The Great Derangement 137, 139, 142–3, 173–4
Guattari, Felix 19, 20–2, 150
Gulliver's Travels 105
Gun Island 29, 137, 139, 140, 143, 146–7, 188, 191
   synopsis 147–80
Gygi, Fabio R. 17

Habiby, Emile 80
Hall, Matthew 14–15

Haraway, Donna 24, 150, 206–7 n.2, n.3, 208 n.1, 212 n.1, n.2
Harrington, Anne 69
Hayot, Eric 62
Heart of Darkness 49–50
Heidegger, Martin 66–7
Henderson, Linda Dalrymple 54, 99–100, 133
Herkimer diamonds 23–4
Hernandez, Jaimie 196
The Hidden Keys 103
Holmes, Sherlock 62, 82
How Forests Think 11–12, 174
The Hungry Tide 6, 29, 65, 139, 145–6, 148–9, 163, 180, 211 n.3
hybrids, human-animal 11–12, 15, 24, 208 n.7
hypercubism 99–102, 108, 204

ibises 191–3
immigration 137–8
immunity paradigm 137–8, 157, 178–9
'Imperative to Re-imagine the Planet' 9
In an Antique Land 149
Indigenous peoples 182–3, 187–90
interanimism 10–24, 207 n.5; *see also* animism
Iran 70
"Is There Such a Thing as Animism?" 16

jaguars 11–12
Japan 17–18
Johnson, Ryan 55, 62–4, 81–2
Joukhadar, Zeyn 29–30, 191–6

Kafka, Franz 13
Kant, Immanuel 8, 10
Kimmerer, Robin Wall 1, 20, 23–4, 187, 203
Kluwick, Ursula 210–11 n.1
Kohn, Eduardo 11–12, 22, 174, 194
Kurniawan, Eka 26–7, 33, 34–7, 51–2, 64, 66

Latour, Bruno 5
law 108–9
Lazarillo de Tormes 105
Leenhardt, Maurice 195
Lehman, Rhoda 80
Lem, Stanislaw 182
L'Engle, Madeleine 133, 204

Lindisfarne, organization 204, 205
Lisbon earthquake, 1755 7–8, 10
The Lives of Animals 13
Li, Victor 211 n.2
Lloyd, G.E.R. 63
Lovelock, James 147, 204, 205

Malaya 41–3
Malloy, Vanja V. 52–3, 54, 74–5
Manasa Devi, deity 147, 150, 166, 176, 188
Man Tiger 26–7, 34–7, 38–9, 51–2, 66
Marder, Michael 5–6, 14, 21, 206–7 n.3
Marx, Karl 60, 64
Massumi, Brian 20–1
Mathematical Carnival 107
messianism 144–5, 146, 211 n.7
Millennial Monsters: Japanese Toys and the Global Imagination 17
Miller, Stuart 41
Mimica, Jadran 18, 194–5
Mistry, Anupa 196–7
Mohawk people 23–4
multidimensionality 5, 62–4, 100, 112, 151; *see also* dimensionism
Murakami, Haruki 1–2

Nancy, Jean-Luc 135–6
Nayar, Pramod K. 211 n.4
The Night Tiger 26–7, 33–53, 106, 141
nonhuman 26; *see also* animals
Norbu, Jamyang 62
Novel Creatures 208 n.6
The Nutmeg's Curse 10, 16, 19, 30, 181–4, 187–8
Nuttall, Sarah 147, 210–11 n.1

'Of a Smallness in the Soul' 102
Ontario, Canada 28–9, 112
The Open, Man and Animal 85
Orientalism 15
Origin of the German Trauerspiel 180

Paradiso 105
Pasolini, Pier Paolo 101, 104
Pastoral 103
Pavel, Thomas 60
Peirce, Charles Sanders 11
A Perfect Night to Go to China 102
The Perfect Order of Things 102

perspectivism 22–3
physics, quantum 54
planet-thinking 3–10, 22, 23–4, 204–5;
    see also Gaia
plants 14–15, 114–15
Plant-Thinking, A Philosophy of Vegetal Life 14, 21
play 109–10
politics 27–8
portals 3, 24, 61, 92, 106, 157, 165–6
Potnia Theron, deity 150
predators 11–12, 22–3
preternatural 139–40, 142–3, 148, 150–1, 162–5, 211 n.4
Primitive Culture 16
Problems of Dostoevsky's Poetics 108
puma 11–12

quantum physics 54
quartz 23–4
Quincunx Cycle 100–1, 103–4, 106, 110, 141

race 102–3
Rajiva, Jay 145, 146
Ray, Sangeeta 6–7
realism 104–7
"Reclaiming Animism" 18, 162
Redhill, Michael 103
refugees 33–4, 83–6, 137–8
relativity 53, 75, 99–100
rhizomes 19, 20–1, 23–4, 150
Riemenschnitter, Andrea 206 n.1
Ring 103
the road 111–12
Robbins, Bruce 208 n.1
Runa, people 11–12, 194
Rushdie, Salman 206 n.1

Said, Edward 15
Saussy, Haun 55, 60–2, 65
science 1, 20, 54
Sea of Poppies 80, 149
The Shadow Lines 6–7, 8–10, 65, 148, 149, 163, 179
Sirató, Charles 2, 20, 27, 54, 56–8
Skeat, Walter William 42
solar eclipses 74–5, 99–100, 112, 203
Solaris 182
Sorcerer to the Crown 41–2

sound 196–7
spacetime 19, 53, 57, 58, 94, 110–11;
    see also time
The Spell of the Sensuous: Perception and Language in a More-Than-Human World 19
spiralling time 30, 189–90, 195
spirit realms 3, 199–202
spirits 1, 3, 33–8, 189–91
spiritualism 81, 100
Spivak, Gayatri 5, 6–7, 9, 208–9 n.2
Split Tooth 29–30, 196–202
State of Exception 108, 109
Staying with the Trouble 24, 150, 212 n.1, n.2
Stengers, Isabelle 18–20, 162
"The Storyteller" 3–5, 7–8, 207 n.4
supernatural 18, 199, 207 n.5, 210 n.1;
    see also preternatural
surrealism 2, 27, 52–3, 54–5
sweetgrass 23–4
Syria 137–8

Tagaq, Tanya 29–30, 196–202
Taüt (bird) 86–7, 88–90
techno-animism 17–18
Teorema (Theorem) 104, 105
tesseracts 99, 204
Thiem, Mathieu 207 n.5
The Thirty Names of Night 29–30, 191–6
Thompson, William Irwin 203–5
A Thousand Plateaus 19, 21
tigers 13, 34, 37–9, 42, 51–3
time 24–5, 30, 33–4, 59, 110–12, 189–90, 195; see also spacetime
Titan, Samuel 4
Torok, Maria 209 n.3
transitioning, transsexuality 193–4, 196
transmigration 81–2
Trudeau, Pierre 123
Tsing, Anna Lowenhaupt 206 n.2, 210 n.2
Tu Weiming 47–8
two dimensional 72–4
Tylor, Sir Edward 16

Uexküll, Jakob von 2, 11, 27, 64, 66, 67–9
uncanny 139–40, 142–3, 148, 150–1, 162–5, 211 n.4
The Unconsoled 105

Van der Vliet Oloomi, Azareen 27–8, 33, 54–96, 106, 141, 167, 188
Varela, Francisco 147
Viveiros de Castro, Eduardo 22–3

Walkowitz, Rebecca 208 n.1
Weber, Samuel 144, 180
were-animals 11–12, 15, 24, 38–41, 208 n.7
"We Refugees" 83–4
What Is a World? On Postcolonial Literature as World Literature 59, 145

Whitehead, Joshua 30, 128, 187, 210 n.3
White, Laura, A, 206 n.1
Whyte, Kyle 24, 30, 188–90
Wilkinson, Darryl 16–17
Winn, Philip 187–8
wolves 208 n.7
worldling literature 34–5, 59–60
world literature 25, 27, 55, 61–4

Yadaw, Sagnik 211 n.3

www.ingramcontent.com/pod-product-compliance
Lightning Source LLC
Chambersburg PA
CBHW071835300426
44116CB00009B/1550